If Jesus Were a Sophomore

If Jesus Were a Sophomore

Discipleship for College Students

Bruce Main

Westminster John Knox Press
LOUISVILLE • LONDON

Unless otherwise indicated, scripture quotations are from the Holy Bible, New International Version, Copyright © 1973, 1978, 1984 International Bible Society. Used by permission of Zondervan Bible Publishers.

Scripture quotations from the New Revised Standard Version of the Bible are copyright © 1989 by the Division of Christian Education of the National Council of the Churches of Christ in the U.S.A. and are used by permission.

Book design by Sharon Adams
Cover design by Jennifer K. Cox
Cover illustration by John Fitzgerald

First edition
Published by Westminster John Knox Press
Louisville, Kentucky

This book is printed on acid-free paper that meets the American National Standards Institute Z39.48 standard. ♾

PRINTED IN THE UNITED STATES OF AMERICA

02 03 04 05 06 07 08 09 10 11 — 10 9 8 7 6 5 4 3 2 1

Library of Congress Cataloging-in-Publication Data is on file at the Library of Congress, Washington, D.C.

ISBN 0-664-22564-0

To my parents
For their enduring gift of roots and wings

Contents

Acknowledgments

I t has been an incredible sixteen years of working alongside hundreds of dedicated college students who have desired to express their changing faith by loving children, teens, and families in Camden, New Jersey. Thank you for your witness of sacrificial service, faithful love, and your willingness to work with joy in some very difficult circumstances. It is a privilege to have been part of your journey.

To the heroic children and teens of Camden, who have allowed me to live and work in your presence: I am grateful for your daily demonstration of true courage and perseverance. Your lives continue to inspire me daily.

Without the remarkable fifteen-year commitment of my colleague Gina Settle, there would be no UrbanPromise Ministries. Thank you for embodying what God can do when collegians truly surrender their lives to the intentions of God and live as disciples of Jesus.

To the one who truly believes in the potential of young adult faith, Tony Campolo: I thank you for your continued friendship and enduring vision to mobilize college students to change the world.

Thank you to my good friend Dr. Paul Keating, who encourages me to write and has spent hours reading and editing my work. You are brilliant and a true encouragement to me.

To my board of directors, the many faithful supporters who fund the ministry of UrbanPromise, and our dedicated staff—thank you for demonstrating God's faithfulness so consistently.

Finally, I am grateful to my most loyal friend, partner, and wife, Pamela. Your outlook on life and laughter has kept it fun.

Foreword

When speaking with college-aged young people, I often point out that the decisions that will structure the rest of their lives will, for the most part, be made between the ages of twenty and twenty-five. In all likelihood, when they will marry, their vocational choices, their spiritual commitments, and their socioeconomic lifestyle will all be set in place during that five-year span. I can sense a tension among young people when I point this out to them, and for good reason. There are few guidelines to direct them in their decision making. Our pluralistic society offers a host of conflicting values laid out for young women and men in smorgasbord fashion, and in an increasingly postmodern culture, one value system seems just as good as another.

A seemingly simplistic answer for Christian young people is often provided by church folks who tell them to ask themselves in each decision-making situation, "What Would Jesus Do?" The letters WWJD seem omnipresent these days as a host of well-meaning Christians try to make statements about the way *they* handle decisions. You see the letters WWJD on lapel pins, bracelets, and T-shirts. Believe it or not, you can buy a $500 pin with diamonds spelling out the letters (even though I'm pretty sure Jesus wouldn't spend $500 to buy one).

While the basic idea of WWJD is good, answering the question that these letters pose is very difficult for young people struggling to work through the dilemmas they face almost daily. To really consider what Jesus would do in a given situation requires a comprehensive reading of the Gospels and an understanding of how Jesus handled things in his day. Using Scripture, one has to try to get inside the head of Jesus and figure out how he thinks (Phil. 2:1). For young people between the ages of twenty and twenty-five, this is especially difficult because these ages were part of the "silent years," a time during which the Bible doesn't tell us anything about what was going on in the life of Jesus. We know nothing of him in these formative years except that he "grew in wisdom and stature and in favor with God and men" (Luke 2:52). How did Jesus understand his "calling"? What did he do with his sexual desires, and did he ever get "turned on" to some girl who might have lured him away from his calling? How did he relate to his parents when he felt they didn't understand him? Did Jesus ever have doubts about his faith, and how did he hammer out the theology that would guide his preaching?

There are those who are shocked that such questions should even be asked. With indignation they exclaim, "You act like Jesus was a human being just like us!" Well, Jesus *was* a human being—though not *just* like us. He went through the same kinds of temptations and struggles that are encountered by every college student—but he never blew it. He was without sin (Heb. 4:15).

If you find that hard to handle, you're not the only one. The first heresy in the early church was not a questioning of the deity of Christ, but of his humanity. The gnostics, who propagated the idea that Jesus only *appeared* to be human but really wasn't, were challenged by the likes of John, who made it clear that, in Jesus, God was made flesh and lived among us (John 1:14).

Because he was human and struggled through the same kinds of decision-making processes that must be endured by every thinking college student, Jesus can be a model for them to imitate. But it will take a lot of biblically conditioned imagination to establish that model for young people who are searching for it. In this book, Bruce Main takes on this task. Bruce draws on his own struggles during his college days, and then examines the ways in which the hundreds of college students who have served with him in his inner-city ministries have worked through the crises in their own lives. He gives graphic examples of how difficult it is to figure out what Jesus would do, and even more difficult to live out Christ's example in one's own life.

What emerges on the pages that follow is not only a fairly clear picture of the imagined lifestyle Jesus would embrace if he were to be incarnated as a twenty-first-century student, but also good biblical and theological justification for the verbal pictures Bruce draws for us.

First of all, Bruce picks up on Jesus' preference for the poor. He points out that starting with his inaugural sermon (Luke 4:16–22), Jesus brings "good news to the poor." Bruce sees the poor as a special people whom Jesus' followers are expected to serve and defend. Furthermore, Bruce is convinced that the primary basis upon which people will be judged on judgment day will be how they responded to the poor. It is not that he is teaching a "works salvation." Bruce is too orthodox for that. It is rather that he knows that salvation comes only by having a personal connectedness with the resurrected Christ. He has picked up the truth grasped by St. Francis of Assisi, that the poor are sacramental, and that Jesus mystically presents himself to us through them. In a mysterious way, Jesus waits to be loved in the poor, and if we do not love Jesus in the poor, then we cannot say that we have a personal relationship with him.

This Franciscan insight is the raison d'etre for Bruce's own ministry, UrbanPromise. Over the years, Bruce has called college-aged young people, from across America and from overseas, to join him in his ministry located in Camden, New Jersey. He calls them to serve with him, not just because the children and teenagers of Camden need help, but because Bruce knows what will happen to these collegians when they encounter the resurrected Christ through the people they meet on the streets of Camden. In this book he gives us a host of stories providing evidence that young people go through life-changing transitions as they experience Christ through battered children, delinquent teenagers, foul-mouthed gang members, and drug-deadened mothers.

The concept of praxis plays a heavy role in Bruce's thinking. He is convinced that learning what Jesus would do in any given situation cannot be an academic process. Instead, it requires reflection in the context of action to learn such things. Ministry among the poor is so essential for experiencing Jesus, learning his ways of doing things and answering the real questions of college-aged young people, that Bruce expresses genuine regret for those who fail to accept his invitation to serve among the poor.

As you read through this book, you will discern not only the footprints of St. Francis, but also the impact that the life of Dietrich Bonhoeffer has had on Bruce's life. What is supremely evident is that Bruce intensely identified with Bonhoeffer's definition of Christian discipleship. He buys into Bonhoeffer's famous line, "When Jesus calls a man, he bids him come and die." During his years of doing ministry with young volunteers, Bruce has seen what happens to those who shy away from the high cost of discipleship. He understands that for college students today, as for Dietrich Bonhoeffer, following Jesus may require sacrifice. It may mean bucking the desires and plans that parents may want to impose on the young recruit for kingdom work. It may mean sacrificing a romantic relationship that interferes with a calling from God. And most of all, following Jesus definitely will require abandoning the lifestyle that is being prescribed by the culture via the media. In this book, Bruce clearly sets forth that to do what Jesus would do, if Jesus were a college sophomore (or freshman, or junior, or senior) today, requires radical commitment.

Bruce tells of the many young people who come to work with him on the streets of Camden but give up when they realize how hard it is to do what Jesus would do in the difficult situations in which they find themselves. He talks about those who go away sad, like the rich young ruler described in Mark 10, because the sacrifices required are too great for them. He talks about those who just cannot go all the way for the long haul.

As I read what Bruce had to say about commitment to ministry, I was reminded of the verse from the book of Isaiah that reads ". . . but those who hope in the LORD will renew their strength. They will soar on wings like eagles; they will run and not grow weary, they will walk and not be faint" (Isa. 40:31). This verse points out how so many of us start off in ministry like soaring eagles. We have an enthusiasm that seems to have no limits. We are thrilled and excited by the work we have to do. But it is not long before that original burst of enthusiasm disappears and we have to settle down into the routine and sometimes mundane tasks that ministry requires.

Ministry can be hard and the appreciation received can be little. The hurts can be many and the discouragements painful. There come those times when we are slowed to a walk, as the verse suggests. Can we keep going, even then? How we answer that question determines the nature of our commitment. The Bible says, "But he who stands firm will be saved" (Matt. 24:13). That's what Bruce believes.

When Winston Churchill was asked after the Battle of the Bulge if the British soldiers were braver than the German soldiers, he replied, "No! The German soldiers were just as brave as the British soldiers, but the British soldiers were brave five minutes longer." Bruce would like that story, because he has seen the fantastic fruit of those young missionaries who have "hung in there" when things got discouraging and come out as "more than conquerors." He teaches those who join him in ministry the truth of this verse: "Let us not become weary in doing good, for at the proper time we will reap a harvest if we do not give up" (Gal. 6:9).

Finally, I like what Bruce has to say in this book because he refuses to substitute religiously prescribed piety for true spirituality. He has seen too many volunteers for ministry come to Camden with legalistic formulas for Christianity and a language dripping with shibboleths that reek of a "holier-than-thou" superiority. With James, Bruce believes that true religion is to visit the orphans and the widows in their affliction (James 1:27). He is tired of those narrow-minded religionists who discount the spirituality of those who do not express their theology in certain specified phrases, or whose lifestyle does not conform to their own culturally prescribed dictates. His is a spirituality that comes out of a heart and life that loves justice, does mercy, and walks humbly with one's neighbors. "And what does the LORD require of you? To act justly and to love mercy and to walk humbly with your God" (Mic. 6:8).

There is much that Protestants and Catholics can learn from each other. Charismatics and old-fashioned Calvinists can teach each other many things, and liturgical ritualists and traditional freewheeling advocates of the new praise music need to learn to understand and appreciate each other's different worship styles. Bruce's ministry through UrbanPromise has made such learning possible for the young men and women who minister with him, and as you read about his ministry you will find yourself getting into that same inclusive ecumenical mindset.

This book is not just for collegians. People of all ages who are trying to figure out what Jesus would do in the complexities of our everyday life will find it extremely helpful. Bruce Main shows us what an anointed imagination can do, what learning about God in praxis is all about, and what a solitary life can accomplish when committed to Christ.

Tony Campolo
Eastern College
St. Davids, PA

Introduction

I pray that all those young people who have graduated
do not carry just a piece of paper with them
but that they carry love, peace, and joy. . . .
That they become the sunshine of God's love to our people,
the hope of eternal happiness and the burning flame of love
wherever they go. That they become carriers of God's love.
That they are able to give what they have received.
For they have received not to keep but to share.

Mother Teresa

Little is known about Jesus between his birth and thirty
years of age. Only Matthew and Luke make an effort to
record the awesome marvel and miracle of his birth. Even after
Joseph and Mary left Egypt and returned to settle in Nazareth
there is little biblical information about Jesus' formative years.
Luke does give us a glimpse of a precocious young boy who baf-
fles the religious elders. But besides this reference to a kid who
can go toe to toe with the teachers of his day, the Scriptures are
strangely silent about the teen and young adult years of Jesus.

Fortunately, orthodox Christian faith holds the belief that
Jesus, throughout his life, experienced the fullness of human
existence. Think of it—Jesus did not drop out of space like a
supernova on his thirtieth birthday. He was born at a real time
in history, in a real place—a place we can still visit. He ate food
and wore clothes. Jesus had a real job as a carpenter and certainly
got blisters on his hands. Jesus lived the common life of the people of his day. This is one of the most intriguing and important
Christian beliefs. We hold to what we call a "fully God/fully
human" doctrine. That means that Christians who hold to this
doctrine believe that Jesus did not magically skip over his
teenage years, move brain-dead through his twenties, and arrive
at his thirtieth birthday totally empty of cultural, religious, and

living experiences that shaped his personhood. Since Jesus was fully human, then all of his experiences—the teachings at the local synagogue, his earthly parents, the birthday parties he attended, the local gossip—must have played a part in shaping his personality and character, which ultimately prepared him for his three-year ministry. The experience of Jesus' life prior to his recorded ministry must have affected his personality, his methods of handling situations, his attitude toward people, his worldview, and his intellectual development.

The writer of the letter to the Hebrews builds on this doctrine of full humanity and contends that "we do not have a high priest who is unable to sympathize with our weaknesses, but we have one who has been tempted in every way, just as we are—yet was without sin" (Heb. 4:15, 2:18). This biblical writer affirms that Jesus was tempted in every way. We can conclude, based on this Scriptural affirmation, that if Jesus was tempted and can truly "sympathize" with our weaknesses during all stages of our lives, he must have experienced the fullness of childhood, the fullness of the teen years, and the fullness of what it means to grow into a mature adult. If Jesus experienced the fullness of these stages of life, then he must have experienced some of the growth pains and temptations that accompany these periods of our development. To me it is very affirming to know that Jesus can identify with me at any stage in my life. Although his culture was significantly different than ours, Jesus still experienced some of the pains and joys of growing into a mature adult.

Since the teen and early adult years in a Christian's life are key stages for establishing personal values, convictions, and a life calling, I have often wondered how Jesus' faith developed and changed as he physically grew and matured. Did his knowledge of Scripture increase? Did his prayer life become more disciplined? As Jesus entered into his adolescent years and began to shed some of his parents' faith—the things he learned in the synagogue—and discover a faith of his own, did he go through times of questioning the traditions of the Jewish community? Did questioning take the form of "rebellion" (not sin—there is a difference) as he sought to establish his relationship with God outside of parental participation? (The Temple scene in Luke, with Jesus talking to the elders, almost implies a kind of rebellion. Jesus was just a few years ahead of most of us.) Further, did Jesus serve God with acts of compassion, justice, and mercy prior to the years of his recorded ministry? If so, did those acts of service affect the way he exercised his ministry later in life?

This side of heaven we will never be able to answer these questions. But if we ascribe to the doctrine that Jesus was fully human (in the broadest sense of the term), I believe we have the right to ask the questions even if it makes some people within our faith communities a little uncomfortable. It is healthy to ask questions! One of the reasons so many college-aged students leave the church and find little connection with the body of Christ is because they do not find the church to be a safe place to ask tough questions. Perhaps this is why more and more college students are visiting chatrooms on the Internet for their spiritual nourishment. When they are online, students can enjoy anonymity, interact honestly with other spiritual seekers, and not be ostracized from the community for raising issues that church is afraid to address. Stripping Jesus of his superman status, through the asking of questions, can be a threatening enterprise to Christians who want to elevate his divinity and not embrace the weaknesses of his humanity.

The result of asking questions about the growing up of Jesus should not push collegians away from the Gospels. It would be a shame to see the "twenty-something" crowd interpret the absence of Gospel material in Jesus' late adolescent and young adult years as a sign to put one's faith on hold. Although activity during these years is not documented, I would like to believe that when the Scripture says Jesus grew "in wisdom and stature," he used every opportunity, every experience, and every stage of his life to develop his relationship with God and develop his skills, gifts, and talents as a human being. If Jesus approached his life in this manner, then the college student who seeks to grow as a disciple should be asking, "How would Jesus want me to use these critical years to prepare myself for a lifelong service to God? And how would Jesus want me to use this period of life to develop the disciplines, the principles, the knowledge, and the experiences necessary for a life of vibrant, well-grounded Christian service?"

When you begin to ask these questions, exciting things take place on many levels. During these critical college years, as you begin to prepare yourself for a life of dynamic service for God's kingdom, you become increasingly open to the movement of God's Spirit in your life. As you begin to take steps toward discipleship in the areas of prayer, spiritual discipline, service, and risk-taking, God will meet you and open new doors that you never knew existed. On another level, it is in the process of preparing yourself to be used by God that your faith becomes more deeply personal. Often when students have been raised in a church family, with the expectations of attending church and meeting a certain code of behavior, faith is not really personal. But when you begin to move beyond the expectations of your parents and church leadership and make decisions based on what you sense God is calling you to do, your faith moves to a whole new level. Rather than wrestling with the question "What do my parents want me to believe?" or "For the sake of fitting into my church, what should I believe?" you will begin to ask, "What do I believe?" and "How would Jesus want me to live out my faith?"

For many students this period of self-examination can be an agonizing experience. For the first time in your life, your worldview is altered and the security of your inherited faith is challenged. An agnostic professor may challenge your convictions in a philosophy class. A biology teacher may undermine your whole notion of the creation account. Evidence of Christian involvement in evil institutions like slavery and apartheid may cause you to question your heritage and history. All of a sudden Sunday school answers do not matter. Real answers must be found. Faith, for the first time, must be rediscovered, not just accepted because Mom, Dad, Pastor, Coach, or Teacher said it was a good thing.

The process of discovering a personal faith is crucial, slow, and often painful. When the term "personal faith" is used, I do not want to limit the idea to the present evangelical notion of asking Jesus to be your "personal savior." For the purposes of this book, a personal faith means the formation of a faith that is developed independently from the inherited faith of parents or significant authoritarian voices. Personal faith is something that is conceived through experiences, discussions, learning, and revelations from God's Spirit. A personally owned faith is something that results from a student taking the time to sit down and ask, "What do I really believe?" and "How is my belief going to affect the way I live my life, choose my career, and invest my time and life energies?"

The college experience is often a critical period of life for the formation of belief and the maturing of faith. For those who have the opportunity to attend college, this time can be conducive to reflection, learning and piecing together a new faith puzzle that will guide you and become a picture of what your faith walk will look like for the remainder of your life. For many students a career has not begun, a family has not been birthed, and, happily, a mortgage has not been obtained. A degree of freedom is enjoyed like no other period in life. Unfortunately, many students do not take advantage of this transitory time. Even with relatively few responsibilities, incredible freedom, a chance to reflect and think, and a growing distance from parental expectations, this crucial period of life evaporates quickly. I believe this time of life is unique, a special gift from God that must be used wisely and strategically.

I remember my sophomore year in college. It was that year that my faith was sent into upheaval. Yet at the same time the words of Jesus spoke to me as never before. I began to seriously ask myself what kind of Christian I wanted to be—or whether I wanted to be a Christian at all. Everything seemed to be up for grabs. As I began to ponder my faith and consider what it meant to be a disciple of Jesus, I knew some serious life decisions had to be made. Up until that point I had never thought about what it meant to be a real disciple of Jesus, and to allow every aspect of my life to fall under the Lordship of Christ. I was a Christian. I had said "the prayer." I had been raised in the church, and I was certain that my eternal salvation had been secured.

But then I entered my sophomore year. Everything began to unravel. All of the sudden I became aware that the world was bigger than my immediate surroundings. There were problems in this world that were growing each day. Poverty, injustice, racism, violence, and a host of other issues were affecting the lives of God's children. The questions I had to ask were, "Is there any connection between my faith and these growing social issues? Should my newly discovered faith have anything to say about these problems? Is Jesus really the answer to the problems in the world? Or is Jesus just a coping mechanism?"

I discovered that by trying to make faith practical and active during the college years my spiritual growth and future life plans were significantly and positively affected. Through service projects in Mexico, summer internships in the innercity, and ministry teams in local prisons, I soon discovered that my faith was most vibrant and most real when it was at work serving the lives of people who were hurting, who were poor, and who were disconnected from the church. It was through these experiences that relationships with other believers were formed, and my convictions, values, and life direction crystallized. To a large degree, involvement during those years of my life created a foundation on which I now live my life. Without those experiences and opportunities to deepen my faith, I doubt that I would be engaged in the work I do today. I am grateful for those life-shaping experiences.

How Did Jesus Spend His Early Adult Years?

When Jesus was finally called to begin his full-time service to God, there appear to be many qualities and characteristics established in his life that helped fulfill his calling. Jesus knew the Old Testament Scripture—he had obviously studied. Jesus woke up early in the morning and prayed—he had established discipline in his life. Jesus related well to all kinds of people—he had not lived in isolation and sheltered himself from the world. Jesus spoke in stories, parables, and a language that people understood—he had learned to communicate. Jesus knew the terrain of his geographical area—he had traveled the roads and paths of Palestine. Jesus understood the problems with formalized religion—he knew how to challenge its bankruptcy. Jesus knew the culture, the people, and the religious orientation of his world. By the age of thirty, Jesus had acquired the earthly skills and spiritual knowledge needed for God to bring about the kingdom through him. Jesus used his early adult years to prepare himself for public ministry.

If Jesus were a sophomore, freshman, junior, or senior, I believe he would use these years to cultivate lifestyle patterns that are consistent with the values of God's kingdom. These lifestyle patterns would develop a firm foundation for a life of commitment and service to God. Jesus would use his college years to enrich his faith, develop a clear sense of his life mission and vocation, and build good friendships that would encourage him in his calling. Jesus would get to know a broad spectrum of people so he could exercise tolerance and build unity and peace between people who are different. Jesus would spend time with the poor, he would grow in wisdom, and he would deepen his relationship with God. In short, Jesus would use this important period of life to equip himself as an effective kingdom worker. Like an athlete who practices through the repetition of exercise, Jesus would establish healthy kingdom behaviors that would guide him for the remainder of his days.

These are significant years of life that can never be recaptured. Sharon Parks, a prominent scholar on faith development in young adults, calls our college and university years the "critical years." She says that the ages between nineteen and twenty-four are "the birthplace of adult vision and the power of ongoing cultural renewal."[1] Parks contends that these years must not be wasted, as they are critical to our future and the future of our world. Forging this "adult vision" begins today as you give your classes, your relationships, your work, your experiences, and your time to God and ask for God's creative and empowering Spirit to take the experiences of your daily grind and transform them into behaviors on which a foundation for ongoing discipleship can be established and a kingdom vision for your life can be crafted. Therefore, *If Jesus Were a Sophomore* is *not* just a book for the college sophomore. It is a book for *any* young adult who desires to capture this important season of life called early adulthood for God's purposes and begin to put in place the building blocks for a future of faithful discipleship. The following pages are stories and ideas that I hope will provide guidance as you put this process into motion.

Note: When I was in college I was recruited by Tony Campolo to lead a ministry in Camden, New Jersey, called UrbanPromise Ministries. After graduating from college, a number of college-aged adults and I decided to move into the heart of one of America's most under-resourced cities and initiate a number of ministries directed toward urban children and teens. This "founding" group of college-aged adults were from different countries and represented numerous Christian denominations. What united the group was a common desire to live out our faith practically and make a difference in the world. Since those early days UrbanPromise has grown into a dynamic, holistic ministry providing programs that encourage academic achievement, develop life-management skills, equip for spiritual growth, and encourage the development of Christian leadership among inner-city children and teens. This mission is fulfilled through the operation of alternative schools, job-training programs, small-business development, summer camps, after-school programs, college-readiness programs, teen-mother counseling, and a host of other programs. UrbanPromise in Camden works with over seven hundred different youth on a daily basis during the course of the school year. Our forty full-time staff also host between sixty and ninety college students on a yearly basis who travel from all over the world to serve as both summer and year-round interns. These students engage in neighborhood-based, cross-cultural ministries daily and have the opportunity to reflect academically on issues of poverty, missions, personal spirituality, race, and urban youth ministry. UrbanPromise has also expanded into other under-resourced communities in Toronto, Vancouver, and Wilmington, Delaware. If you would like further information, please visit our Web site at www.urbanpromise.com.

Remember:

> I long to accomplish a great and noble task, but it is my chief duty to accomplish humble tasks as though they were great and noble. The world is moved along, not only by the mighty shoves of its heroes, but also by the aggregate of tiny pushes of each honest worker.
>
> Helen Keller

Questions for Reflection

1. How do you think Jesus would have spent his "college years"? What would have been his commitments? How would he have approached learning? What classes would he have taken? With whom would he have spent his time? What extracurricular activities would have occupied his free time? How would he have grown?

2. Is the idea of Jesus growing as a person, or being subjected to some of the growth pains you experience, difficult for you to embrace? If so, why? How do you deal with the tension between the humanity of Jesus and the divine nature of Jesus?

3. Do you feel you are maximizing your college years? Are you developing the kind of behaviors, patterns, habits that will help you live a life of discipleship after you graduate?

4. Do you view your college years as a special gift from God? Do you have a sense of urgency as to how to use this period of your life? How can you better utilize this time period?

5. Identify some areas of your life in which you need to grow.

Prayer and Meditation

Lord,

Thank you for this unique period of life.
Thank you for the privilege of school and learning.
We acknowledge that most of our world will never have this
    opportunity.
We are grateful for Your goodness.
We are reminded of our responsibility to be good stewards of
    Your gifts.

Help us to use this time wisely.
Help us not to waste this special period of our lives.
Help us to open ourselves to the work of your Spirit in our life.
Help us to develop the kinds of behaviors and commitments that
    will lead us to a life of faithful discipleship.

We pray that our lives will bear much fruit.
We pray that when we graduate we will not just carry pieces of
    paper.
We pray that we will be carriers of Your love, Your peace, and
    Your joy.

Amen

Chapter 1

Growing Behaviors:
Becoming Spiritually Big

Our deepest fear is not that we are inadequate. Our deepest fear is that we are powerful beyond measure. It is our
light, not our darkness, that most frightens us. We ask
ourselves, who am I to be brilliant, gorgeous, talented and
fabulous? Actually, who are you not to be? You are a child
of God. Your playing small doesn't serve the world. There
is nothing enlightened about shrinking so that others
won't feel insecure around you. We were born to make
manifest the glory of God that is within us. It's not just in
some of us; it's in everyone. As we are liberated from our
own fear, our presence automatically liberates others.

Nelson Mandela

When they saw the courage of Peter and John and realized
that they were unschooled, ordinary men, they were astonished and they took note that these men had been with Jesus.

Acts 4:13

On Becoming Big

The year was 1960. The city was the cosmopolitan port of
New Orleans. Supreme Court Justice Judge Wright had
just passed a law stating that schools could no longer be segregated
on the basis of skin color. The reaction of people in parts of the
southern United States was intense, emotional, and often cruel.

The William Frantz Public School became the centerpiece
of the issue for the nation when the first African American child
enrolled in this all-white school. As a result, white parents
pulled their children from the roster in an effort to boycott the
legislation that had just passed. As the nation watched on television, an absolutely incredible scene unfolded.

Each day a little six-year-old girl named Ruby Bridges would
make her way to school. On both sides of the street, parents

yelled obscenities and threw food at this precious girl in a white frock and pigtails. Surrounded by twenty federal marshals, Ruby faithfully made her way through the hostile crowd to a school that had been abandoned by all the white students.

In the North, a young Harvard psychiatrist named Dr. Robert Coles took a keen interest in this little girl. As a scholar and therapist interested primarily in how children in crisis cope, Coles was eager to find out more about this little one who found herself under the microscope of the nation. He traveled to New Orleans to meet Ruby and began the process of trying to understand how the first-grader was processing this horrific experience.

One of the first exercises Coles had Ruby perform was to draw pictures with crayons of her daily experience. Each day after school Ruby would spend time with Coles and put her child-like impressions and thoughts on paper. He quickly noticed that when she drew pictures of herself, these caricatures would be very small and often incomplete. Limbs would be missing. Often her face would have no features. Oddly, the caricatures of other (white) children in the pictures were always much larger than Ruby's self-portraits and full of features and color. Coles found the contrast fascinating.

In addition to observing the drawings, Coles took time to talk with her teachers. Somehow he had to figure out how this six-year-old could deal with such stress and yet continue to persevere. The answer to this question came one day when a teacher informed Coles that early that morning Ruby had stopped at the top of the stairs, turned to the crowd, and mouthed some words toward her hecklers. According to the teacher, this action had sent the crowd into a hysterical frenzy. The marshals could hardly maintain control.

That night Coles asked his young student about the incident. "Why," asked Coles, "did you stop at the top of the stairs, turn to the crowd, and mouth some words?" The response caught Coles by surprise. In the sincerity and simplicity that can come only from a six-year-old, Ruby responded by telling Coles that each morning, before she began the trek down the street toward the school, she would say a short prayer for the people in the crowd. She had forgotten to pray that day and decided that she had better do it before she entered the building.

Not believing that this six-year-old child had the capacity to really pray, the somewhat cynical Coles continued to probe. "What did you pray, Ruby?" "I pray," whispered Ruby to Coles, "'God, forgive them for they know not what they do.'" Coles

was astounded. Here was a six-year-old girl, under intense persecution, uttering the same words Jesus cried as he hung on the
cross. Somewhere in her brief life, young Ruby had picked up
this traditional Christian prayer of forgiveness. She was using
the prayer because she had heard her minister say that we are to
pray this way for our enemies. Although skeptical about issues
of a religious nature, Coles began to marvel at the faith of this
young girl.

Over a period of weeks, Coles noticed another theme emerge
in the drawings of Ruby. As this little girl persevered each day,
her drawings began to change. Slowly her self-portraits began
to expand in size. Slowly arms, legs, and facial features appeared.
Over time, the hecklers in the crowd, who once dominated the
portraits, were drawn smaller. Ruby's pictures of herself began
to grow in relationship to the size of the white people in the
crowds. Her crayon self-portraits were more fully human. Her
face now had features like a nose, a mouth, and eyes. A once bald
head was now covered in thick, dark hair. The pictures reflected
that something incredible was taking place.

When Coles probed Ruby for an understanding of the
changes in the drawings, she articulated a powerful revelation.
When the morning walks through the hostile white crowds
began, Ruby had subconsciously thought that her actions were
wrong and that she was inferior to the hecklers. In Ruby's mind
the crowds were justified in their outrage. Over time, however,
Ruby's perception of herself began to change. Slowly Ruby
began to realize that there was nothing wrong with her attendance at the Frantz Public School. Her fears of these frightening people dissolved as she prayed and confronted her enemies
each day.

Ruby's pictures revealed a great deal of truth. The crayon
drawings communicated the inner transformation of a young
girl who looked at fear, faced it, and became a bigger person
because of it. By stepping out each morning and facing this ugly
crowd—a crowd that would intimidate most adults—she grew.
Ruby slowly saw through the threats and became a model of
courage for which a whole nation could look to for strength to
fight the racist laws of the South. Originally Ruby had looked
up at these "giants" each day with a sense of inferiority and
shame. Soon she realized that they really were not giants! They
were simply insecure people who were afraid to lose their power
and place in society.

By not cowering away from crisis and difficulty each day,

Ruby developed the behavior of bigness. This timid, scared little girl gained confidence each day as she walked into the crisis and consequently established a pattern in her life that would foster growth in her as a person. Ruby did what most Christians would never do. Instead of avoiding crisis, she faced crisis. Unfortunately, in our contemporary Christian culture we have been seduced to believe that Christian faith is about avoiding crisis. Jesus is sold to us as a vendor of "personal blessing," one who eliminates pain and takes away our problems. From birth we are raised to think that the sole objective in life is to get a good education, get a good job, and then live a life that has a minimum of crises. Life is to be lived as safely and securely as possible. Unfortunately, walks down safe and easy roads do not create opportunities to grow as human beings and grow in our faith. I like Erik Erikson's definition of crisis when he claims,

> I must briefly define this ancient little word. In clinical work (as in economics and politics) crisis has increasingly taken on half of its meaning, the catastrophic half, while in medicine a crisis once meant a turning point for better or for worse, a crucial period in which a decisive turn one way or another is unavoidable. Such crises occur in man's total development sometimes more noisily, as it were, when new instinctual needs meet abrupt prohibitions, sometimes more quietly when new capacities yearn to match new opportunities, and when new aspirations make it more obvious how limited one (as yet) is. We would have to talk of all these and more if we wanted to gain an impression of the difficult function—or functional unity.[2]

Erikson looked at crisis in a much more positive light than we often do. According to Erikson, people need crisis in order to become "whole" people. When Erikson uses the term "functional unity," he refers to people who develop a strong identity and a strong faith, and who can stand against the "disorder, dysfunction, disintegration, and anomie" of our modern society. It is this "functional unity" that creates "the strong person" whose life is marked by an ever-deepening integrity of one's life and one's faith.

Ruby's experience of crisis in 1960 began the process of shaping a remarkable young woman. This crisis was, as Erikson describes, "a crucial period in which a decisive turn one way or another was unavoidable."[3] But it was this crisis that created a moment for Ruby (even at six years old!) to move to a place where she could think more deeply about herself, her faith, and her changing world. It was also this crisis that created a moment for her country to examine itself and begin to take some national steps toward healing and wholeness. A "decisive turn" took place in young Ruby's life. Through crisis, and through the interaction of her faith in the crisis, Ruby grew from a fearful little girl with an inferiority complex to a person who demonstrated tremendous inner strength and determination. Ruby had become a bigger person.

Tiny Churches, Tiny People, Tiny God

Our calling as Christians is to grow as people. God did not create us to stagnate and live in fear of change. God created us to become "big" people of faith. But we all know that growing and becoming big can be a painful process. For many the transition from high school to college is initially filled with anxiety and fear. New people, new classes, and new ways of doing things can all be intimidating. But to grow, one must step out and confront the fear. Everybody knows what happens to those who never move on from one stage in life to another. Friends who still hang around their high school campuses long after graduation are people who are not confronting new challenges and growing as people. Robert Bly, in his insightful little book *The Sibling Society*, argues that one of the problems confronting our nation is that people are not growing into mature, well-integrated, whole adults. We are increasingly becoming a society of adolescents where fewer and fewer examples of fully grown, fully matured people can be found. People are avoiding personal growth because it involves pain, confrontation, and responsibility.

One only has to look at dying churches to meet people who are afraid to grow. George Barna claims that "having studied thousands of churches and tens of thousands of church-goers over the last two decades, I am convinced that most Christian churches in this country lack the vision, leadership, passion, plan and resources to adequately satisfy people's spiritual hunger in ways that are relevant or satisfying."[4] In short, the church lacks big people—people who have the capacity to change, to dream, and to adapt. Barna goes on to say that the church is operating about fifty years behind the culture. He further adds that "we are faced with a daunting challenge: change quickly and significantly or fade from the scene."[5] But change for small people is frightening. To keep up with the ever-changing landscape of our society means living with a degree of discomfort. Barna is not optimistic for the church's future because he meets a church full of people who resist change and growth. He meets small people.

I remember sitting down in a South Jersey diner a few years ago with two members of a dying, inner-city church. One of the members, a deacon, had attended the church for forty years. He liked tradition. He liked the hymns sung a certain way. The other member was new to the church and had quickly found herself drawn to lead worship. She was a terrific pianist and had the potential to be a great worship leader.

"Perhaps we can pick the hymns up a notch," suggested Ms. Smith, the new pianist, between bites of pie. "Having livelier music might attract more people."

"No way," responded the deacon. "God knows that those hymns can only be sung one way!"

Unfortunately, the faith of the deacon had become so tied to "the way" things had been done that he could not make an adjustment that might help the outreach of the church. The bigger picture of reaching people had been lost in the focusing on small things like the cadence of a song. For this church leader, hymns could be sung only one way. Paul's idea of becoming "all things to all people that I might win a few" was not within his capacity. He had allowed his faith to be placed in the box of his tradition, his culture, and his emotional disposition. Because his God was so tightly restricted to the confines of his perspective and experience, he could not entertain the possibility that God might want to see some changes in the church in order to reach a changing community. Since he could not entertain the idea that God was bigger than his hymns and ritual, he could not adjust to the changing community that God so desperately wanted to love. Consequently he continued to help the church become increasingly irrelevant and detached from the people in the neighborhood. He was small, his God was small, and the church continued to grow smaller each day!

"Big people," on the other hand, are people who are willing to face their insecurities, adapt to change, and open themselves to becoming people who will allow themselves to be stretched. "Big people" are willing to invite a little crisis into their lives because they are willing to obey the prompting of the Spirit, step out of their safety zones, and experience a little discomfort. In a rapidly changing world, there is no greater time in the history of the church for the up-and-coming generation to let go of their security blankets and begin a faith journey that involves risk, pain, joy, and sorrow.

Bible Big

When we meet Peter in the book of Acts we have to ask ourselves, "Who is this guy?" "Where did he come from?" We meet a Peter who is now healing people. We meet a Peter who is now standing in front of political and religious leaders and defending Jesus. Peter is in and out of prison. Peter is a courageous man. Between the coward we meet in the latter part of Luke and this man we meet in the early part of Acts who is not afraid to die for Jesus, the reader witnesses a remarkable transformation. Peter has changed from a timid man to a man of enormous faith and courage.

The personal change is remarkable. This is the same man of the Gospels who saw miracles but did not really understand. This is the same man who heard parables but did not comprehend. This is the same man who ran when called to take a stand for his friend and teacher. And now the public looks at him in amazement. He has grown. He has become big!

So how does Peter move from being a spiritual half-pint to being a person who people look to with amazement? And, in turn, how do we move from being spiritually small people to people who are big in faith? Peter became "big" because he did not give up. After Peter denied Jesus, he repented of his sin, moved beyond his shame and embarrassment, and allowed himself to be filled with God's Spirit. Unlike Judas, who also denied Jesus, Peter was able to accept the grace of God. He did not wallow endlessly in his guilt. Not only did Peter accept God's forgiveness, he then began to take courageous steps of faith in Christ's name. In the chapters leading up to Acts 4:13, the reader meets the man Peter who is emerging as the leader of the early church. Peter is devoting himself to prayer (Acts 1:14), preaching (2:17), healing (3:7), getting arrested (4:3), and defending his faith (4:8). With each act of obedience, Peter grows. With each confrontation, Peter develops confidence. Through prayer, through preaching, through crisis, through difficulties, Peter's new faith is forged. Despite his slow start, Peter becomes the man on which Jesus Christ builds his church.

Real Students, Real Growth

The mission organization I work with—UrbanPromise—is committed to bringing college-aged students to the inner city for a year. One reason we provide this opportunity is because

God can use experiences of being immersed in new cultures, within new socioeconomic groups and potentially dangerous environments, to develop courageous and active faith in college students. With uprooted lives, and all their security blankets removed, an opportunity to take "the decisive turn" is created. With "props" stripped away, God really begins to make the changes necessary for a pilgrimage toward "bigness." One of our interns, Michelle, recently wrote the following:

> This past year of working with the poor has shattered the neatly constructed box I had created for my faith and God. Previous to this year, theological questions were dismissed as irrelevant to daily life and ignored in the hope that they would simply disappear. Although I had moved away from the faith constructs of my upbringing, my concept of God and faith remained essentially as a box. Both consciously and subconsciously I limited the power and magnitude of God and God's impact upon every aspect of my life. During this past year, this box has been effectively and thoroughly destroyed, and as a result, I feel like much of my year has been spent reconstructing a new and radical image of God.

Michelle's ministry experience caused her to grapple and struggle with questions regarding the God of her upbringing. Her confrontation with injustice, human suffering, and oppression caused her to reevaluate her Christian faith. This intense questioning and crisis of faith caused her to rethink many of her convictions and life goals. She is a bigger person. Her knowledge of God is growing.

Darla, another intern with our programs, went through a similar struggle when confronted with some of the harsh realities of the inner city. Like Michelle, Darla also experienced a crisis of faith, which ultimately led her to become a bigger person of faith. She wrote in her diary:

> So I found myself in the inner city one summer . . . Never knowing exactly why I was going, but feeling God leading me there, I trusted that it would become clear to me as time went on. If anything, however, it became less clear. I did not know why I was there and what I ought to be doing; I did not even know who this God was who had presumably led me there. I could not reconcile all of the senseless suffering I saw with my understanding of a good and sovereign God. How could I thank God for all the blessings in my life, and not hold God responsible for the lack thereof in others' lives? How could I pray? My faith in prayer presupposed a God willing and able to intervene

directly in the course of human history; how could I believe in and trust and love a God with such power who continued to let children suffer? Yet even as I raged against God, I began to suspect that in some small way my own heart's cry was a part of God's response. I now feel called to ministry because even when I cannot fathom the reasons behind it, I continue to believe in the enigmatic power of the Holy Spirit. Even when the pain in the world seems too much to bear, I am able to believe that God has the power to move the world because I can see that God has the power to move me.

Both Michelle and Darla came out of their year in the city bigger people. They took a risk to come to a foreign place. Both came out of fairly affluent middle-class backgrounds. Both students had been raised in the church. But it was not until they were faced with the difficult daily circumstances of the urban poor that their personal faith began to become transformed. Let's face it: When a Christian begins to allow him- or herself to be challenged by the radical claims of the gospel and the injustices of the world, it can be threatening and uncomfortable. But real growth is always uncomfortable. In order for our concept of God to grow and our faith to become "big," we must be willing to put ourselves in situations that shake us up.

I like the way Clark Pinnock sums up this journey toward "bigness" when he writes, "It's a long and painful process of growing into the full stature of Christ, but once we commit ourselves to God's program God will not stop for anything else. God really intends to submit every fibre of our being to God's life which shares God's power, God's knowledge, and God's eternity."[6] More than ever the kingdom needs young people who are willing to grow in the "full stature of Christ." It is when we grow into the full stature of Christ that mountains will be moved and the power of God will be released in our lives in unprecedented ways.

Why Is It Always the Tough Stuff?

It is difficult to understand that obstacles and difficulties can be used by God to make us into bigger Christians. It is always a real test of faith not to give up in the midst of difficult experiences and instead to use them as opportunities for growth.

A few years ago I was running a Bible club for young people. Shortly into the Tuesday night session two twelve-year-old boys began to disrupt my lesson. After trying to quiet them for the third time, I kindly asked them to leave the building and wait in the parking lot until the club meeting was over. When they resisted my request, I begrudgingly handed the meeting over to another staff worker, politely escorted them to the door of the church, and saw them out into the parking lot. I thanked them for coming and invited them to return when they could control their tongues.

Just as I was closing the door one of the little boys turned to me and yelled at the top of his lungs: "Fuck off white scum, fuck off!" "Excuse me?" I responded, rather shocked. "Fuck off! Fuck off! Fuck off!" continued the young boy with seething anger. I approached the little boy and asked him to apologize for the statement. Instead, all I received was the continued barrage of verbal assaults as he backpedaled to the edge of the property. He did not let up. All the way down Westfield Avenue the young boys screamed obscenities at me.

When I finally retreated back into the church, I felt as if I had been coated with a film of anger and rage. Each obscenity had stuck to me like a wad of mud. In the eyes of the young boys, I was perceived as the enemy. I was the white man who represented all that was bad about their family, their community, and their broken young lives. I was the one who had oppressed them. I was the one who was to blame for the absence of their fathers. I was responsible for the conditions in which they lived.

At that moment part of me wanted to just pack it up and quit. I had felt personally attacked. My role, my mission, and my calling were all brought into question by the obscenities of these little boys. Questions of self-doubt began to fill my mind: Maybe I wasn't supposed to minister in this community. Perhaps the smiles and the hugs from the other kids were just a mask. What did they say behind my back? Perhaps there was someone out there who could do a better job.

Consequently I decided to go to some of my African American friends and ask them how they would interpret the situation. I relayed the story, told them how I felt, and asked what they would do. Fortunately my friends were very honest. They shared about white racism and challenged some of my own prejudices. They also shared about the 14 million impoverished kids in America who have all but lost hope and blame a system that favors the privileged. These same friends gave me valuable insight into the frustrations of parents who are trying to raise good kids in communities that are dangerous and have inadequate educational systems, unhealthy environmental hazards, and few parks and recreational facilities. They opened my eyes to how racism has had a direct impact on inner city communities.

In the end, the experience proved to be significant in my development as a person and as a minister. I learned, with some pain, that the last thing the inner city needs is a bunch of white folk who think they can come in and change the world. I needed to learn that real, long-term ministry involves building trust, exercising humility, listening actively, and practicing patience. Real ministry involves taking some shots and experiencing criticism, but it also involves staying committed over a period of years so that relationships can move beyond the color of our skin. In a strange way the crisis created by the two little boys at the Bible club became an opportunity for learning and growth. By understanding some of the dynamics behind the four-letter words I was able to become a bigger person.

Redefining Big

In 1997 the world lost a very big person. The irony is that the physical stature of Mother Teresa of Calcutta was very small. In photographs next to other politicians and celebrities, Mother Teresa seemed frail and dwarf-like. Bent over, thin, and barely five feet tall, this tiny nun from the slums of Calcutta could move the hearts of thousands with her words. Powerful world leaders would listen to her concerns and act on her insights and humanitarian suggestions. Despite her human weakness and her lack of physical power, Mother Teresa moved the world closer to the heart of Jesus.

How did Mother Teresa become a spiritual giant, a "big" woman of faith? Mother Teresa became spiritually big because she became worldly small. She let go of worldly and personal agendas and embraced a kingdom agenda. It was in the embracing of God's agenda that she became big. And the embracing of God's agenda often meant committing to activities that were perceived to be of no importance by contemporary culture. Mother Teresa was faithful in little things. She loved until it hurt. She gave until she was empty. She even said, "There are no great acts; just small acts filled with love." Mother Teresa sought out crisis, human suffering, and people who were nobody to anybody. She confronted powerful people in her humility, and the power of God moved through her in mighty ways. It was through her faithful obedience to Jesus Christ that she became a person whom the world could not ignore.

The life and witness of Mother Teresa confirmed Jesus' definition of what it means to be a big person. As a matter of fact, in many of Jesus' teachings there are suggestions that the way to become big in the kingdom of God is to do the opposite of what the world defines as big. It is the last who shall be first. It is the humble and meek who shall inherit the earth. It is the servant who will be exalted. It is the weak and the poor who shall experience the power of God. By following the Jesus way of doing things we are slowly transformed into "big" people who have the capacity to do big things like move mountains and change our worlds.

To be a Christian means accepting an invitation to travel on a journey toward bigness. To be a Christian means saying yes to crisis, yes to hardship, yes to all those things that create "big" people. When we read the biographies of great figures of faith—Dorothy Day, Oscar Romero, Mother Teresa, George Mueller, and Dietrich Bonhoeffer, among others—we find that all of them had one thing in common: Their lives were full of crisis. Yet it was through this crisis and hardship that these people became giants of faith who did remarkable things in the name of Jesus.

If Jesus Were a Sophomore

I wonder how Jesus would react if he visited a few Christian clubs on a typical university campus? As he observed the Baptist Student Union, the InterVarsity Fellowship, the Fellowship of Christian Athletes, and the numerous other fellowships that meet regularly, what comments would he make? What challenges would he speak to those who make up these fellowships? What would he affirm? What would he critique?

I imagine that groups which insulated themselves from others on campus might raise some concerns for Jesus. People who have remained in their Christian incubators might evoke some challenging words from Jesus. Can you imagine Jesus giving the year-end wrap-up speech to a Christian fellowship group?

Jesus takes the microphone and begins.

"Thanks for the invitation to address your group tonight."

There is a noisy excitement in the group. The energy level is high. The worship band has set the mood by closing out the praise time with twenty verses of "He Is Lord."

"You have met together for the entire year," he continues. "I celebrate and applaud your commitment. You've sung your fill of worship songs. You've heard great speakers challenge you with biblical insights. You've spent time outside the meetings together, eating pie and drinking coffee until the wee hours of the morning at the local Denny's. I'm glad to see you support one another."

By this time the group members are feeling pretty good about themselves. The meeting has a celebratory nature. It is a time to reflect and remember all of God's blessings over the past year. But the Speaker is just getting warmed up.

"But how many of you have really grown in faith? How many of you have grown as my disciples? Sure you've gained a few spiritual pounds. You've digested a lot of data. You can quote a few more verses than you could eight months ago. But have you really grown? Have you put yourself in situations where you've been broken, challenged, and stretched because of your belief in me?"

The room is now strangely silent. There is little movement in the group.

"Look around you. This is basically the same group you began the year with. It reflects little diversity. Are there any new believers? Have you reached out to those who look and believe differently than you? Have you gone places where you are uncomfortable to go?"

By this point the group is under deep conviction. The Speaker is speaking truth.

"I'm afraid you've become a social club. You've created a comfort zone. You've made a little cocoon. Instead of using this group as a community that launches people into places where my light and love need to shine, the group has become an end unto itself. You've used this group as a shield to protect yourself from difficulties that come with the call of discipleship. How can you grow if you never put your faith into action? How can you grow if you do not follow the example I set with my life? You must understand that true growth involves far more than simply acquiring more knowledge about the Bible and spending more time singing songs about me. True growth comes when you throw yourself into situations where I'm the only thing you've got to hold onto. True growth takes place when you engage in conflictual situations because of me. Christian faith is not about making life easier. It is not some spiritual tonic that will help solve all your life's problems. Truly walking in my footsteps will cause you problems. Big problems. But it is through these problems that you will grow and experience God in ways that you could

never imagine. I leave you with these parting words. Grow! Risk! Step out in faith! Become a big person!"

The students are left stunned. The Guest Speaker has made his point. He walks off the stage.

I have to believe that a visit from Jesus might be the best thing for some of us and for some of the fellowships we attend. Jesus would spur us on to break free from our protective cocoons and place ourselves in situations that would create the kind of dissonance needed to nudge us out of our complacent worlds and into a place where we could experience the faithfulness and power of God in new and dynamic ways.

Lest we interpret this call of Jesus to personal growth incorrectly—through a kind of nihilistic, "X-Games" lens—it is important that a distinction is made between reckless, self-serving thrill seeking and acts of faith-filled discipleship. Jesus would not be calling us to jump off bridges with bungee cords attached to our legs while chanting "Trust in the Lord!" He would not be exhorting us to ride our mountain bikes down ridiculously steep and dangerous terrain, believing that we are truly "riding by faith and not by sight." There is a distinct difference between searching for a greater and more intense adrenaline rush and the taking of selfless risks for God's kingdom. The first quest serves the self. The first quest only meets the needs of the self and seeks to fulfill the self. The latter kind of risk-taking serves and betters the lives of others while stretching us as children of faith.

The Gospels are a powerful reminder that Jesus and his disciples were people who did not fear growth, confrontation, and difficulty. In the book of Luke, we learn that Jesus grew in "wisdom and stature." We often overlook this fact that the son of God actually grew and that Scripture says he continued to grow. Becoming a bigger person was part of the Jesus agenda.

Since Jesus modeled a commitment to growth in his own life, I believe Jesus would challenge college students to develop behaviors that would lead them to become people who are big in the kingdom of God. Jesus would encourage students to break away from lifestyle patterns that lead to personal and spiritual smallness and find places and situations that would create the kinds of crisis needed to really develop as kingdom people.

Jesus wants our notion of discipleship to continually deepen. Jesus wants our ability to walk in faith to become riskier and more expansive. Jesus needs a new generation of college-aged disciples who do not live in fear of the world, but who have learned to confront the world and in doing so have realized that they possess the strength and power to change the world. Jesus needs a new generation of "ordinary" students, equipped with a set of behaviors and commitments that foster personal growth, whom the world will look at with "astonishment" because of their courage and say, "These men and women have been with Jesus."

Remember:

What a great gift it would be if we could see a little of the great vision of Jesus—if we could see beyond our small lives! Certainly our view is very limited. But we can at least ask him to call us out of our small worlds and our self-centeredness, and we can at least ask to feel the challenge of the great harvest that must be gathered—the harvest of all nations and all people, including the generations of the future.

J. Heinrich Arnold

Questions for Reflection

1. To what moments, in your college experience, can you attribute significant personal and spiritual growth? List these experiences. In listing these experiences or moments, can you discover any themes, patterns, or events that might help you in developing growth behaviors for the future?

2. If you were to draw a "picture" of yourself last year and compare it to a "picture" of yourself this year, would there be any significant changes? Like Ruby Bridges, would you portray yourself as being a bigger person? Would your perceptions of the obstacles and challenges in your life be drawn any smaller?

3. Are there small things ("security blankets") that you are hanging on to that inhibit God from doing a big work in you? If so, what are some of those things? List them. Talk about them.

4. Who are some of your heroes of faith? Are they "big" people? Can you share anything about the decisions these people made throughout their lives that have helped them grow? What were their defining moments? What crisis did they have to go through?

5. What are some practical steps you (or your fellowship group) can take to move out of your "safety zone" and into zones where you will be challenged to grow? List these steps.

For the Leader

Ask your group the following question: If Jesus were to make a surprise visit to your fellowship, small group, or club, what do you think he would say? What concerns would he express? What would be his challenges to the group? How would he nudge the group members toward greater growth? Ask everyone to write down his or her thoughts on these questions and then share them with the group.

Prayer and Meditation

Lord,

I confess my fear of growth. I acknowledge my fear of change.
Give me the courage to persist through the pain of growing.

Create situations and events from which I can be stretched.
And fill me with the big vision You have for my life.

Identify the security blankets to which I cling.
Give me the faith to release these things that keep me small.

I pray for the day when I might live by faith and not sight.
I pray for the day when I might have the ability to move mountains,
Love unconditionally, serve joyfully,
    and abandon myself completely to You.

Amen

Chapter 2

Worldly Behaviors:
A Worldly Spirituality

Spirituality is about all of life and all of who we are. It has to do with moments of retreat and rush-hour traffic, with periods of silence and the noise of little children, with the communion table and the work bench, with hushed Sunday worship and frantic family dinners. The promise of "God with us" is not confined to the mountaintop. It is, in fact, an invitation to "know Christ and the power of his resurrection" right where we are.

Simon Carey Holt

Making Space for God

I had divided the staff into small groups. Borrowing a quote from a writer on spirituality who encouraged disciples to make space for God in the daily routine of life, I had each person in the circle answer the question, "How would you make more space for God in your day-to-day life?" Surprisingly the group stumbled into a rather lively discussion about what they thought making space for God really means.

To my right was Claire, a collegian from a fairly conservative evangelical church in the Midwest. Claire's response was that to make space in her life for God, she would need to disengage from activity and find more solitude. Claire needed more quiet times, more devotional minutes, more time to just be with God. She wanted to find time when her thoughts could be completely directed to holy things like "the Word," her "daily bread" devotional, and her collection of praise and worship music. By creating an environment of "isolated holiness," Claire thought she would become a more attractive target for God's periodic releases of the third member of the Trinity. Like standing in the middle of an open field during a lightning storm, in isolated communion with God, Claire thought she would stand a greater chance of getting hit with a bolt of juice from the Holy Ghost.

To my left was twenty-one-year-old Lucy Jones from Seattle, Washington. A self-confessed coffee addict and body piercer,

Lucy had only recently come to faith. After a little dabble in Buddhism and a few seminars on New Age philosophy, Lucy somehow landed on Christianity.

"Making space," began Lucy, "means trying to see more of God in my daily activity. In the complexity, hecticness, and confusion of each day, I want to see God's Spirit at work." I could tell that the group was a little taken aback by the response. Between the puzzled looks of perplexity creasing their foreheads, I sensed the group's dissonance and anticipated the coming questions: Can people make space for God in daily life by just looking at their daily routine differently? Can a person really connect with God in the presence of activity? The discussion began to heat up.

Those in the group who had been raised on a diet of finding and experiencing God in more "reality-free zones" like church, Sunday school, and quiet times argued that the way to really open oneself to the work of the Holy Spirit is to carve out more time in one's waking hours for distraction-free time with God. "Busyness, interruptions, and too much talking," they argued, "is a type of enemy of God—a kind of seducer who lures people away from their first love."

But Lucy held her ground. She did not want to cut back on her ministry duties, she did not want to turn away a teenager who needed someone to talk to in the middle of the night, and she certainly did not want to wake up an hour earlier each day. She wanted to find God in the *doing* of life. Somehow her faith depended on finding God intertwined in the relationships she was creating. In a room full of screaming kids, Lucy wanted to see God. In driving a van full of teenagers to choir practice, she wanted to see God. In her weekly trip to the Laundromat, she wanted to experience God. In the sounds of the blaring stereos and the high-pitched screams of car alarms, she wanted to somehow hear the voice of God. Could she? Was it possible?

Difference of Theology

The positions argued by the two different groups represent two very different theological positions. These two opposed positions are very connected to how we interpret God's activity and how we understand spirituality. One position holds to the idea that God works best when God does not have to compete with distractions. Real spiritual growth takes place in isolation. Our models include the desert fathers, the monastics, Jesus in the garden, or even Oral Roberts locked up in his prayer tower at Oral Roberts University. This position contends that when worldly cares and concerns can be locked away in a closet for a few minutes each day, the chances of meeting God are much greater.

Part of this theological position is fueled by ancient Greek philosophy, which split life into the sacred and the secular— matter and spirit. For Plato, what really mattered was the spirit of the human being. The body was simply a cage holding the spirit until it was released at death. The residue of this philosophy has seeped into our Western theology, and we continue to uphold the notion that "spiritual stuff" is both separate and better than the stuff of the "world." There is the stuff of God—like hymn singing, devotions, and chapel—and there is the stuff of "this world"—tulip planting, screaming kids, dirty city streets, and baseball. For some reason "the stuff of this world" proponents do not view matter as something that God can penetrate and work through. Because stuff of this world can so easily become distorted, abused, and used for evil purposes, it is believed that the best thing to do is avoid it. Better to play safe, avoid any temptation, and carve out moments of "purity" where we can be sure to find God.

But do we only find God in isolation? Do we only find God when we put on our reading glasses and press our noses up to the onion skin paper, red-lettered NIV, NASB, NRSV, RSV, New English, New King James, or Old King James version of the Bible? Or is God continually creating, continually revealing, continually speaking in the midst of daily activities, mundane chores, commonplace interactions, and water fountain conversations? Are these also conduits through which God works and speaks? Therefore, is "making space" for God less about restructuring our daily schedule and more about restructuring the way we look at life? Does "making space" have less to do about time with God and more to do with seeing God?

Where Are the Stories?

Every few weeks I ask our staff for stories about what God has been doing through and in their ministry. Often the results are discouraging. Sure, there are a few cute stories about what children have said. Someone might share how a little boy or girl has given his or her life to Jesus. But stories about God moving in unusual and creative circumstances are rare. Until recently I have not been able to understand why so few stories are generated. Why are the only stories worth telling stories about how many kids came to the altar on Wednesday night? Why are the only times when God moves those times when a church service is particularly emotionally charged? Why are the only miracles worth noting the miracles of someone speaking in tongues or being miraculously delivered?

I would contend that there is a direct correlation between so few "stories" and how we view the activity of God. Is God at work in the day-to-day grind of life, or is God only at work during those times of being set apart? If we simply view God's activity in terms of what has been defined as sacred activity, the result is daily life without any sense of the divine. One of the great travesties of so much evangelical spirituality is that it continues to suggest that the best place to meet God is on some space station halfway between heaven and earth. Put on the Christian praise tapes and escape the world!

The consequence of this kind of spirituality is that our lives become devoid of stories—great stories of God's movement in the ordinariness of our circumstances. If God's only activity is measured by how many say the sinner's prayer, or how many respond to an altar call, or how many dance to the music of the worship band, or whether the lyrics of my favorite Christian rock group made me cry, then we will miss the really great stories. We will miss seeing the relentless activity of God at work right under our nose. Our theology will continue to blind us.

Confessions of a Closet Jesuit

The best thing that ever happened to my spiritual life was being introduced to a bunch of Jesuit priests who minister in the city. A born-and-bred evangelical, I was always taught that the Catholics were good people with really bad theology—heretical theology at that. The doctrine of Mary would throw my Baptist friends into a tirade. A priest with the power to absolve sins? Come on, only Jesus could do that! And the crucifix! Why would they leave Jesus on the cross when he has risen?

One of my first encounters with the Jesuits in my city was hearing about a special mass that was held at Holy Name Church each spring. It was a mass for the children of a baseball league they had started. A special mass for kids playing baseball! They had crossed the line, I thought to myself. Sure enough, on opening day each spring, two hundred little boys and girls marched into the vacuous sanctuary of Holy Name Church in their sneakers and uniforms, baseball gloves clutched under their arms, their hats on backwards. The kids would take communion and then be sprinkled with holy water. After bestowing a special blessing, Father Clem and Father Rick would lead a processional through the streets of North Camden to the playing field. Should baseball come into the sanctuary? This was pushing it.

Then I learned that up until four years ago there was no Little League baseball in North Camden. In one of America's poorest communities, kids had nothing to do but hang out on the streets. There were no bowling alleys, no soccer leagues, no swimming pools. Just lots of concrete and nothing to do. Believing that children are close to the heart of God, and believing that God wants nothing more than to see children laugh, play, and exercise their small bodies, one of the priests decided to get some baseball gloves and bats donated and start a league. The rest is history. When kids thought of baseball, they thought of church. When kids felt the leather of their gloves against their sweaty palms, they remembered Father Rick blessing their gloves. Baseball was no longer just a game. Baseball was God-activity.

My next encounter with the Jesuits was at a Good Friday service. Instead of meeting in the church, like I had always done, the priests made a big wooden cross and marched through the neighborhood with their congregation. With somebody dressed like Jesus carrying the cross, a throng of people would weave through the crowded city streets. They would stop at various locations, read Scripture, and pray. At a corner where a kid was shot the month before, the priests and the people prayed for the child and for the family.

The next stop was a corner that was notorious for drug dealers and gang bangers. Again the group would stop and pray. They prayed that God would redeem and cleanse the corner from the evil. They prayed that the government would increase efforts to stop the trafficking of drugs. Next was a boarded-up, abandoned house. Here they prayed that the house would again become a home. They prayed for the groups in the city who worked on housing issues. They prayed for credit unions who offered low-income mortgages to needy families.

This was church? On Good Friday? When I finally conjured up the nerve to ask one of the brothers why they take "church to the streets," he responded, "Because it is in the streets that we find Jesus. Wherever there is brokenness and pain we find the Lord." It was a Good Friday service that I will never forget.

And then I understood. I understood why, within the Catholic tradition, Jesus was still on the cross. I understood why, wherever there is brokenness, poverty, and pain, there is usually some extension of the Catholic church. Jesus, our Emmanuel, did not resurrect simply as a sign for us to abandon the world and pursue God in far-off places. Jesus resurrected on a cross so that we would be reminded that in the midst of pain, despair, and suffering, God's Spirit overcame the power of evil and chaos by resurrecting Jesus. The Jesuits believed that that resurrection power is still at work in the bleakest of human conditions.

Jesuit theology is rooted in the thinking and spiritual disciplines of St. Ignatius. Ignatius believed that God could be found in all situations. Even in the most painful and deplorable of human conditions, Jesus could be seen if only our eyes were open to seeing. For Ignatius, space for God was not made by removing ourselves from the world. Making space for God was developing a discipline of seeing God at work in the midst of daily life, especially where life is most difficult. For Ignatius, all of life is a spiritual activity.

Jesus in the Wiping of Noses

The son of a friend of mine was in a tragic swimming accident between his eighth and ninth grade of school. He broke his neck, and in an instant my friend Susan's son was a quadriplegic. Determined to do the best for her son, Susan decided to enroll him in a Christian high school. She thought this would be a place where she and her son could find the kind of support needed to succeed. He would receive more love. Children would be less likely to tease him. He would be surrounded by people who loved God.

She set up a meeting with the principal and the key teachers. When she arrived at the meeting, she was asked a number of questions by the faculty. She felt a lot of tension in the room. There was a distance, a lack of warmth. She did not sense that the school wanted her son. The last straw came when one of the teachers, who had earlier seemed repulsed by the thought of the student holding a pencil in his mouth, asked, "And what would we do if your son sneezed?" In Susan's words, "That's not the kind of thing a mother wants to hear after finding out her son is a quadriplegic." She promptly got up and left. On the way out, her son's therapist, who was not a Christian, commented, "I wouldn't even send my dog to this school."

Susan began calling around to other schools in her community. Not having much luck, she finally called a Jesuit high school. After explaining the situation to the head priest, she was surprised when he invited her and her son to come and check out the school. He was warm. He welcomed the prospect of having a quadriplegic student in his school.

Susan and her son arrived at the school. As with the other Christian school, she met with some of the key faculty. But this time she sensed a totally different attitude. Rather than being seen as a liability to the community, the prospect of having a quadriplegic student in the school was perceived as a blessing. It was an opportunity for the community. Finally, after the teachers had explained a little about the school and had talked about their curriculum, they turned to the son and asked, "Do you have any questions for us?" Remembering the teacher from the Christian school, Susan's son looked at the committee and said, "What would you do if I sneezed in your class?"

One of the brothers leaned forward, looked Mark in the eye, and with tenderness and compassion whispered, "We would, of course, wipe your nose."

For the next four years Mark attended the school. Because it was a three-story school with no elevators, the wrestling and football teams were conscripted to carry Mark up and down the stairs each morning, at lunch, and after school. Mark eventually graduated. Mark went on to college. Mark succeeded because he was embraced by a community of faith.

Why did one Christian community view Mark as a liability and the other view Mark as a blessing and an opportunity? Again, I believe the way we treat one another can be directly related to our spirituality. If we believe that Jesus is met in the wiping of noses and in the drool of a very dependent young boy, then we will embrace him into our community because we want to see and experience Jesus. If we believe that God is present in the suffering and pain of people, then we will not turn away people who suffer.

But if our theology claims that God is only met in places that are set apart from the rest of the world, then kids like Mark might be viewed as a distraction to our pursuit of God. Because of the additional time demands and inconveniences associated with people of need, dependents like Mark are perceived as an obstacle to getting at God. Furthermore, places of poverty, pain, and chaos might be avoided because God is perceived to be "absent." To illustrate, I remember a young woman from Canada who arrived for a summer of service in the inner city. By chance I happened to read a postcard she was sending to her friends. She wrote, "I can't wait to get out of this living hell. Satan is victorious in this place." She ended up leaving early and not fulfilling her commitment. Sadly, she never allowed herself to see God at work, even in the most desperate of situations. Put bluntly: The way we think about spirituality affects the way we serve Christ.

A Possible Contradiction

It is important not to negate the importance of solitude, silence, and isolated prayer. All these spiritual disciplines are critical for disciples to grow in Christian commitment and life. Even those who are most engaged in the stuff of real life, like the Jesuits, spend time in stillness and quiet prayer. What is important is that a kind of spirituality is developed that finds God in both the quiet of "the closet" and the interaction of daily life. Making "space" for God is more than just carving out more quiet times. Making "space" for God requires a new orientation of how and where we seek to find God.

One discipline I have found helpful is to take a few minutes at the end of each day and write a brief story of how I saw God move in my interactions with people. I try to pick one episode or one snapshot in the midst of my busy day to meditate on and record. After recording the event I then ask, "What could God have been trying to say through this encounter?" or "What new characteristic did I learn about God through this event?" or "What biblical principle was amplified and made real in this brief moment in time?" I have found this exercise to be one of the most exciting spiritual discoveries for me. As one would view a roll of film frame by frame, I have begun to see each minute of each day as a small, but important, picture that is used to communicate God's ever-present creative activity in my life and in the world.

Let me share from a few of my journal entries:

December 3, 1999 1:45 P.M.

I'm sitting in a little office next to the sanctuary. Next to me is Scott, a young man who I have watched mature over the past ten years. He is about to get married. I'm the pastor, he is the groom. Nervously we wait for his bride (who is an hour late!) to show. Since we have time on our hands, we begin to talk, pray, and reminisce about our years together. It is a wonderful moment in time. A sanctuary full of people waiting. Music playing. And we have time to share stories.

"Tell me again how you met Juanita," I ask Scott.

"Do you remember when I was in South Africa?"

"Yes," I nod.

"Well, I was jumped by a guy with a knife. He stabbed me and tried to kill me. I ended up in the hospital for a couple of months."

The story was becoming clearer to me.

"Guess who my nurse was?" he smiled.

We both have a good laugh. God has a great sense of humor. How ironic. The act of evil committed against Scott has been transformed into something beautiful. An act of violence and hatred has brought two committed Christian young people together in marriage.

Scriptures are again lived out before me. I am reminded of Paul's admonition to the church in Rome: "All things work together for good for those who love God." Once again, the Scriptures are fulfilled before me. What is God teaching me? The Scriptures are not just empty words. The Bible is not just an antiquated historical document. The Word of God is living. The promises of God are again fulfilled.

November 24, 1999 3:20 P.M.

I've just finished a wonderful Thanksgiving meal with some friends and their guests. After dinner I engage in conversation with a man named Mau. He is a Vietnamese refugee who has built a wonderful life for himself and his family in the United States. He is not a Christian.

His story is fascinating. As a young boy he fled his country by boat during the communist takeover of his country. While in a refugee camp in Southeast Asia, his family was sponsored by a Lutheran pastor to come to the United States. A particular church provided a home and an opportunity for his family to get started in this country. I would have thought that this act of generosity would warm him to the Christian faith. I sense a bitterness.

When I probe for more details, I discover that the Lutheran

pastor eventually did something that Mau thought was extremely dishonest and deceptive. The actions of the pastor hurt Mau's family.

For the past twenty years Mau has been closed to anything about God. Why? Because the one "man of God" he knew was dishonest. Mau asks me, "Why would I want to join a movement where its leaders do not act out what they preach?" I try to explain that this one Lutheran pastor is not representative of all Christian leadership. But it is hard for Mau to understand. Mau has integrity. Mau's word is as good as a contract. "Why do I need God if I have more integrity than a pastor?"

What is God teaching me? What is my lesson? As a leader I must be careful. I must realize that my actions may lead people either closer to God or further from God. I must understand the weight of leadership. My actions do matter.

December 6, 1999 9:03 P.M.

I'm loading the dumpster next to our offices. It's a dark, cold December night. From across the street comes a voice, piercing the crisp night air.

"Rev. Bruce, is that you? Rev. Bruce is . . . is . . . that . . . that you?"

Slowly coming toward me is the small frail body of a woman. It's Rhena. Rhena is a woman I have known for a number of years. Her life is chaotic. She lost custody of her children because of a drug addiction. She is always desperate, living on the edge. She gets close to me. Because of the reflection of the street lamp, I am able to look into her terrified eyes. They have that frantic look—like a deer mesmerized by the headlights of an oncoming car. I can tell she is scared. Before she makes her usual request, I decide to be proactive.

"Rhena, would you like to come inside? We've just been decorating for Christmas. Have some hot chocolate, a few cookies?"

She follows me to the front of the building and we walk through the front doors. Immediately we are enveloped by a cacophony of sweet smells, brights colors, flashing lights, and the sounds of Christmas carols against the background laughter and chatter of our staff. I notice Rhena's eyes filling with tears. For the next hour, Rhena eats Christmas cookies and drinks six cups of hot cocoa. I can tell she is relishing the moment.

The next morning my secretary buzzes me about 10 A.M. "Bruce, there is a Rhena in the lobby. She needs to see you."

I hesitate. "Okay, send her down."

I meet Rhena at my office door. She reaches out for my hand.

"Thanks for last night. Thanks for inviting me in. My life was unraveling again. When I walked through the doors I sensed peace. I felt peace. Thanks."

Rhena turns and leaves the office.

What can I learn from this encounter? What is God trying to teach me? How can this interaction help me grow in faith and love? I first reflect on God's incredible grace and love for all of creation. God's grace extends to even the most messed-up, dysfunctional people. Rhena needed to come into "the Inn" and experience the peace of the Christ-child. God, in God's wonderful grace, led Rhena to us. And, for a brief moment in her chaotic life, she experienced God's grace in a special way. The Christmas message is for everyone, not just those who can find their way to a church. There is room for everyone in the Inn.

If Jesus Were a Sophomore

If I had an opportunity to go back in time and spend a week with Jesus I wonder if I would be disappointed. After walking miles and miles along dusty roads, shucking grain in farmers' fields for dinner, rowing across bumpy bodies of water, and listening to the disciples moan and complain, I can imagine the following dialogue:

"Jesus, when are we going to get to the spiritual stuff?" I begin.

"This is the spiritual stuff," he replies. I'm startled and caught off guard.

"But what about the miracles, Jesus? You know, the stuff I read about in the Gospels. I mean, all we've done today is wash some feet, eat breakfast with a sleazy tax collector, and counsel some woman about her promiscuous sex life. We haven't even had a good night's sleep—we can't even find a place to lay our heads! Animals have better accommodations than we have had, Jesus. What's so special about this?" comes my reply after a hot and exhausting week.

"The miracles are the exceptions, not the rule," replies a patient Jesus. "The problem with the Gospels is that the writers took three years of my ministry and reduced it to a highlight film. I wasn't doing miracles twenty-four hours a day. Time passed between the miracles."

"Well, what about worship, Jesus? You know, shouldn't we get some guitars and spend some time praising God?" I ask.

"How about if we make our whole lives an act of worship?" responds

Jesus. "Sure, you can wake up with me at sunrise and come and pray, but why don't we allow God's Spirit to enter into all that we do today?"

Invite God's Spirit into all that we do, I think to myself. I guess that would include all the ordinary stuff too.

"I'll give it a try, Jesus. I'll give it a try."

Simon Carey Holt put it wonderfully when he wrote, "I have long been fascinated with the domestic nature of Jesus' spirituality. Time and time again in the Gospels, Jesus embraces the most ordinary of circumstances and places, finding within them rich sources of spiritual meaning." Holt continues by adding, "Of course, moments of withdrawal are an important aspect of Jesus' relationship with the Father, but they are always the exception. Jesus spends the largest part of his time in the most everyday settings—homes, neighborhoods, and marketplaces—identifying and responding to the presence of God."[7]

It is interesting that Jesus did not call his disciples to the desert. Rather, he modeled the spiritual journey by living in the heart of daily reality. Jesus' spirituality was not a spirituality of isolation. Jesus' spirituality was found in boats, in vineyards, in graveyards, and in the marketplace.

God can teach us something through every moment of every day. Sometimes our most profound spiritual discoveries are not found during our daily devotions or locked in the prayer closet. Our most profound and important spiritual discoveries can be found in reflecting on the events of our day and asking God's Spirit to use those events to teach us important life lessons and reveal spiritual insights. It is in the middle of our daily routines—our conversations in the coffee shop, a late-night walk under the stars, an unexpected meeting with a professor, dissecting a part of God's creation in biology, or an introduction to a new novelist—that God wants us to take note and discover some new aspect of what it means to be a growing Christian. I believe Jesus would encourage collegians to begin the process of finding God in daily life. I believe Jesus would want young adults, beginning to take their spiritual journey seriously, to cultivate the behaviors of seeing God at work in the most mundane of human activity.

Remember:

If we view everything and everyone, every event and every structure, as capable of reflecting God . . . then we begin to look at the sacramental dimension of life in a different way.

Robert Banks

Questions for Reflection

1. How do you "make space" for God? Do you meet God "away" from the mix of life? Or do you seek to find God's presence in all aspects of your daily routines?

2. List five situations, encounters, or events that have taken place in the last twenty-four hours. Ask yourself: Was God part of these activities? Did you invite God to participate in these activities? Do you think God was trying to teach you something from these encounters? What can you do to try and see more of God in the ordinary stuff of life?

3. St. Ignatius developed a discipline called the Examination of Conscience. He challenged his followers to spend ten minutes at the end of each day to reflect over the day's events. He first asked God's Spirit to settle and calm him. Second, he spent a few minutes thanking God for the little gifts he had been given—specific things. Third, he reflected on the various events of the day and asked this simple question: "Was I open to God who is always there with me?" If he was not open to God, he asked for forgiveness. Spend some time performing this exercise.

4. Write down an event or encounter from your day. Reflect on this moment and try to discern if God was trying to teach you something through it. Write down your reflections.

For the Leader

Ask your group the following: What do you think it would have been like to spend a week with Jesus and his disciples? Ask the group members to share what they would struggle with most. Ask the members to discuss how walking with Jesus on the hot, dusty roads of Palestine might help them to integrate more of God into the ordinary aspects of their lives.

Prayer and Meditation

Lord,

Sometimes it is so ordinary to live in the muck and mire of life.
Sometimes I just want to hang out on the mountaintop, and live
in the ecstasy and glory of Your presence.
Protect me, Lord, from using my faith to escape this world.
Shield me from the temptation of dividing life into that which is
spiritual and that which is earthy.
Help me to see You at work in ALL aspects of life.
Help me to believe that You are more interested in how I treat
my neighbor than how excited I get during worship.
Help me to invite You into the most ordinary of my daily routines.
Help me, Lord, to listen to my life.
Help me, Lord, to hear Your voice and experience, Your revelation
through the people and circumstances of my day-to-day
existence.

Amen

Chapter 3

Gratitude Behaviors: Cultivating an Attitude of Gratitude

Joy is the most infallible sign of the presence of God.
Leon Bloy

This is the day that the LORD has made, let us rejoice and be glad in it.
Psalm 118:24

God in the Waves

The great reformed theologian John Calvin had an amazing view of God. Calvin believed that God was so intimately connected with creation that nothing happened without God's involvement. According to Calvin, the world was not simply created by God millions of years ago and then left spinning throughout the universe. Not only did God create the world, but everything that happens within the world happens because God wills and enables it to happen. Calvin's theology leaves little room to chance. But Calvin did more than just throw around lofty adjectives to describe God, such as "sovereign," "omnipotent," and "omnipresent." Calvin challenged Christians to buy into his concept of God and make this concept of God an existential reality in their lives. Calvin believed that if Christians really believed in a God who was intimately involved in every aspect of creation, the way Christians lived out their lives would be different from those who did not believe.

In Calvin's best-known work, *Institutes of the Christian Religion*, he describes a God who begins each day by literally dragging the sun across the sky. The rising of the sun in the morning and the setting of the sun each evening all connect to God's activity. Therefore, every new day is a gift from God. Furthermore, every wave crashing against the beach is mysteriously drawn in by God, and every wave returning to the ocean is somehow released by God. Human beings, Calvin contends, are given each breath by God. When our lungs expand it is God

41

pushing in the air. When our lungs retract God is present and active as the air is released. Even when our hearts push blood into the outermost areas of our body, God is actively stimulating the heart and other necessary body parts to keep the blood flowing. Nothing, absolutely nothing, happens because of chance or luck. Everything happens because the God of the universe causes it to happen.

The theology of John Calvin makes some Christians nervous. This kind of theology raises difficult questions about God—questions like: If God is involved with every act of the world, what about natural disasters? Why does God allow evil? Can God prevent accidents? The questions are endless. If one wants to read through a thousand pages of tough theological thinking, he or she may be able to find some answers. What is interesting, however, is that in the midst of all of Calvin's theologizing his message to the Christian community is clear: Because nothing happens by chance, the appropriate response from the Christian is to live a life of continual thanks and gratitude. At the heart of the Christian life, exclaimed Calvin, should be the behavior of continual, ongoing, uninterrupted thanksgiving and gratitude expressed to God.

Obviously not everybody—even those within the Christian community—can buy into Calvin's explanation of how the world functions on a day-to-day basis. People are ready to accept God as Creator, but how the intricacies of life on our planet play out on a daily basis is still a profound mystery to many. People believe in God, but they are not ready to consent to the fact that God makes everything happen. It is fascinating, however, that the secular science community is becoming increasingly aware of the precise order and balance within the world and universe. Joseph Campbell, for example, who by no means is an evangelical Christian, commented that scholars in the field of science are becoming increasingly convinced that "whatever name you want to give to the higher power, there is a master planner who has left nothing to chance." Calvin may be closer to the truth than many give him credit for. Consider the following information given from a wonderful Brennan Manning sermon called "Healing Our Image of God."

1. If the slant of the earth shifted less than one degree from its present position, the vapors from the ocean would move both north and south, piling up huge continents of ice.

2. The weight of this planet has been estimated as six trillion tons. Despite this massive amount of weight, the earth is per-

fectly balanced and turns on its axis at the rate of 1,000 miles per hour. This travel adds up to approximately 25,000 miles per day, close to 9 million miles per year. Considering the enormity of our planet rolling at this considerable speed, revolving around the invisible axis and being held by an invisible hand of gravity are quite extraordinary feats.

3. Consider the sun. Every square yard of the sun's surface constantly emits an energy level equivalent to something being propelled at 130,000 miles per hour—that is comparable to the power of 450 eight-cylinder automobiles in every square yard of the sun's surface. Scientists say that if the sun's interior were completely filled with coal, the entire supply of coal would have been burned up in the first 5,000 years of the sun's existence. Radiocarbon dating tells us that the sun is a relatively young 4 to 5 billion years old. If we covered the sun's surface with a 50-foot-thick sheath of solid ice, this frozen cover would melt in approximately 60 seconds.

4. Within the animal kingdom there is an order to life that is absolutely remarkable. Potato bugs and canaries hatch in 14 days; chickens hatch in 21 days; ducks and geese hatch in 28 days; mallards hatch in 35 days; parrots and ostriches hatch in 42 days. Everything hatches in multiples of seven. Is this chance? Or is there a design to the universe?

The royal albatross bird, found in the South Pacific, has an 11-foot wingspan. This bird can fly 600 miles with fewer flaps than it takes a sparrow to fly across the street. Furthermore, the albatross can sleep while it is flying. Because of a special device in its brain, the albatross can adjust its flight patterns as the wind changes without even waking up! The most amazing aspect of the albatross is the built-in desalinization process that can produce fresh water from salt water on long trips. While countries in the Middle East spend millions of dollars to perfect this process and produce factories that can extract dangerous salts, God has already perfected this device in the albatross. Is this just a result of Darwin's "survival of the fittest," or is there a creative God behind all these incredible intricacies?

5. In a book called *The Computer Age*, a modern scientist decided to try to calculate the value of a single human brain cell. The scientist put a price of 5 cents on each of these cells. He then priced the connectors at one penny. With the brain being made of over 10 million neuron cells, the final cost for one human brain would be 1 quintillion dollars! This is more than the net worth of many countries in the world.

By spending a little time reflecting on the natural world, one begins to see some incredible traces of order and balance. Whether it is the hatching patterns of ducks and birds or the precise slant of the earth, it all seems a little too complex to believe that it just happens by chance. What the scientists share with us and what theologians like John Calvin espouse force us to look at our lives as a miracle and a gift. We must ask the question: If God is really this intimately involved in the ongoing creation of the world and in the sustaining of our lives, then must we not begin to live our lives in a perpetual state of gratitude because each breath, each sunrise, and each heartbeat is given to us by God? If both science and theology dictate that there is an incredible order to life and that the handprints of God are evident everywhere in creation, then we must begin to view our lives through this same lens. Believing that our lives are given by God, sustained by God, and ultimately taken by God should profoundly affect the way we live our lives and the attitudes we hold toward life. Psalm 118 helps give further clarity to this idea.

Psalm 118

The writer of Psalm 118 majestically coins the words, "This is the day that the LORD has made; let us rejoice and be glad in it." This verse of Scripture has been sung frequently in worship services throughout the Christian community. Psalm 118:24 is one of those famous verses that everyone has heard several times. Unfortunately, it is seldom understood within the broader context of the psalm.

Throughout Psalm 118 we read about a man who has been to the brink of death. Earlier in the psalm, the psalmist claims that enemies "swarmed around me like bees." The psalm suggests that the writer comes very close to death. He was surrounded. He was as good as dead. To really understand what was happening in the psalm, picture yourself completely surrounded and backed up against a wall. You look to your left—an army is closing in. You look to your right—there is a mass of soldiers moving forward. Straight ahead there are hundreds of fierce-looking soldiers getting closer and closer. Behind you is a sheer mountain wall. There is no escape. You close your eyes and wait for the predictable outcome. The footsteps come closer and closer. You close your eyes and begin to cry out to God. Louder and louder you cry! Finally you pause, look up, and see that the army has been diverted. Just before you were to breathe your last breath, the impending army was sent in a new direction. Your life has been spared from the jaws of death. Life takes on a whole new meaning.

It is at this point that the psalmist cries, "This is the day that the Lord has made!" The only reason why the psalmist can make this statement with such passion is that his life has truly been given as a gift from God. There is no reason for him to be alive. He was a dead man and God somehow gave him another shot at life. Because of the absolute assurance that his life is intimately attached to the hand of God, this man's life is changed forever. His response for another chance to live, breathe, smell, walk, and smile is one of rejoicing and gladness. He will pray prayers of thanksgiving. His life will be an expression of gratitude to God.

For those who have had a close encounter with death, the impact these encounters make can be very profound. Life, after a brush with death, is looked on with completely new eyes. It can be one of those moments that changes the entire course of your life. A few years ago one of our college interns was held up at gunpoint in a carjacking. The experience affected his life profoundly. This is what D.J. wrote:

> They told me to lie face down in the middle of the street. The asphalt was cold and hard. The gun was placed firmly against the back of my head. They told me to give them the keys to the car. I fished around in my pockets for what seemed like an eternity looking for them. . . . I was left lying there in the middle of the street, unharmed, but with the sensation of the gun's barrel so strongly implanted on the back of my head that I can almost feel it now as I write this some years later. . . . I would not want this to happen to me again, but the fact that it did happen forced me to face some fears and wake up to some realities that hitherto had only been ghosts in my imagination. The first thing it taught me is that God is real. This is something that as a Christian I "know," but often it is not something that I feel. But having gone through that experience, I have a different perspective. In moments of doubt, I can recall myself lying face down on that street and praise God for what God did. . . . I thought I was safe because I was twenty feet from a lighted house filled with a dozen other missionary friends, but God showed me that no walls of our own making, no camaraderie or fellowship can save you in the end. God will be there with us.

D.J. encountered the notion of death in a way he had never experienced. The experience, however, shaped his life and gave him a renewed perspective on faith and the role that God plays in giving us life. D.J. will never be the same. When he begins to take life for granted, he will remember the night he lay on the cold asphalt of Thirty-second Street, wondering whether he would see his friends again. D.J. will remember that God gave him another chance to live. His response will be a response of praise.

Why Are Our Lessons So Difficult?

A middle-aged man named Jack used to hang out on our campus just outside of the library. Jack would take a bus to campus each day, sit on a little wooden bench, and wait for students to come to the library and study. I used to dread trying to get past him. I was always greatly relieved when he had already snagged another student. If Jack got you by the arm it would be at least a half hour of your time. For "busy" students this was seen as a tremendous inconvenience.

Jack was severely challenged. His legs and arms spoke of the tragedy of a disfiguring disease in his life. Walking was a great chore. His speech was barely audible. Jack's hygiene also reflected the difficulties he had washing his hair, shaving his face, and brushing his teeth. Patches of unshaved facial hair, yellow teeth, and greasy hair all made Jack appear dirty and disheveled.

One day I was sitting in the cafeteria, enjoying my egg-and-cheese omelette and reading the daily sports page. The coffee was particularly good, and I was really enjoying my few moments of solitude before the day was to begin. Out of the corner of my eye I saw Jack walk through the cafeteria door. I quickly raised my newspaper another notch, hoping he would not see me. I was too slow. He was on his way to my table.

Slowly Jack dragged his twisted body across the cafeteria and plunked himself down on the chair across from me.

"Gooooood . . . moooooorning," he stammered. I dropped my paper reluctantly and returned the greeting.

He asked me what I was doing. I told him that I was really enjoying reading the paper and eating my eggs. He did not get the hint.

"Did . . . did . . . did you take a shower this morning?" I could tell that he had not. His hair was matted.

"Yes," I replied with little thought.

"Did . . . did you thank God for your shower this morning?" continued Jack.

I pondered for a minute. I did not usually thank God for showers. "No," I confessed.

"Did . . . did you shave this morning?" The splotches of missed haired on his face revealed that he had tried to unsuccessfully.

"Yes," I answered again, stroking my smooth chin which I had shaved that morning with such ease.

By this time in the conversation, I knew what was coming. I knew that Jack would be coming back at me with another statement of indictment.

"Did . . . did you thank God for helping you shave this morning?"

I had to confess it again: "No."

Then out of the blue, like a voice of one of the prophets of old, Jack commanded me to get down on my knees—in the middle of the cafeteria! I could not believe it. There, in front of all my professors and all my peers, I was being instructed to get down on my knees by this severely disfigured man. I had no choice. I had to do what he instructed me to do.

I got down on my knees. I was embarrassed. I felt as if every eye in the school was on me.

"God, I . . . I . . . I pr . . . pr . . . pray," began Jack in a loud, slurred voice that seemed to reverberate throughout the cafeteria, "that this man would become grateful for what you have given to him. Heeee . . . lll . . . ppp . . . help him to rejoice continually that he . . . he . . . he can sh . . . sh . . . shave with ease and wash his hair."

Jack continued to pray for me. He prayed that I would be grateful for the things I took for granted. He prayed that I might be thankful for all the little things God had given me. He prayed. And he prayed. When he finally finished I got up. He turned and slowly limped out of the cafeteria.

When I reflect on my experience in school, the event with Jack in the cafeteria stands out like no other event. Of all the learned professors I sat under, of all the scholars and thinkers I took notes from, the moment with Jack in the cafeteria was probably one of the greatest learning experiences of my life. The humble had taught me a tremendous lesson. It was the voice of the weak that convicted me of my sin. The "unlearned" and the "uneducated" had given me my most valuable life lesson. I learned that day that life is not by chance and that God had given me some amazing gifts and abilities. I needed to be grateful.

Infectious Rejoicing

We are not called to live stupidly and put ourselves in grave danger just so we can learn to be grateful people. But we are called to live lives that reflect a deep sense of gratitude for what God has given us. We may never have a gun pointed at our head, but many of us have great health, food, shelter, and a host of other luxuries that many others in the world do not share. The fact that we are in university or college is a display of our amazing privilege. Looked at in perspective, less than five percent of the world's population will ever have the luxury of pursuing a college degree. In many inner-city communities in this country, more than 50 percent of the students drop out of high school between the ninth and twelfth grades. College is a privilege. We are a blessed and privileged people.

The classic devotional book *Closer than a Brother* tells of a little monk named Brother Lawrence who washed dishes in a Swiss monastery. The amazing thing about Brother Lawrence is that he did not care about the specific task he was called to do. What he cared about was how he used the task to grow closer to God. Life tasks were not what gave Lawrence his identity and worth. Whether he washed dishes, preached sermons, or wrote books, it really did not matter. All aspects of his life were done to the glory of God. While washing dishes this monk "practiced the presence of God" by continually thanking and praising God. Lawrence disciplined himself to become a person who continually practiced the presence by cultivating a spirit of thankfulness in his life. As a result, Lawrence became a legend throughout Europe. People sensed a joy and an aliveness in Lawrence that compelled them to travel great distances to be with him and learn from him. Somehow in the menial tasks of day-to-day existence, Lawrence was able to transcend the mundane and connect with God in a very real way.

This kind of discipline does not always come easily. It is difficult to discipline one's mind to think of the good things in one's life rather than the negative and cynical. With so much distraction and negativity in our world it is next to impossible to develop this life of continual praise and gratitude. One practical way to help develop this discipline of cultivating an "attitude of gratitude" is to create a journal that forces you to focus on specific things you are thankful for. Go spend ninety cents on a rule-lined book and let it become your "Gratitude Journal." At the end of each day, take twenty minutes reliving the day to find things in that day that you can be thankful for. It is amazing that even the worst of days can turn into times of praise when we look deeply at our lives and begin to see the amazing presence of God's hand in sustaining our lives and giving us what we need. The great Catholic writer Thomas Merton captured the essence of looking for God's involvement in our day when he claimed,

> Life is this simple. We are living in a world that is absolutely transparent, and God is shining through it all the time. That is not just fable or a nice story. It is true. If we abandon ourselves to God and forget ourselves, we see it sometimes, and we see it maybe frequently. God shows Himself everywhere, in everything—in people and in things and in nature and in events. It becomes very obvious that God is everywhere and in everything and we cannot be without Him. It's impossible. The only thing is that we don't see it.[8]

As mentioned in the last chapter, St. Ignatius was another Catholic saint who encouraged his followers to do the same in a daily exercise called the Examination of Conscience. Ignatius challenged his followers to take ten minutes at the end of each day to review the events of that day. He wanted his people to look for God's presence in each of those events. In relationships with others, in the observation of nature, and in the special blessings of food and comfort, Ignatius wanted his followers to thank God for provision and wanted to make sure that God had been invited into the moment. Ignatius wanted his followers to get out of the rut of taking things for granted. He encouraged his followers to praise God for the smallest, most ordinary things—jam on toast, warm running water, a simple smile from a stranger. Ignatius believed that people, by developing this kind of behavior, would begin to see God more regularly in the small events of the day as they were happening, and take time to thank God for all the little gifts. Ignatius wanted Christians to break out of their blindness and self-centeredness. He wanted Christians to become grateful people.

Teaching Gratitude

When I used to work with high school kids, I would do a little exercise that would attempt to help adolescents develop an appreciation for their youthfulness and health. I would create situations for the young people that reminded them of how fortunate they were. My middle-class students could be so spoiled and selfish that I needed to jar them into realizing the blessings of God in their lives. One exercise I did was to put popcorn kernels in their shoes and have them wear old eye-glasses. I would then take them to a shopping mall and have them walk for a few hours with sore feet and blurred vision. When they finished the evening and complained bitterly about the experience, I would remind them how many elderly people in our country live like that each day. I would remind them of how fortunate they were to be able to walk anywhere at any time and not be handicapped by their vision and foot problems. The kids would always go away at the end of the night feeling a little more grateful for their health and youthfulness.

Attitudes Matter

The apostle Paul is another who makes a big deal about our attitudes. Frequently throughout his letters, Paul calls the people within his churches to "rejoice" in their circumstances, and to "give thanks" for whatever might be put in their paths. Paul calls Christians to be the kind of people who look for the good in every situation. The apostle Paul was on to something. He knew that one of the ways Christians can authentically witness to the world is by the way they view life and respond to difficulties. To the church of Philippi, Paul says, "Rejoice in the Lord always. I will say it again: Rejoice!" (Phil. 4:4). He continues by saying, "Do not be anxious about anything, but in everything by prayer and petition, with thanksgiving, present your requests to God" (4:6). To the church of Thessalonica, Paul encourages the saints to "Be joyful always; pray continually; give thanks in all circumstances, for this is God's will for you in Christ Jesus" (1 Thess. 5:16–18). If more Christians begin to truly cultivate a spirit of gratitude and thankfulness for their lives, people will be drawn to Christ, not because of a well-articulated altar call, but because they sense and see a response and joy toward life that is real. If the church was full of people cultivating this attitude of gratitude, the good news would not need to be "sold" and "marketed." People would be drawn to people of faith because of the good news they witness across their faces and the difference in their attitudes.

If Jesus Were a Sophomore

If Jesus were to trail you for a day—you know, like a shadow— what would he see and hear? If he eavesdropped on your coffee-bar conversations, listened to your phone calls, overheard your chitchat in class, and watched the way you interacted with people, what would he observe? What would his feedback be to you at the end of the day?

Let's imagine this really happened and, at the end of the day, the two of you meet in your dorm room to debrief.

"I've been with you today," he begins.

"Kind of a lousy day," I candidly report back.

"I don't know about that," comes the familiar Voice. "It all depends on how you look at things."

"What do you mean? All that could go wrong did go wrong. Extra assignments. A long line for the showers in the morning made me late for breakfast. By the time I showed up they had stopped serving the hot entrees. All that was left were the breads, cereals, and fruits. My roommate tied up the phone line with his Internet research. I missed a call from my best friend. What was good about today?" I grumble as I finish my litany of complaints.

"Have you ever stopped to ponder the miracle of your life?" shoots back the Voice. I detect a little irritation. "Did you know that less than 5 percent of the world's population will ever have the opportunity to attend college? Did you know that many of your inner-city high schools will graduate fewer than 50 percent of their students? The fact that you're in college is a miracle. A privilege. I'm not trying to dump a guilt trip on you, but maybe you should look at the bigger picture. Maybe you should embrace the extra assignments as a gift."

"A gift?" I think to myself. Obviously he doesn't have to do the work I have to do. But his point does make me think.

"And about the food," he continues. I can sense that he's just getting warmed up. "Breads, cereals, and fruits? That's a feast to most of the world. You've got your health. You're not going to die or get sick if you miss a meal. You need to be grateful for what you do have."

By this point I'm feeling a little guilty about my attitude. I don't sense he is trying to make me feel guilty. I sense that he is lovingly trying to expand my view.

"You've got a couple of choices. You can choose to complain or you can choose to be grateful. You can look for the negative in things, or you can try to see the miracle and blessing in things. You can let your circumstances control you, or you can try to rise above them and seek God's blessing in them," he wisely counsels.

I think long and hard about the day. The more I reflect, the more I am able to see the abundance of blessings and privileges I have been given. My Mentor clears his throat and makes his final recommendation.

"Try to cultivate a spirit of gratitude. Look for the little gifts you receive every minute of the day. They are from God. It will revolutionize your life."

I turn out my lights, lay my head on the pillow, and think, "Tomorrow will be different."

An attitude of gratitude is a behavior that takes time and discipline to cultivate. In a world becoming increasingly cynical and skeptical of God's presence and involvement, it is critical that the up-and-coming generation view their lives as sacred and special because of the ever-present activity of God. The behavior of gratitude needs to be exercised through the activity of seeing God in the intimate details of life and responding to the awareness of God with praise, joy, and thankfulness. This way of responding to life is not the natural response of our human condition. It takes a conscious commitment to live life in a way that seeks to find God at work continually and praise God continually for this work.

In an age that can often be marked by cynicism and joylessness, Jesus calls college students to become counterculture people who have cultivated an attitude of gratitude in their lives. Jesus calls college and university students to begin the process of becoming people who, even in the most dire circumstances, rejoice and find God's involvement in all aspects of life. The mark of Jesus' kingdom is rejoicing and joy. When the apostle Paul asks the church of Galatia, "What has happened to all your joy?" (Gal. 4:15), he asks the congregation because they had lost their distinctive marking. Let us all work toward securing our distinctive mark of joy, gratitude, and rejoicing.

Remember:

How many joys are crushed under foot because people look up at the sky and disregard what is at their feet.
                                    Johann Wolfgang von Goethe

Questions for Reflection

1. Do you believe that gratitude should be a discipline that you should try to cultivate? If not, why? If so, how do people begin to cultivate this discipline in their lives?

2. What are five "gifts" you have received today (little things) that you have not taken the time to thank God for?

3. What stands in the way of you becoming a more grateful person? How can these obstacles be eliminated from your life?

4. Who do you know who embodies an "attitude of gratitude"? Talk about that person. Share a situation that you observed where you saw the person exercise this discipline.

5. Start a "Gratitude Journal" today. Record things for which you are grateful.

For the Leader

Ask each member of your group to give a report based on this question: If Jesus had "shadowed" you today, what would he have observed? What would he say about your attitude?

Prayer and Meditation

Lord,

I confess that I often miss the wonder of my life.
I confess that I often fail to see all the wonderful gifts I have
    been given.
I confess that my attitude is often conditional and not rooted in
    the miracle of my life.

Peel the blinders off my eyes so I can see ALL the gifts you have
    given me.
Grant me the discipline of gratitude so I will not be controlled
    by my circumstances.
Help me to embody Paul's challenging exhortation to "Rejoice
    always."

I want to be marked by a spirit of gratitude, Lord.
I want to be known as a truly grateful person.
May Your Spirit nudge me toward this place.

Amen

Chapter 4

Commitment Behaviors: Learning to Commit

Who are the healers who manage to turn people around? Not pinch-hearted bureaucrats. Not paper pushers. Not people competing for power. Not size, not funding, not buildings make a difference—it is soul touching soul that changes lives. The one who won't give up is the one who makes the difference.

Mary Taylor Previte

Commitment and Jesus: Forgotten Friends

It was an interesting Bible study. None of the members were Christians. What began as a series of casual lunch discussions soon evolved into an in-depth study about the life and teachings of Jesus. Let me explain.

On our campus were numerous international students of many faiths. Even though it was a Christian college, many Buddhist and Muslim students had been accepted by the admissions department. Many felt it was a move to bolster sagging enrollment. Whatever the reason, some students and faculty were up in arms about the policy. After all, they argued, how could a Christian college allow students of different faith on campus? The inclusion of the Buddhist and Muslim students was seen as an invasion into the insular bubble of Christendom that some were trying to preserve. Fortunately, most students and faculty did not hold to this sectarian and exclusive view. Rather, they viewed the inclusion of non-Christian students as an opportunity for ministry and outreach.

Every day the international students would gather around two or three tables in the back corner of the cafeteria. Sadly the American Christian students never mixed and shared fellowship with the students from Iran, China, Korea, Taiwan, and other Middle Eastern and Asian countries. Although the students rubbed shoulders in the food lines and lived in the same dorm complexes, they knew little about one another. Geographically they were side by side, but emotionally and socially they were worlds apart.

The international students seemed afraid and insecure. In a new country, miles from home, security and belonging were found in likeness. At the same time, few American students conjured up the courage to cross the invisible border. After watching this phenomenon play out day after day, I finally decided to step out of my comfort zone and become a little adventuresome. Instead of sitting at my normal table, I ventured across the cafeteria to this "strange new land" to have lunch with a group of Taiwanese students. I was a little nervous. After all, how would I be welcomed? Would I even be allowed to place my tray at their table? I took a deep breath, calmed my nerves, and proceeded toward my destination.

First glances implied reservation and caution. The bewildered students were a little surprised and shocked to see a Euro-American cross the invisible "international border" and venture into the Northeast Asia corner of the cafeteria. Perhaps they thought I was lost and had taken a wrong turn. Though still tempted to head back into the "heartland" where everybody looked and talked as I did, I kept my bearings and headed for my destination. Politely, the students waited for me to recognize my error, turn around, and make a quick exit from their territory. "Can I join your table?" I asked, to their bewilderment and surprise. With smiles and affirming nods the group motioned for me to sit. The journey was a success. The adventure had just begun.

From that day forward I was a regular in the international section. Quickly I moved from tourist status and became part of their community. While the names of my American friends were Frank, Tom, and Randy, my new friends had names like Ming, Moon, and Abdul. It was a new world: a United Nations microcosm in a sea of white, middle-class college students. Lunchtime discussions changed from talk about college football and dorm life to politics in Asia, differences between democracy and socialism, and current events from different parts of the world. I asked questions about social problems and family structure in their country and they, in turn, asked questions about American behavior. After a few months of gained trust, we began to talk about religion, faith, and Christianity. The discussions were lively and interesting. I enjoyed my new friends and they seemed to enjoy me.

One day the discussion rolled around to Jesus. My non-

Christian friends fired tough questions at me: How could Jesus be the son of God? Did I really think Jesus was killed and yet rose again from the dead? Was Jesus the only way to heaven? Day after day, between bites of meatloaf and tossed salads, I did my best to answer their thought-provoking questions. Questions beyond my ability to answer I would take back to my dorm room and reflect on for the next roundtable discussion. One memorable day, when the discussion became intense, I suggested we conclude the dialogue later in the evening. They would bring the refreshments and I would bring my Bible. Together we would try to figure out some of the answers to these difficult questions.

To my surprise they all showed up. It was the first Bible study I had ever led in my life, and the audience was an eclectic group of non-Christians, atheists, Buddhists, and Muslims. Only God knew what would happen next.

For the next four months we read through the Gospel of Mark. Each week we would look at a particular portion of Scripture that would give a glimpse into the life and teachings of Jesus. Most of the students had heard the name of Jesus around campus, but they had little knowledge as to who he was and what he did during his three-year ministry. They were curious. They had a keen interest in knowing what Jesus said and commanded his followers to do. They wanted to know how Jesus lived his life and how Jesus would address issues in our present world. They wanted to know what it would take to follow him—what they would be called to do, what they would be called to believe, what they would have to give up, and what commitment would define their lives. Since these young people had not been raised in a Christian culture and saturated with Bible verses, everything was fresh and new. The teachings of Jesus jumped off the pages and penetrated their hearts in powerful ways. I ended up seeing Scripture in ways that I had never seen. I was now reading the Bible through their eyes. The Word was fresh and new.

When one of the students read that it was "better to cut off your hand if it causes you to sin," they were perplexed and amazed at the seriousness of Jesus—they were also concerned that Jesus might demand the same from them. When one of the students read about how Jesus said that fathers, mothers, sisters, and brothers must not stand in the way of following him, they all wondered how these teachings would fit into their Eastern culture, where the family and allegiance to parental authority was so important. This small band of "seekers" pondered the words and teachings of Jesus and began to truly count the cost of what it would mean to become a disciple. None of these young men or women was going to follow a man who was so demanding, so challenging, and so radical if they were not ready to really make a genuine commitment. With every new idea they asked questions, sought clarity, and desired to know what specific verses really meant for their lives.

Because of their child-like naïveté toward the Scriptures and their observations of American Christian faith, what perplexed the group was the apparent disparity between how Jesus called his followers to live and how the Christian students actually lived their lives on campus. When they heard students complain about food, they wondered why these American students were not more thankful. When they saw students turn their backs on the needy and poor, they wondered how that action matched what Jesus taught about the poor. They would ask me, "Jesus tells his followers that they should visit those in prison; why don't the Christian students go visit those in jail?" Or "Jesus says we should forgive those who do wrong against us; why don't the Christian students forgive one another?" And "Jesus says that we commit murder with our words; why do these Christians talk about others the way they do?"

It was difficult responding to some of their questions. They were right in their critique. For the first time Scripture was being revealed to them, but they were not seeing it lived out in the behaviors of those around them who were supposedly Christian.

Working with a group of students who had grown up outside the Christian culture was an eye-opening experience. It was a breath of fresh air. As those students wrestled sincerely with the claims of Jesus, they were holding a mirror up to myself and my fellow students on campus. Because they had not been steeped in the trappings of our contemporary Christian culture, my new friends were confronting a gospel that was not skewed by the "subculture" of Christianity. They were hearing the words of Jesus for the first time and letting his life and words shape their idea of Christian discipleship. In their minds, making a commitment to become Christian would not be a decision of convenience. It would not be taken lightly. Taking this step would mean abandoning old beliefs, letting go of some of the customs of their parents, and, in some cases, losing their families. These students were truly counting the cost.

So often those who grow up in Christian homes, or grow up

in a Christian-friendly culture, never really have to count the cost. Christianity becomes something people grow into. Like Little League baseball or going to school, Christianity becomes one more activity that fills a slot in our weekly schedule. In the words of J. D. Smart, Christianity becomes a kind of "civil religion."[9] It has lost its prophetic, counterculture edge and has become a birthright for Americans. But for this group of students, who had not grown up contaminated by this civil religion, they were slowly "counting the cost" to determine whether a commitment to Christ was worth the sacrifice.

Finally one Thursday night, near the close of our study, one of the students raised his hand. "We've talked among ourselves," he began as the others in the group nodded with approval, "and we feel as if we understand what Jesus desires for his followers. We are ready to commit our lives to him." I was stunned. Amazed. I knew it was authentic. After four months of intense study, I knew they understood the ramifications of their commitment. So, with heads bowed, this group of non-Christian, atheist, Buddhist, and Muslim students gave their lives to Jesus. No one had been manipulated. No one had made an emotional decision. They had each thought the decision through and had decided it would be worth the sacrifices. They were not looking for cheap grace. They really wanted to make a radical conversion to a new style of living. For the first time in my life I was part of the conversion experience of people who had really tried to understand the dimensions of Christian commitment *before* they made their commitment. They had, in the words of Jesus, counted the cost and decided it would be worth the rejection and losses they would encounter in their lives.

Learning Commitment

Church history shows us that it is through committed people that lives are changed. Whether we look at the life of the German martyr Dietrich Bonhoeffer; the El Salvadoran priest Oscar Romero; the advocate for the poor in New York City, Dorothy Day; or Father Damien, who brought good news to the leper colonies in the Hawaiian Islands, we find brothers and sisters whose commitments were tried and challenged. The cost of following Jesus for each of these saints was intense and demanding. It was persecution and death from Hitler for Bonhoeffer, intense ridicule and eventual assassination for Romero, harassment and imprisonment by the federal government for

Day, and personal sickness and loneliness for Damien. But in all of these examples, it was the perseverance and commitment that enabled these disciples to change their communities and their world. It was their stubborn unwillingness to capitulate to the pressures surrounding them that kept their testimony alive and vital for the larger church body.

Ultimately it is the committed person whom God can infuse with the power of the Spirit and use to express love and justice in the world. It is the committed person who gives an enduring witness to the kingdom of God in the world. Throughout the Scriptures there is example after example of people who faithfully commit to living out the call and commission of God in their lives, regardless of what that commitment entailed. Abram packs his bags and leaves his city to follow the voice of Yahweh—his commitment is based on a promise. Noah stays committed to God's call to build a boat—the process takes over one hundred years. Daniel is so committed to spiritual integrity that he allows himself to be thrown to the lions. Jeremiah preaches to his people for over twenty-five years, is unsuccessful at converting his nation, and is persecuted for his message. But he stays committed. These honest records of faith, passed on to our generation through the Holy Scriptures, reveal testimony after testimony of committed people.

One of the most gripping biblical examples of commitment is Jesus in the Garden of Gethsemane. It is in the garden that we meet our Lord in anguish, wrestling with God over the prospect of going to the cross to fulfill his mission. In addition to capturing a living example of the power of commitment, this snapshot of Jesus displays a powerful contrast between a man committed to obedience and his disciples, who have little sticking power when the going gets tough. The Gospel writer Mark records this riveting scene that ends up changing the whole course of human history: "Going a little farther, he [Jesus] fell to the ground and prayed that if possible the hour might pass from him. 'Abba, Father,' he said, 'everything is possible for you. Take this cup from me. Yet not what I will, but what you will.' Once more he went away and prayed the same thing" (Mark 14:35–39).

Jesus agonizes over having to die. So often Christians overlook this part of Jesus' life. We have become so focused on the actual crucifixion that we forget this scene of Jesus wrestling with a very difficult decision. Many people imagine that Jesus just jumped up onto the cross without any kind of struggle of the will. Many people have the notion that, since Jesus knew he had to die, there was no real difficulty in consenting to the decision of voluntarily hanging spread eagle on the cross. But in this scene we meet Jesus, in the fullness of his humanity, struggling with his commitment. Earlier in the passage Jesus cries, "My soul is overwhelmed with sorrow to the point of death" (v. 34). The narrative reveals a very human man who is depressed and overwhelmed with the prospect of dying.

Despite his very human struggle, Jesus does not waver from his commitment. The Gospel of Mark probably demonstrates the depth of this struggle best by recording that three times Jesus went out to pray through his decision to obey God. Mark reveals that the decision was not easy. While his disciples slept, Jesus struggled to maintain his ongoing commitment to obedience. Yet at the end of this struggle, Jesus comes to the place of saying, "Yet not what I will, but what you will" (Mark 14:36c). It is at this point that Jesus surrenders his agenda and maintains a commitment to total obedience. It is this deep commitment to the agenda of God that eventually overrides how Jesus felt ("My soul is overwhelmed with sorrow to the point of death," Mark 14:34) and what Jesus desired ("Take this cup from me," Mark 14:36), and helps him to fulfill the call of dying on the cross.

It is on his knees in the Garden of Gethsemane that Jesus connects with all those who have given their lives to following the will of God. Christians may not be physically crucified like Jesus, but Christians are called to surrender their entire will and being to whatever God calls them to. In many respects we all kneel with Jesus in the Garden. We are all confronted with situations that call us to surrender our lives in order to live obediently before God. It is at this intersection—between God's will and ours—that we must decide if we will remain committed to God's agenda for our lives or live out our own agenda.

Courage for Commitment

I often wonder if Jesus drew any of his strength and perseverance to remain committed to God's plan from the rich biblical tradition of those who maintained their faithfulness. When Jesus was tempted to get up off his knees and run, did he recall how things must have looked for Daniel in the den of lions? Or Shadrach, Meshach, and Abednego in the fiery furnace? Or the prophets like Jeremiah, who preached for decades without a convert? David confronting Goliath? As a boy Jesus was steeped in the traditions of the Old Testament—those stories of faithful servants who lived courageously for God. Stories of regular people who experienced the promises of God because of their steadfast commitment to the voice of God must have rolled around in the memory banks of Jesus as he lived out his calling. These same stories not only inspired Jesus but have helped thousands of Christians live out their calling over the past centuries. These stories of faithful, committed people inspire other followers of Jesus to live as faithful, committed people.

Unfortunately we live in a culture that has reduced the concept of commitment to almost nothing. Marriages break apart because people have decided that feelings override commitment. Corporations pay allegiance to the profit margin rather than staying committed to faithful employees. People make fewer commitments to churches. Commitment is a dying idea. Commitment to God and to a lifestyle that is inspired by the life of Jesus has become increasingly foreign. Yet more than ever, the Christian community needs young people who do not have a conditional commitment to Jesus, but who are willing to give their entire being and life to following Jesus in this world. The church needs people whose understanding of discipleship is much deeper than simply reciting a prayer for eternal security. The church needs a new generation of young people who are committed to a life of service and sacrifice regardless of difficulties and challenges.

A Ten-Minute Gospel

Part of the reason why the concept of a costly commitment to Christ is in such peril is because of the present evangelical tendency to define the message of the gospel in terms of what is culturally acceptable. At some point in the history of North American Christianity, the true gospel message was hijacked, stripped of its meaning, and then re-dressed in clothing that would fit more appropriately within our culture. What we have done, in short, is reduce the gospel message to a ten-minute prayer for an eternal life insurance policy, and we have neglected all aspects of what it means to truly follow this man Jesus. Recently this ten-minute gospel and ten-minute commitment was made evident at a staff meeting. Let me share a story:

Everybody had just sat down when his arm shot up with alarming speed. I braced myself. Another Monday morning staff meeting, but today's would be far from normal. I had decided to "break the ice" and asked for feedback on our weekend activities—our first junior staff training session. It was obvious that Brian had something urgent to share.

"If we're going to be frank, I need to say a few things." He had our attention. "I thought the program yesterday was an abomination to the name of the Lord. References to Christ and our mission as a ministry were simply an appendage to the program. I was embarrassed to be there!"

Our staff was stunned. They had been thrilled by what had happened the previous day. Many were ecstatic about the new relationships they had formed and were anxious to begin the journey where, as the Spirit allowed, they would share their faith with the kids. Brian's words left them dumbfounded and stunned.

Over two hundred teens, mostly non-Christian, had turned out for the first of eight sessions in preparation for our summer jobs program—a program that included evangelism, discipleship, leadership training, and a host of other activities. Explicitly Christian songs had been sung, Scripture had been read, challenges to community responsibility—clearly rooted in our Christian faith—had been offered. But "the gospel," in Brian's mind, had not been presented.

"Perhaps," finished Brian, "we can take ten minutes at the next training session to present the gospel."

On this particular day, our young, earnest brother demanded more time and attention be given to the name of Jesus and the gospel. In his eyes, the Christian songs and challenges were not enough. For Brian, only an explicit presentation with an invitation counted as the gospel. "And so," he requested, "the gospel should be given ten minutes." Then our claim to be a Christian ministry would be fulfilled.

Presenting the Gospel

What is "the gospel?" Gospel means "good news." On one level, this good news has been told in the four New Testament accounts that share the "Gospel" name. Their story is a simple one: incarnation. God gave God's self to us in the form of God's son, Jesus Christ; Christ was killed, and rose again; and his life, death, and resurrection mean new and eternal life for those who believe. Can these four books be reduced to ten minutes? Can we take three years of recorded life and reduce "the gospel" into a neat, ten-minute presentation? And if we can, can we really tell the story?

Moreover, isn't the good news God's reaching out to us? Isn't it the demonstration that God does indeed love us that makes the incarnation become decidedly good? This realization frees us from the legalistic obligation of telling the entire story of the Gospels in order to present the gospel. When possible, of course, we ought to share as much of the story of our Lord as possible. But the core of the story—its essence—demands much less, and much more, than a detailed historical account of the life, death, and resurrection of Christ.

The danger lies in imagining that the précis of the good news, containing only as much content and soul as a press release, does the job. The Gospels show that Jesus and his evangelists did not reduce his message to a pithy sales pitch or an advertising slogan to be shared through the streets of Jerusalem. They could have massaged his message into an instruction manual or a brief sermon and everyone could have memorized it. And, with a little training and a quick pedantic beat, we could all have had the gospel down to a slick presentation—perfect for those who like a ten-minute gospel.

But the fact that the writers of the Gospels made painstaking attempts to give their readers such accurate details, stories, and content suggests that a formulaic version of the "good news" would never do. The whole story was, and continues to be, important because it is more than a story—it is a model, a lifestyle, a person.

Real Decision

The good news is that the gospel is something to be learned through experience. It is a journey that started with a call to follow, learn, and risk. The initial gospel commitment was to a relationship, and it was through a relationship with Christ that the early disciple would find out what made God's entry into the world so decidedly good. "Follow me," said Jesus at the seashore, "and I will make you people who can fish for other people." The emphasis was on the active verb *make*. A Christian is at once re-made and being made, and is being sent into the world to be of value to others looking for God.

And of course, the making of a disciple demands not one but many recommitments. After three years of following Jesus, the disciples had to decide whether the news they preached was really that good. Since their friend and leader told them he was the Promised One, the Messiah-hung-on-a-cross, they had to choose between identifying with this criminal on a cross and his message, or their old lives as fishermen. It is crucial to realize that they really did not have to accept Jesus as Lord, as King, as Messiah, as Savior, and as God's son until his death and resurrection. Christ's painful death created a moment of decision for those who knew him, his resurrection gave them hope to believe, and the Spirit gave them the power to follow. Here, the disciples had to ask, "Was this man the gospel, the good news?" And if so, were they willing to risk their lives for what Jesus taught, lived, and modeled? Confronted by their risen teacher, they had to make a decision. It was at that moment their faith could finally be reduced to a decision that could be made in minutes—perhaps even ten.

But this point of decision happened after three years of training, modeling, and most important, relationship with both Jesus and one another. As they faced the hard choices of following Jesus, they did not face them alone. Their choice not only was an "informed" one, but was rooted in their experience of Christ, their faithful, trustworthy, and gracious friend.

The earliest Christians had been part of the gospel experience. Jesus had invited them to participate in this gospel experience, and because of this participation, they could make the kind of decision that would be needed to keep their new faith alive and vibrant. If these men and women had been asked to make the decision based on a ten-minute snapshot—for instance, on the way to Jerusalem with people waving palm branches and singing "Hosanna, Hosanna"—they would have responded with a resounding YES! If the decision of the disciples had been based on a "ten-minute" glimpse of Christ's life on a hillside with thousands gathered around him, clamoring for attention, and eating his free food, I am sure that they would have all claimed Jesus as Lord—without hesitation.

But Jesus himself rejected such an appeal. "Count the cost," he told those who would follow him.

Who enters a marriage based on a ten-minute phone call? Only the desperate. Who makes an important investment based on a ten-minute glance at a glitzy brochure? Only the ignorant and the greedy. Who goes into battle without adequately sizing up the enemy? The vanquished. No important decision is ever made and fulfilled unless there is adequate thought and experience put into it. The early disciples decided to call Jesus Lord because they had lived with, served, and watched the gospel be incarnated, come alive, in front of them!

Too many religious leaders offer a something-for-nothing gospel designed by marketing experts rather than the costly, committed call of following Jesus. And too many of our converts reflect our quick-sell approach. People who make a decision to follow Christ based on a ten-minute presentation of the gospel will often (happily, not always!) make a ten-minute commitment.

Jesus' road to the cross was not an easy journey. It was a journey that demanded total commitment, incredible focus, and unmatched perseverance. His life was met by opposition because he was willing to confront the status quo, challenge those with power, and befriend the masses. As followers of Christ, why should we expect anything less from ourselves than from our leader? Unfortunately, the cultural trappings of our faith have led us to believe that it is an easy road filled with rewards and blessings along the way. The rewards and blessings may come, but we do need to realize that a life of discipleship will be one of commitment, struggle, and perseverance.

Learning Commitment

If college and young adulthood are critical years for shaping us into the kind of Christians we will become later in life, it is important that the discipline of commitment is established during this period of our lives. It is crucial that the fundamental building blocks of what it means to keep commitments be put into place. Like a foundation that supports a large building, the ability to keep commitments becomes the foundational structure on which our faith, our relationships, and our vocations are all built. Without the ability to fulfill commitment, our faith will crumble when the going becomes difficult. John Stott puts it another way when he claims, "Christians are like chocolate soldiers; when they get too close to the flame they melt." Committed people do not melt when they encounter the "flames" of life. Committed people endure and become stronger.

The biblical theme of perseverance is helpful in understanding the nature of a committed life of discipleship. In order to fulfill and maintain a commitment to discipleship, the follower of Jesus is called to persevere. Commitment and perseverance go hand in hand. The ability to persevere in difficult, trying circumstances enables us to keep our commitment. Daniel Taylor, in his outstanding book *The Myth of Certainty*, perceptively writes that "perseverance means carrying on in the face of obstacles, continuing in what one is doing despite unfavorable circumstances. The marathoner perseveres despite a protesting body, the sculptor perseveres despite the unyielding stone, the husband and wife persevere despite the strains of marriage."[10] It is the person who perseveres, according to Taylor, who eventually tastes the joy of finishing the race, experiences the satisfaction of creating a beautiful piece of art, or enjoys the blessing of a unified family.

The Bible is full of examples of people who persevere. Two thousand years later we are all thankful for people like the apostle Paul who persevered and kept his commitment to the call of God. Paul was always running into problems—he was shipwrecked, beaten, imprisoned—because of his unwavering commitment to preaching the gospel. It was a tenacious commitment, coupled with the Holy Spirit, that enabled Paul to plant churches and win new converts to Jesus Christ. And, if we took the time to trace the roots of our faith, we would find that we are somehow linked to the faithful witness of Paul. Our lives have been changed because of the commitment of a faithful brother centuries ago. One must ask: Where would the church be today if Paul had not persevered? Would the Christian church even exist if the apostle Paul had not faithfully and diligently stayed committed when times were very dark and very bleak? It was an unyielding commitment to follow Jesus, at all cost, that motivated Paul to write letters from prison to struggling churches and preach the life-changing message of the gospel to those in need.

A Model of Commitment

I remember hearing the great missionary Richard Wurmbrand speak. Wurmbrand is one of those great saints of the Christian church who labored faithfully for years during the Communist rule in Romania. His faithfulness to Jesus ultimately led him to fourteen years in solitary confinement for refusing to let a totalitarian government silence his witness. As Wurmbrand described his little cell—dark, dank, and claustrophobic—to a captivated audience at my seminary one day, I wondered if I could stay committed in a similar situation. As he shared, with vivid description, that the only color he would see each day was the green mold on his stale bread, I was amazed at how this man persevered and continued to share the joy and love of God with those who tortured and beat him. Somehow, by the grace of God, Wurmbrand persevered. He stayed committed and ultimately made a difference for God's kingdom by changing the lives of fellow prisoners and inspiring thousands of persecuted Christians worldwide through his testimony and the creation of a ministry called The Voice of the Martyrs. Wurmbrand's unique message of love and forgiveness has brought thousands of people to a deeper understanding and knowledge of Christ as well as informing many in the Western church of the persecution of Christians worldwide.

The Habit of Commitment

It is important for collegians to realize that commitment and perseverance do not simply show up one day when we are thirty or forty. Commitment is learned. Commitment is learned in a person's day-to-day living and carries over into how we exercise our faith. As an athlete builds strength and endurance each time he or she lifts weights or exercises, likewise a Christian learns the discipline of commitment each time he or she is faithful in the little things of life. How individuals keep their appointments, return their phone calls, answer their correspondence, pay their bills, and fulfill their responsibilities all figures into how Christians fulfill commitment throughout their lives. Patterns of commitment and perseverance developed early in one's life will help sustain a vital, obedient, and committed life of discipleship as one grows older.

In his autobiography, *A Long Walk Home*, Nelson Mandela describes how the habit of commitment can be developed even when a person is imprisoned. Even though he was significantly limited in what he could do to overthrow the system of South African apartheid while in prison, Mandela did maintain little acts of activism while detained. He kept a rigorous schedule. He exercised. He kept abreast, as much as he could, with the things going on outside the prison walls. And he fought for issues of justice for the men inside the prison. Mandela claims that maintaining a commitment to his ideals and convictions, even on a small and restricted scale, kept him prepared for when he was released. Mandela did not put his commitment to the cause of apartheid on hold for two decades because of his confinement. Mandela knew that commitment needs to be practiced. Like a muscle that will grow flabby if not exercised, the ability to maintain commitment will vanish if it is not maintained. What some would claim as wasted years, Mandela used to prepare himself for the possibility of one day being released. As we all know, Mandela has gone on to be an effective leader both in his country and in the world.

He has changed the course of history, even though he spent the prime years of his life in prison.

During one's college years, it may seem that the small and insignificant decisions—like taking classes that make us think rather than assure the easiest grade—do not mean much in our spiritual journey. But it is these little decisions not to cut corners and take shortcuts that ultimately shape who we become. Pushing ourselves to do the best possible research on a paper—when we know we can get by with doing little—helps create patterns of perseverance that will help us become committed people later in life. Getting up for classes in the morning—when we know it will not matter if we skip—helps in developing the disciplines needed to sustain a healthy spiritual life that will last for the long haul. It is through these commitments to the everyday small things that we prepare ourselves for the bigger things that God will bring our way. Our college years can be an instrumental training ground for learning the disciplines that help us to keep commitments.

Urban Training Ground

Every summer our mission organization hosts between sixty and ninety college students from all over the world. For months these students prepare for their summer of service in the city. They raise money, they sublet apartments, they have their families pray for them, and they get their home churches to commission them. They come with huge expectations, wide eyes, and a desire to serve God. The reality of city life can be a jolt to their romantic notion of serving God.

The day after the students' arrival I can always spot those who are struggling. Their eyes are bloodshot, their faces pale. At every opportunity they are on the phone calling home. Inevitably they will find their way to my office. I know the words before they are mouthed: "I don't think God is calling me to stay!"

I have learned to hate that line. First, it is bad theology to blame something on God that God is not responsible for. I have real problems believing that God would open doors for students to travel across the country, would meet their financial needs, would provide opportunities to serve and love needy kids, and then disclose upon their arrival (when it begins to feel a little uncomfortable), "You're not supposed to be here!" When in Scripture has God called anyone away from something because it gets too difficult?

Those who end up leaving always make me sad. I am saddened not because I lose a volunteer. I am saddened because I believe a pattern of quitting and not sticking with commitments can quickly gain a foothold in a person's life. Once bad patterns are given the opportunity to flourish, they are extremely difficult to reverse. As I follow the lives of those students who bailed out before fulfilling their commitment, I frequently see patterns of noncommitment in all aspects of their life. Those who struggle and stick it out, on the other hand, always give me hope. They give me hope because their willingness to persevere is a starting point for a life of commitment. Furthermore, this commitment to persevere can birth a lifestyle that faces difficult obstacles and experiences triumphant and personal growth in the end. As these students maintain their commitments through these fires, I watch their confidence grow as they look to their future.

A few summers ago a college senior named Leslie arrived from a university on the West Coast. I could tell she was struggling. She must have cried the entire first two weeks. I had never seen a student so depressed. She desperately wanted to leave. She thought she needed to go back to California. I encouraged her to stay. She had had a pattern of quitting in the past. This time she decided to confront her demons and stick it out. I believe it was the most important decision of her life—not only because she has done great ministry with our organization, but because she broke a negative cycle that had a grip on her life. Now, four years later, this young woman has undergone the most amazing transformation. She has faced past hurts, she has grown in her faith, and she has found a joy like she has never known. And she has blessed many, many inner-city kids with her love and compassion. This all happened because she chose to stop running, kept a commitment, and let God do a work in her life.

If Jesus Were a Sophomore

I sometimes wonder what it would have been like to have Jesus sit beside me in one of my college classes—especially a church history class. I could just imagine fifty-plus students feverishly taking notes, trying to keep up with a professor who is attempting to cover the time from Peter to Martin Luther and the Reformation in a fifty-five-minute lecture. Suddenly Jesus puts up his hand. The professor, somewhat irritated that someone would dare interrupt his flow of information, acknowledges the waving hand in the back of the room.

"Yes? Do you have a question?"

"I was wondering if I could make a comment," asks Jesus.

The room goes completely silent. After all, there is an unspoken rule in this class that questions are only tolerated (and only asked by the brave); student comments border on heresy. The much-published, distinguished professor takes off his glasses and squints his eyes, trying to see which student has the audacity to make a comment.

"If you must, go ahead," barks the professor, obviously irritated.

"As you were running through the names and dates of significant people in the history of the church," continues Jesus, "I couldn't help but think of the stories of some of these people. They weren't just names. They were people with families, with potential careers, and with real lives. Peter was hung upside down on a cross because of his commitment. James and John were killed because of their unwavering devotion. Those early Christians in Rome—the ones you just mentioned as an afterthought in your lecture—they were burned alive, eaten by lions, and publicly humiliated. They lost everything."

"What's your point, young man?" says the professor. He is not to be upstaged.

"My point is this—there would be no church history to teach if it were not for ordinary people who gave their lives for My sake. It is because of their commitments—commitments unto death—that you can stand up in front of this class today and have anything to say. The story of My church is a story of ordinary people who would not give up and would not compromise. I just think they deserve more than cursory mention. Their stories should be sources of inspiration for those who are trying to live as disciples."

The history of the Christian church, taught by Jesus, would be a course worth taking. I can only imagine the passion with which it would be taught. His perspective on the whole evolution of Christian faith would be awesome. But equally impressive would be his perspective and insight on what could have happened to the whole Christian movement if certain people had not remained faithful and kept their commitments.

Just think if the disciples had broken their commitment to be faithful witnesses of the good news? Just think if, after Jesus was crucified, the disciples hit the road and never availed themselves to the power of God's Spirit? Just think if Peter and Paul punted when things got tough? Just think if those in the early church in Rome renounced their faith and went back to their old lives when persecution came their way? It is hard to imagine how history would be different. It is probable, however, that the Christian church would have never made the inroads it has made. We must realize that our lives are radically changed because early followers of Christ kept their commitment. You and I know about this man Jesus because a group of people, centuries ago, were willing to stay committed at all costs.

I often wonder how different the world would be if all students who committed their lives to Jesus during their college years did not give up on their God-given dreams and visions when things got difficult. Would the history of our world be significantly better if more Christian students established patterns of commitment that enabled them to persevere when the trials, temptations, and "cares of the world" began to sidetrack them? Would there be less suffering in the world if students who began their faith journey with a burden to end poverty kept true to their calling? Would there be fewer environmental problems in our world if students who had begun their discipleship pilgrimage with a commitment to caring for God's creation had not capitulated to the temptations of money from corporations who care more about the bottom line than their communities? Would there be less crime among youth in our cities if students who had met Jesus in college and developed a heart for urban America had not lost their passion when better job offers, promising more money, came their way? I believe the world would be a much better place. But without the discipline of commitment firmly established in the lives of student disciples, thousands of potential world-changers have lost their vision and life mission. They have succumbed to mediocrity and status-quo religion.

Every time a commitment is broken by a disciple of Jesus Christ, God's work in the world is interrupted. Every time a disciple goes back on a promise and chooses to do his or her own will, the momentum of God's movement in the world must find a new channel to work through. God has chosen to use people to change the world. Therefore, God needs people who will remain committed and will persevere, even when things get difficult.

Jesus stayed committed unto death. Young college-aged disciples, navigating their way through this unique developmental stage of life, need to take advantage of this gift of time and cultivate commitment behaviors that will help sustain a life of passionate and faithful discipleship. J. Heinrich Arnold voices a powerful warning when he contends, "We must be faithful to the end. For a Christian the most dangerous time is the middle of life. At the beginning, when our faith is new, God may seem especially near to us. After a few years, however, lukewarmness often sets in. If we are dedicated, God will carry us through our middle years, though we must still be watchful. But let us not have fear. If we are true to God, nothing can separate us from his peace."[11]

Arnold appropriately warns that the middle years of life can be times when vibrant discipleship can slip into complacency. Arnold would also argue that it is essential to use the early adult years to develop the discipline of commitment.

The message of Jesus to collegians: Use this period of life to build a foundation on which a life of faithful discipleship can be built. Like the parable of the wise man who built his house on the rock because he heard the Word of God and acted on it, Jesus encourages all his would-be followers to act on his words by developing one of the key behaviors of discipleship—commitment!

Remember:

I have walked that long road to freedom.
I have tried not to falter; I have made missteps along the way.
But I have discovered the secret that after climbing a great hill, one only finds that there are many more hills to climb. I have taken a moment here to rest, to steal a view of the glorious vista that surrounds me, to look back on the distance I have come. But I can rest only for a moment, for with freedom come responsibilities, and I dare not linger, for my long walk is not yet ended.

Nelson Mandela

Questions for Reflection

1. In what areas of your life do you most frequently break commitments? List them. Ask yourself, "How is the breaking of these small commitments affecting my ability to keep bigger commitments?"

2. Who is the most committed person you know? Talk about that person. What makes that individual a committed person? How do you know he or she is a committed person?

3. What Christian missionaries, pastors, or disciples do you admire most? What kinds of commitments have they made throughout their life? At what points in their life were they tempted to break their commitments? What has been the "fruit" of their faithful commitments?

4. List a few commitments of yours that are presently being challenged. How can you keep these commitments even in the face of being challenged to break them?

5. Are there ever commitments we should break? If so, what should be the criteria for breaking commitments?

For the Leader

Have your group imagine and talk about the following: If Jesus were a student on a university campus today, what might be his primary commitments? How would he express these commitments in his daily life?

Prayer and Meditation

Lord,

I confess that I do not always see the connection between my daily behaviors and my long-term commitment to You.
I confess that my vision for my life is often limited.

Help me to see the connections between my daily commitments and the kind of committed person You need me to become.
With each commitment I keep, use it to strengthen me when things get really tough.

Lord, I do not know what You have in store for my life.
I do know that I will be tempted, challenged, and persuaded to abandon my commitment to You.

When those times come, I pray that Your Spirit will grant me the strength, the grace, and the courage to remain faithful to the call You have placed on my life.
When those times come, please bring to mind those Saints who did not let go of Your hand and whose lives were ultimately fruitful for Your Kingdom.

Thank you for your commitment to the Cross
And the redemption and salvation You have given to me because of that commitment.

Amen

Chapter 5

Friday Night Behaviors:
Managing My Relationships

> The attraction to the opposite sex is natural, but it is not
> sufficient ground by far on which to marry or found a fam-
> ily. It is quite natural that when a man loves a woman, he
> wants to know if she is the "right" one. There is only one
> answer to this question: both must feel that a marital rela-
> tionship will lead them nearer to Jesus.
>
> I can well imagine—in actual fact, I know it for sure—
> that the right choice for a spouse is not the one who is most
> attractive erotically, but the one whose companionship will
> lead both partners closer to Jesus. If marriage is based only
> on physical attraction, it will go to pieces easily.
>
> J. Heinrich Arnold

Whatever Happened to Dating?

It was a Friday night that few of our staff at UrbanPromise
would ever forget . . . especially the women. It was "women's
night out." The men were responsible for planning a night out
for all the women on the team. There would be no "pairing" or
"couples." Just a good ol' fashioned group date. Everybody
would be treated the same. It didn't matter how one dressed,
how much one weighed, or how comfortable one was in relat-
ing to people of the opposite sex. There would be no pressure.
Every woman on staff would be spoiled and treated like royalty.

The eight women on our team were escorted to the "date"
location in an old, beat-up, fifteen-passenger church van. With
the setting sun reflecting off a small lake, the arrival set the tone
for the rest of the evening. As the women stepped off the van,
they were immediately greeted by two male staff dressed in
tuxedos and were escorted along the lakeshore toward an out-
door gazebo. One could see smiles begin to stretch across the
faces of our female counterparts as they got closer to their destination.

To override the background symphony of chirping crickets
and bullfrogs, the sweet melancholy sound of a baritone voice
began to filter down from the grassy knoll to their left. As the

women craned their necks toward the source of the familiar voice, they saw their fellow staff worker, Chris, singing choruses from famous Broadway musicals. With the last flickers of natural light disappearing behind the distant foothills, an ambiance of romance was created. The women stood and cheered as Chris concluded each selection from *Cats*, *Phantom of the Opera*, and *Les Misérables*. It was shaping up to be a glorious night.

Upon the conclusion of the music, the women were guided up the stone steps to a small bluff overlooking the Pennsylvania countryside. With carefully placed candles spread around the blankets on the grassy landing, the women could hardly contain their excitement as they nibbled on freshly cut strawberries and cheeses.

While the women were enjoying their hors d'oeuvres, another of the men on staff began to pluck away at his guitar and hum familiar tunes. Hors d'oeuvres were followed by the main course—carefully prepared shish kebabs barbecued on an open grill. Everything about the evening was a hit with the young women. Each additional surprise was met with cheers of approval. Laughter filled the air. All the tiredness of the day's work had been forgotten. Any tensions among staff workers were distant memories. Every woman had been swept up into the moment and fully enjoyed the attention.

After dinner the men all took turns sharing an encouraging word about each of the women. Rick shared poems. Chris had specially chosen words that highlighted a certain characteristic of each of his female colleagues. Keith had meaningful and fun stories. Every woman was affirmed for the positive attributes she brought to our small community. Nothing negative was shared. The night had been crafted to be intentionally positive.

While dinner was being cleaned up by a few of the men, the women were led to the small stone chapel just off the lake. There in the silence of God's holy place, poetry from some of the great Romantics was read: Wordsworth, Byron, Shelley. Poems pontificating the virtues of love and commitment were read with passion and feeling. At the end of each reading the women cheered wildly and gave thunderous rounds of applause. They felt special. They felt cared for. Each woman in the circle had been lavished with attention. For some, this was a new experience.

When the evening was finished and we all started walking back toward the van, I noticed Mary trailing behind. Mary, the one who always seemed so confident and self-assured, was crying. For a moment I thought that we had blown it. I thought that in our attempt to include everyone equally we had some-how left her out. "Did she not get a rose?" "Did she feel that the words shared about her were not encouraging enough?" I retraced all the events of the evening. I could not think of any oversights. I was sure that we had covered all the bases. Finally I asked her what was wrong.

"Mary?" I stumbled. "Was something wrong with the evening?"

"No, no, no," she answered through her tears.

"What's the matter, then?" I nervously prodded.

"It's just that I have never been treated before like this by any man. I have never been around men who have treated me with such love and dignity. My father was abusive. My dating rela-tionships have been disastrous. I just did not believe that men could ever treat me this well. I've been selling myself short all these years."

We walked for a while, not saying a word.

"Can I do anything to help?" I said, trying to break the awk-ward silence.

"No, no. I just think that tonight has shown me that I need to change the kind of people I date and what I look for in a man," she concluded.

We walked back to the van in silence.

For the remainder of the summer the women talked about their big "date night." They talked about how they had never had so much fun and how they had never felt so affirmed. The women talked about how great it was not to feel pressured into getting romantically involved. There was a safety and freedom within the group.

For Mary and others on staff, the experience was the begin-ning of a healing process and a starting point for developing healthy relationships. The "group dates" that continued throughout the summer became moments when healthy friend-ships between Christian men and women were allowed to develop. A new model of dating had been created. For some, this was revolutionary.

Jesus on a Friday Night

It is presumptuous (and probably heretical) to imagine that Jesus ever went out on a date, especially since dating was not part of the customs of his world. In Jesus' world, marriage rela-tionships were arranged between families. It was not left up to the discretion of hopelessly romantic, hormonally charged young adults. Parents helped to choose the mate for their children. Interestingly, much of the world still operates on the pre-arranged model and has a higher rate of success than most American marriages. It is safe to say that Jesus was spared the agonies and heartaches of failed dating relationships.

Understanding the nature and character of Jesus, however, can probably help us understand how Jesus might approach the issue of dating. Since Jesus' life was a continual testimony of affirming the worth and dignity of other people, it is likely that Jesus would not support relationships that demeaned or devalued other people. Dating to "get" something or dating for self-serving purposes would be out. Because Jesus' central life preoccupation was growing in his relationship with God and giving witness to God's kingdom, any relationship that did not lead him closer to God or help him fulfill his purpose of sharing God's good news would be avoided. The more we read of Jesus, the more we see and realize that Jesus was concerned about holiness and righteousness. "Blessed are those who hunger and thirst for righteousness," claimed Jesus in his famous Sermon on the Mount. It is probably safe to assume that Jesus would speak against any relationship that did not help encourage people to move in the direction of holiness and righteousness. Furthermore, since Jesus healed and encouraged people toward health and wholeness, relationships that foster dysfunction and brokenness would be antithetical to his message. Jesus would probably encourage his followers to cut off these relationships before they ever got started. In all interactions with people Jesus sought to bring health, wholeness, peace, and a closer connection with God. Any dating relationships that did not uphold these characteristics would probably not fit into Jesus' pattern of relationships and dating.

When we look at the Gospels more closely and observe Jesus' interaction with women, these relational patterns are affirmed through his actions. By talking to the Samaritan woman at the well (a cultural taboo in his day), Jesus affirmed the worth and importance of both women and those of another race. By protecting the adulterous woman from being stoned to death, Jesus demonstrated the compassion and forgiveness of a God who loved her, despite her actions. By allowing women of "ill repute" to share their love by washing his feet with expensive perfume, Jesus made a profound statement that women are not to be defined by their occupation; rather, their worth is drawn from the fact that they are made in the image of God. By sharing the message of the resurrection at his tomb with women, Jesus reminds his listeners that women have full participation in the sharing of the good news story. Throughout the Gospel accounts, Jesus repeatedly reveals the relational patterns of love, forgiveness, compassion, dignity, and affirmation of every person regardless of race, gender, and occupation—especially women.

With these relational patterns so obviously and visibly demonstrated in Jesus' lifestyle and relationships, it is fair to conclude that Jesus would not support a dating system that destroys the self-esteem and emotionally cripples those who participate in the system. These kinds of relationships are not part of God's plan for Christians. God wants what is best for the children of God in all areas of life. How then, as young adults living in a country that promotes a certain system of dating, do we build relationships with those of the opposite sex that reflect the patterns found in Jesus' relationships?

No-Dating Policy?

A few years ago I conducted a survey with our college volunteers who had served time with our ministry. We asked each of these collegians if they thought a "no-dating" policy among other college volunteers, while serving with the ministry, was a good idea. The response of the students was a complete surprise to those on our leadership team. Almost 100 percent of those interviewed thought that a "no-dating" policy was a good idea. The reason for such an overwhelming response was that most students wanted to be in a place where they were "safe" and did not have to worry about the advances of certain individuals who were looking for a date . . . or a spouse. Those polled felt that dating relationships on staff detracted from community life. When people coupled up, others in the group were left out. The opportunity to build a strong sense of community among staff was diminished. Dating, determined the college students, worked against the establishment of Christian community. Christian community, determined the college students, was far more satisfying and emotionally fulfilling than dating.

When it comes to dating, Christian collegians have a unique opportunity to go beyond the system established by our culture. Because of the potential fellowship with other believers, Christian students have the opportunity to establish something much more fulfilling and healthy than isolated relationships with someone of the opposite sex. Christian collegians have the chance to create places where the dignity and worth of everyone can be upheld and the intimacy and support of a caring community can allow the development of friendships that are fun, healthy, and pure. By creating healthy fellowships of both men and women, where people can relate to one another without the expectation and pressure of moving into isolation, individuals can grow and friendships deepen. "Date-free" spaces can help young adults avoid some of the struggles with sexual temptations and focus on creating friendships that are more communal in nature.

Christian collegians should not forsake the ritual of dating and building relationships with those of the opposite sex. But Christian collegians should raise the bar on dating and take it to a whole new level. The world should be able to look at the way Christians date and say, "That is something I want to be a part of!" Group dates, like the evening described in the first part of the chapter, are a wonderful event for everybody involved. All the participants finished the night feeling special and affirmed as God's children. No one left the event feeling demeaned because he or she had compromised values or succumbed to sexual pressure in the heat of the moment. Relationships were strengthened in a healthy, wholesome manner.

Group date nights have now become a tradition in our ministry. Our summer workers have come to realize that the best way to build relationships with those of the opposite sex is to do it in a forum where everyone is on equal terms. Staff have learned that being a real lover means learning to love those you do not necessarily find sexually attractive. Preparing oneself to be a true lover means learning to love all people. Consequently, every Friday night is either a "guys' night out" or a "women's night out." Group dates are planned weeks in advance. Ironically, as time goes on these "dates" usually get better, because a healthy competition develops. The men and women try to outdo each other. Each Friday night as the summer progresses, the staff serve one another more sacrificially and more creatively. As our staff workers get better at serving their brothers and sisters on the team, I am convinced the Spirit slowly crafts them more into the likeness of the One who came to serve.

Equally Yoked

Growing up as a young Christian, I had always believed that when the apostle Paul talked about not being "yoked" with unbelievers (2 Cor. 6:14) he meant exclusively that a Christian should never consider marrying a non-Christian. I wonder if this is a somewhat limited understanding of the passage?

There is another twist to the often-quoted verse of Scripture that is many times overlooked, especially by biblical literalists who see things only in black and white. Since the term "Christian" today can mean anything from someone who was baptized as a baby and has no interest in actively growing in his or her relationship with God, to someone who is daily putting his or her life on the line to share the gospel, perhaps the interpretation of this passage needs to be expanded to mean that serious disciples of Christ should hook up only with other partners who share the same passion and commitment for God. When Paul talks about being "unequally yoked," was he speaking only in terms of believers and unbelievers? Paul would probably espouse that the premise for a relationship should have more to do with the level of commitment and less to do with doctrinal claims. If our intent is to serve Jesus wholeheartedly—go wherever he asks us to go and lay down our lives as a "living sacrifice"—then we need to find someone who shares these same convictions. If we have one level of commitment and our spouse has another level of commitment, then we will enter into marriage "unequally yoked."

Many potentially great Christian disciples get derailed because of a poor choice in spouse. When we enter into a marriage relationship with someone who has a different commitment level than ourselves, either the relationship will fall apart or the person who desires to serve Christ wholeheartedly will have to compromise his or her witness. A few years ago I saw this scenario unfold before my eyes with one of my staff.

Sandy was beautiful and bright, and she had tremendous gifts for ministry. The children loved her. Teenagers wanted to be her friend. Not only was she good at what she did, but she also had a passion to improve. Every opportunity Sandy was given, she would read books on theology, ministry, or child development to increase her knowledge and effectiveness. She would read the material and then show up at staff meetings glowing because of the new insights she had learned.

Unfortunately she had gotten married right after college. The relationship with her husband had developed in the "plastic bubble" of a Christian college community. Because of the sheltered environment, this young woman had never really seen the faith of her new husband tested. And because Ched acted "the role" of a Christian on the college campus, Sandy assumed that he shared her deep passion and love for urban ministry. I could tell the first day they arrived to do mission work that the relationship was "unequal." Sandy read books and took classes to improve her service; Ched played video games and worked on his car. Sandy spent her extra hours working with teens; Ched spent his extra hours watching television. His heart was not in ministry. He did not possess the same passion to grow. The scales were not balanced. After eight short months of involvement with our ministry, Ched convinced Sandy to resign. To keep the marriage together, she followed his lead. The last news I received was that they were separated. Because of their disparity in commitment, Sandy was in conflict and ultimately distracted from the passion and skills God had given her. The kingdom of God, our ministry, and the kids from our city lost a tremendous servant.

It always breaks my heart to see people marry before they have really discovered who they are and what they want to do with their lives. Marrying someone just because he or she believes in Jesus is not enough. It is crucial that couples have the same level of commitment. If you are in a relationship that is unequally yoked, get out of the relationship. Face the pain now, be courageous, but do not let it drag on another day. The apostle Paul knew what he was talking about. In the end, one of two things happens in unequal relationships: The relationship breaks apart or the committed one is pulled down by the one who does not share the same level of commitment. Seldom does it work the other way.

The magnificent Scottish novelist George MacDonald captured the essence of this marriage dilemma in his novel *The Gentlewoman's Choice*. MacDonald weaves in a strong message to women (which can equally apply to men) about marrying the unequal. MacDonald claims:

> Women are constantly being misled by the hope of being saviors of men! Such is natural to goodness and innocence, but, still, the error is disastrous. . . . It is said that patience reaps its reward, but I fear too many patiences fail and the number of resultant saints is small. . . . It takes God to make a true man. A woman is not enough for it. Marrying a good woman cannot be God's way of saving bad men.[12]

The heart of MacDonald's message is that we cannot save, redeem, or place within our partner a passion for God and

Christian discipleship. Only God and the Holy Spirit can perform this task. MacDonald continues to share his wisdom on the subject by explaining that good people who are filled with "goodness and innocence" need to be particularly cautious that they do not fall into the trap of trying to become saviors. MacDonald claims that it will backfire. He simply affirms that which the apostle Paul wrote centuries ago. Paul's message to those who desire marriage should be seriously considered prior to entering into a relationship. Be wise. Know what you are looking for in a mate. Set a standard and do not waver.

One of my former staff recently called me and asked for advice. She had begun dating a Japanese man who did not espouse Christian faith. She was curious what I thought about interfaith marriages. "He's a great guy. He's kinder, more loving, and more moral than most Christian guys I have dated," she began. "He is supportive of my faith and encourages me to grow. What do you think I should do?"

My friend presented a reality that is becoming increasingly common in a culture where former lines of race and religion are becoming increasingly blurred. She had not intended to fall in love, but they worked on a number of activities together, and their relationship had deepened. Now she found herself struggling for direction.

During the course of our conversation, I found myself raising more questions than giving advice. Realizing that she was deeply in love, I wanted to raise questions that I thought might be helpful for her to ponder as she moved ahead in the relationship and considered the prospect of marriage. As someone who had been involved in ministry, did she want a life partner who could participate with her in Christian ministry? How important was Christian community for her, and how would marrying a non-Christian man affect her interaction with a Christian community? Was she ready for possible alienation from those in her conservative Christian circles? What about children—in what faith tradition would they be raised? Would it be important to have a spouse with whom she could pray? Discuss Scripture? I encouraged her to think hard about these questions, because they would become issues in marriage.

After raising these questions I advised her to find a few other older married couples who had successfully been able to navigate the challenges of an interracial, interfaith marriage and talk to them at length about their relationship, raising some of the same questions I had suggested. Their wisdom and counsel could be very helpful.

Over the years I have found that many dating couples do not take advantage of the resource of older married couples who have been through struggles, have wrestled with the big questions, and can provide excellent insight to starry-eyed, "in love" couples. So often we try to work out our relationship in isolation without the objectivity of outside voices. Perhaps with this advice, the counsel of others, and the guidance of God's Spirit, my friend will arrive at the answer she needs to find for herself.

What Would Jesus Say?

No matter how hard we search the Scriptures and try to make application to contemporary culture, it is still hard to say exactly how Jesus would react and respond in our present context toward the issue of dating. If Jesus were your roommate, for example, it is hard to know exactly how he would advise and guide you in the area of relationships. Again, the best we can do is examine the relational patterns we find in the Gospel narratives and draw our own conclusions. The patterns Jesus demonstrated in his life were that he treated people with dignity, lived a holy life, strove to live obediently to God, and brought hope and healing to people. Any advice Jesus would give us in the area of dating would be filtered through this lens.

If Jesus were our roommate and we were seeking advice from him, I believe his leading questions would always be, "Why are you dating?" "What is your ultimate motivation?" "Is this relationship moving your partner closer to God?" "Is this relationship helping you serve Me more faithfully?" "Is this relationship leading toward marriage?" If you and your partner had no intention of moving toward a life commitment together and in strengthening the service of each other, I think Jesus would advise you to get out of the relationship and keep to group activities. This may sound a little harsh and prudish, but Jesus was often very direct and called people to decision when they were involved in destructive and unhealthy behavior. Couples who stay together month after month without moving toward any kind of deeper commitment (and dating has emotional and physical limitations that can never be understood until marriage) are often developing some kind of co-dependency that is destructive. Instead of creating a healthy relationship with different kinds of people, a couple is consumed with their own relationship. Instead of taking risks and stepping into experiences that are uncomfortable and calling individuals to find new kinds of support, the couple often falls back into what is familiar and comfortable. Instead of going to God for comfort and intimacy in times of isolation and aloneness, couples retreat to each other for support.

Over the years the healthiest college students I have met are people who develop great friendships with a variety of people. Over the years, the healthiest marriage relationships I have seen are between two people who were comfortable in their singleness before they got married. They could be alone. These individuals were secure enough in themselves and confident enough in their identity with Christ that they could be alone. In some ways these individuals heeded Bonhoeffer's warning that "there are Christians, too, who cannot endure being alone, who have had some bad experiences with themselves, who hope they will gain some help in association with others."[13] It is these kinds of people who Bonhoeffer says are usually "running away from [themselves]" and are using their relationship for the sake of diversion. One must be wary of these individuals because they ultimately bring destruction to both relationships and the Christian community. People who bring health to relationships are those who have cultivated patterns of commitment, loyalty, and fidelity in their singleness and then bring these characteristics to the relationship. As single people they have also developed the patterns of commitment in the way they study, in the way they pray, and in the way they work. When they finally take a step toward marriage, they have an array of gifts and disciplines to bring to the relationship. These people who were comfortable and growing in their singleness brought the necessary ingredients to help the marriage flourish.

Time to Oneself

In a powerful book called *Smart Girls, Gifted Women*, Barbara Kerr gives evidence of the importance of people discovering their own identity before they enter into relationships. Kerr explains the common experiences of certain girls who grew into strong women. Kerr studied the adolescent years of Eleanor Roosevelt, anthropologist Margaret Mead, writer Maya Angelou, and a host of others. What she found they had in common was "time by themselves." None of them were popular as adolescents and most stayed separated from their peers, not by choice, but because they were rejected. Ironically, this very rejection gave them a kind of space in which they could develop their gifts and uniqueness. It was not the rejection itself that helped these young women develop aspects of their personhood that some people never develop. The rejection, which many would see as negative, gave these young leaders a tremendous gift—the gift of space and the gift of time alone. Time by ourselves is crucial to developing oneself. Only by developing ourselves first will we truly bring anything of worth to our marriage later in life.

A Model of Commitment

One final reason why it is critical to cultivate these patterns of commitment, loyalty, and individual maturity prior to making a lifetime commitment is the incredibly high divorce rate in our current culture. Unfortunately, the statistics for marriages between people who would identify themselves as active Christians are not much different from statistics for marriages between people who would not identify themselves as active Christians. Most marriages now have about a 50 percent chance of lasting. The price our culture is paying for failed marriages and commitments continues to skyrocket. Most experts believe that increases in youth crime across our country has a direct correlation with what is happening in the home. As North Americans we have forgotten how to keep covenants and vows. We no longer understand the meaning of "until death do us part."

One individual who exemplifies Christian commitment, self-sacrifice, and a true understanding of what it means to be committed in marriage is the former president of Columbia Bible College, Robertson McQuilkin. A number of years ago his wife of thirty-nine years was diagnosed with Alzheimer's disease. This bright, vivacious woman became so incapacitated with the disease that she could not look after herself. McQuilkin was faced with a difficult decision. His ministry and career were thriving. God was obviously blessing his leadership at Columbia Bible College. But his wife was sick and needed constant care. What should he do?

He remembered the vows he had made years earlier— "in sickness and in health"—and realized that he had made a promise before God to care for his wife until death. His resignation from his post at Columbia was painful and difficult, and many people questioned the wisdom of his decision. Now instead of developing an annual $10 million scholastic budget or designing creative programs for students who had to meet the ever-increasing needs of the world, he takes his wife grocery shopping and makes sure that she does not load the carts of other people with canned goods. In the midst of fulfilling this commitment, McQuilkin continues to see his wife as the joy of his life and sees new manifestations of God's love in their relationship.

As we celebrate the lives of celebrities who marry four or five times, true heroes of love are overlooked and lost in the myriad of gossip columns and entertainment show updates. It is the McQuilkins of this world who demonstrate what God desires of Christians.

Signs of commitment can be seen early in dating relationships. If a person does not follow through on promises, cannot maintain friendships with others, has a checkered past of unhealthy relationships, is not disciplined in his or her studies, does not serve others sacrificially, then it is probably a pretty good indicator that these patterns of behavior will appear later in marriage. Yet it is difficult to be objective when we are smitten with love. It is difficult to see the red flags when we are infatuated. It is hard to be completely honest with people when we get into a relationship too deep, too fast. Therefore, it is always in our best interest to take any relationship slowly. And it makes good sense to involve the input of other people who can see things that we are too blinded to see.

Is It Legitimate to Be Single?

One of the worst things to happen in evangelical Christianity, and to a lesser degree in mainline Protestant Christianity, is the lack of affirmation single people receive. Many of my single friends, committed to celibacy and service, are continually viewed as being "incomplete." "When are you going to get married?" "Don't you want a family?" These are the questions they get asked continually.

Rather than embracing singleness as a viable and wonderful lifestyle, these wonderful, dedicated servants of God are looked upon as lacking. Within the Catholic tradition, a call to singleness is often affirmed and protected by the church. A single person can join an order or society in an effort to support his or her very special calling. The Jesuits, Franciscans, Benedictines, and Sisters of Charity are just a few of the orders that support those who feel called to celibacy and service. Unfortunately, this kind of communal and ecclesiastical support is not provided in most Protestant churches.

The apostle Paul has some very explicit words about singleness, marriage, and ministry. In 1 Corinthians 7:32–34, Paul encourages singleness for those who want to serve the Lord with the entire lives. Marriage, claims Paul, divides our loyalties between service to God and service to our spouse. Paul claims, "I would like you to be free from concern. An unmarried man is concerned about the Lord's affairs—how he can please the Lord. But a married man is concerned about the affairs of this world—how he can please his wife—and his interests are divided. An unmarried woman or virgin is concerned about the Lord's affairs: Her aim is to be devoted to the Lord in both body and spirit. But a married woman is concerned about the affairs of this world—how she can please her husband." If you talk to anyone in ministry who is married, they will no doubt tell you of the difficulties, the strained loyalties, and the compromises that are made between marriage and ministry. Scripture affirms that singleness is a very viable option for those who want to serve God wholeheartedly. Singleness is not only an option, it is the preferred option, according to St. Paul. Somehow this message needs to be communicated within the Christian community, so those who sense a calling toward singleness will not be viewed as incomplete and needy people.

If Jesus Were a Sophomore

I wonder what would happen if Jesus showed up on a college campus one Friday afternoon and gathered all the dating couples—who claimed Christ as their Lord—together for a "surprise" meeting. Imagine if all those who attended were invited because they found a special invitation in their mailbox. The invitations were intriguing and hard to resist. Each invitation requested the presence of the particular student. Since they were individually addressed, not every student knew that their partner had been invited. The invitations offered a wonderful surprise to those who found their way to a designated, "out-of-the-way" campus lounge. Oddly, all invitations had been signed by a fellow student with the initials "J.C."

The couples arrive to the meeting in a variety of ways. Some come together arm in arm—unable to peel themselves away from each other's passionate embrace. Others arrive independently, surprised to see their partner in attendance and realizing that they have been "discovered." Up to this point in the relationship their romantic activity has taken place behind closed doors. This public exposure is a little embarrassing.

After everyone is seated, the scene intensifies as a young man walks into the room.

"You all know me," he begins. "You may not recognize me. You all claim to be in relationship with me."

The crowd looks completely puzzled. Bewildered.

"Oh, I'm sorry," says the meeting coordinator. "I'm Jesus."

"Come on. You're putting us on," calls a young man on the front row.

"You look just like us," says another.

"I'm not about to go into a long explanation," replies a smiling Jesus. "Let me just say, many of you are a little perplexed about how you got invited to this meeting. You thought nobody knew about your relationship. Well, guess what? I know . . . everything."

The crowd becomes extremely attentive.

"The reason I've gathered you together is because you are all about to make plans for the weekend. I just want to make sure I am part of the plans. You know, invited along."

"You've gotta be joking!" bellows one student whose boyfriend is so close to her it would take surgery to separate them.

"This is absurd," adds another.

Jesus scans the audience with his eyes. Once again, the entire room goes completely silent.

"No, I'm not joking, and this is not absurd," continues the One who called the meeting. "I want to know if I am part of your plans."

It is interesting to think of Jesus being part of our "dating" plans. For many the idea is a little bizarre. It would be pretty uncomfortable to invite Jesus along on a date. But why is this idea so absurd? We talk about having a "personal" relationship with Jesus. We talk about Jesus being a living Spirit who is intimately connected with our lives. So why is it so absurd to think of Jesus as an actual presence in our dating life? Why is so crazy to think that Jesus is there at the movie theater? The park? The dorm room?

I was recently talking with a college student who was living with her boyfriend in an apartment off campus. She led worship for her Christian fellowship group and was active in missions and various outreach events on campus. As we talked, I realized that this young woman had successfully compartmentalized her life.

She had her spiritual activities—her Christian friends, church, and Bible studies. And then she had this other life. She had invited Jesus into one part of her existence, but she had excluded Jesus from the other part of her life. For a period of time this had worked. Now she was finally beginning to realize that this double life was affecting her spiritual life. She was beginning to realize that Jesus wanted to be invited into all her plans.

Thinking of Jesus as a real person (rather than some abstract being whom we meet once a week at church) can protect us from allowing our faith to become totally disconnected from our daily lives. I think it helpful to ponder the implications of Jesus being a real student on a real university campus today. What would his attitude be toward women on campus? Would he have an opinion about our dating system? Would he speak out against some of the relationships between Christian brothers and sisters on campus? Since we cannot put words in Jesus' mouth—especially words that specifically pertain to dating—all we can do is formulate principles from the words he did speak and the actions he displayed with his life.

The principles we can draw from the words of Jesus are very clear. Jesus calls us to live as holy people. Jesus calls us to uphold the dignity of other people. Jesus calls us to seek the kingdom first, and all (our relationships too) shall be added unto those who follow. Jesus calls us to serve others and lead them into a deeper knowledge of God. These are some of the themes we see at work in the life and teachings of Jesus. These patterns are consistent with his character and the character he wants his followers to incorporate into their own lives and into their dating relationships.

Remember:

We all experience sexual desires, but they . . . can be controlled without damaging us. I have never seen an obituary that gave chastity as the cause of death.

Molly Kelly

Questions for Reflection

1. How has dating and the pursuit of intimate relationships with members of the opposite sex affected your life to date? Have these relationships helped you grow as a Christian? Have they hurt your growth? In what ways have they hurt your growth?

2. Do you feel pressure to date? If so, why? If not, why?

3. What ideas from the chapter do you like? Which ideas from the chapter can help you as you wrestle with areas of dating and sexuality in the future?

4. In what ways can you help create a new model for dating on your campus? Are there activities you can plan that would help Christian brothers and sisters develop deeper relationships with one another and with God?

5. Is singleness a viable option for your life? If not, why? If so, what are you doing to prepare your life for this commitment?

6. Do you think interfaith dating is incompatible with Christian discipleship? Why? Why not? What advice would you give to a Christian brother or sister involved in an interfaith dating relationship?

For the Leader

Ask your group the following: If Jesus called all the Christians together on your campus who were presently involved in a dating relationship, what would he have to say to them?

Prayer and Meditation

Gracious God,

I'm constantly being bombarded with images that are sexual and images that remind me of my incompleteness without a partner.
I have many questions about what You want from me in the area of relationships.
Is there someone out there for me?
What should I be looking for in a partner? How will I know when the time is right?

In the meantime,
Help me to embody the principle of holiness in my life.
Help me uphold all people with dignity and true love.
Help me to serve others first and truly desire to lead all people into a deeper knowledge of You.
Help me to develop myself as Your child, independent and fully confident that I am created in Your image.

In doing these things help me to never let go of the belief that if I seek Your kingdom first,
You will provide for all of my deepest needs.
I move ahead with my life holding to this belief.

Amen

Chapter 6

Parental Behaviors:
What to Do about Parents

"Whoever comes to me and does not hate father and mother, wife and children, brothers and sisters, yes, and even life itself, cannot be my disciple."

Luke 14:26 (NRSV)

The first time I phoned my parents to say I wanted to do mission work I heard a strong "no" and was told to come home. From this it changed to "something you can go and do and get it out of your system." Two years later, they had accepted it as "something God placed and ingrained into my system." Going against my parents' wishes was difficult, but Jesus calls us as Christians to leave our parents, brothers, and sisters. But I think in all of this God has blessed me and my family and brought about reconciliation between us.

Student Missionary

Total Rejection

If you go I will not acknowledge you as my son anymore," chided the father. "I will not allow my son to waste his life on those people!"

At twenty years of age, Stu felt these words cut to the core of his being. Recently out of college, Stu had just secured a great job. He was well on his way to climbing the corporate ladder. His family was excited. Needless to say, Stu knew his father would not be thrilled about his decision to follow God's call. Never did he imagine that his father would react so vehemently against his spending a summer in the inner city. Disowned from the family? Stu began to wonder if he was really hearing God's voice.

Stu was confronted with the most difficult decision he ever had to face. Should he obey the voice of God, or should he obey the voice of his parents? Obeying God's voice would mean losing his relationship with his family. He would not be included in family gatherings. He would be removed from the family will.

The entity that had shaped him and had given him identity and a sense of security was about to be taken from him. Was it worth it? Was this burden being placed on his heart just an emotional response to a well-crafted sermon? Or was it really a call from God?

For weeks Stu wrestled with the decision. At night he stayed up until the early hours of the morning praying, thinking, and reading his Bible. He thought about verses in the Bible that talked about "honoring your parents." He recalled hearing a sermon a few years prior where the preacher claimed that decisions "of the Lord" were confirmed by a sense of peace. In this situation there was no peace—just tension, upheaval, and "unsettledness." Stu was more confused than ever.

The longer Stu prayed, the more he became convinced that he was to make this leap of faith, no matter what the repercussions. Yes, he loved his father. But he also began to realize that there was someone bigger than his father at work in his life. Devotion to God had to take precedence over devotion to family. Stu was a Christian; his father was not. This seemed to be the decisive moment when his father's agenda and the agenda of the kingdom would part. Stu knew that if his faith were to grow, he would have to choose the road of the kingdom. Compromise at this point would surely lead to spiritual death.

The mission experience proved to be critical for Stu. Besides the struggle and pain with his family, the actual work opened Stu's eyes to new realities. Working in an impoverished inner-city community, Stu befriended children and families who lived in deplorable conditions. The new environment was such a vivid contrast to where he grew up that it forced him to ask questions about justice. Meeting children who were basically raising themselves broke Stu's heart as he took on the role of parent, counselor, and mentor. God worked in his life in some amazing ways. His faith was stretched. God honored his decision.

When Stu returned home at the end of the summer his father would not talk to him. He was not invited to family functions. He was excluded from holiday celebrations. And it had been stated that nobody from the family would attend Stu's wedding the following year. Despite the rejection on the home front, the company that had released him for the mission trip rehired him upon his return. Doors began to open in ways he never imagined at his workplace. Day after day employees, many of them non-Christians, would come up to Stu and ask him about his experience in the city. Continually Stu shared his faith and the struggles he was facing with his family. Oddly, the non-Christians at work became an amazing source of encouragement and inspiration during this time.

Stu's faithfulness to God at all costs became a powerful testimony to others—both Christian and non-Christian. Everybody knew what he had given up to serve God. They all watched God change this man in front of their eyes. Even the agnostics were intrigued and began attending prayer and information sessions Stu hosted at the workplace. Stu showed slides and told stories about kids and families living in the inner city. For many people this was their first encounter with a Christian who was trying to live a life of discipleship. Many had heard lots of talk about Jesus in their lifetime by well-paid clergy and television evangelists but were always turned off by their insincerity. There was something real about Stu that nobody could deny.

What Do We Do about Parents?

The greatest obstacle to taking risks for God can be parents, especially Christian parents. Missionaries are applauded for going into the far outposts of civilization to bring the gospel. Bible heroes are taught in Sunday school and pointed to as true models of faith. The disciples are heralded for their willingness to follow Jesus at all costs. But when it comes time for the kids of Christian parents to make the decision to lead a life of radical faith, often that decision is met with opposition. It's okay for someone else's child to be giving his or her life for the cause of Christ in a radical way, but it is not okay when it is their own child. As long as the heroes of faith are kept at a distance, everything is fine. When the "hero" is in the family, things begin to get tense.

I have frequently dealt with students who report that they have tearfully and painfully had to fight their parents to get approval to do a mission project. Rather than walking side by side with their children and becoming part of the exciting things God is doing in their life, parents can often become a tremendous source of discouragement. The parental voice of concerns—practicality, caution, and ultimately disapproval—can become the factor that deters one from stepping out in faith. Comments such as "You're throwing your life away!" "How are you going to pay for school?" "I was hoping you would do something substantial with your life!" and "All the money we've poured into your education, and this is what you have decided to do?" are thrown at students who are trying to respond to the call of God at this crucial period in their lives. Year after year I see what students have to go through to get approval from parents to serve the kingdom in a way that costs something and involves risk. With guilt and lack of support, many students buckle under pressure and never respond to God's urgings.

The Disobedient Child: St. Francis of Assisi

The life of the great Catholic saint, Francis of Assisi, is fascinating. It was assumed that Francis, as the son of a wealthy merchant in Venice, would follow in the footsteps of his father. When the message of Christ began to compel him, Francis changed the course of his life. He asked the question, "Am I to live comfortably in the wake of my father? Or am I going to be obedient to Jesus?"

There was a defining moment between Francis and his father. When the young Francis felt called to help the poor, he concluded that he himself must become poor. That meant giving up the privilege and comfort of his existing life. In a dramatic and symbolic moment Francis stood before his father and stripped off his fine clothing. Naked, Francis handed his clothing to his father and put on sackcloth. To the dismay of his father, Francis embarked on a life of voluntary poverty and turned his back on the family business. Much to the embarrassment of his family, he no longer ate the fine food of the family table, but begged from the people of Assisi for their trash. This was the beginning of a powerful movement of God's Spirit that eventually turned into a revival of the church throughout Europe.[14]

Throughout the history of the church one meets people who face the decision of whether they should listen to the voice of their parents or listen to the voice of God. How different would the world be if St. Francis had not acted against the desires of his father and abandoned all for the cause of Christ? Because he chose to make this radical departure from his upbringing, St. Francis has inspired millions of people throughout the centuries to share with the poor. An entire holy order called the Franciscans was created to provide a community for men who desired to live out the vows of poverty, chastity, and service to the poor. This order continues today by deploying thousands of monks into the world to spread the joy and love of Jesus as St. Francis shared the joy and love of Jesus.

Had St. Francis just listened to his father he would have become another rich merchant who attended church once a week and held positions of status and power within his community, but he would have been quickly forgotten. Instead, St. Francis has lived on over centuries of church history as a model of total devotion to Christ, inspiring people to love the poor, love God's creation (he talked to the birds and animals), and be "a clown for Christ" (Francis invented the "clowning ministry"). St. Francis lived a life that has had eternal significance.

Who Is My Mother? Who Is My Brother?

Surprisingly, Jesus has a few things to say about family. In a patriarchal society where parents (especially fathers) had a much greater authority than today, Jesus' words about this issue are even more radical. In Matthew when Jesus is confronted with the information that his mother and brothers are waiting outside to see him, Jesus responds that "whoever does the will of my Father in heaven is my brother and sister and mother" (Matt. 12:50). It is in this statement that Jesus redefines family. Biological connections are not the only criteria defining family for Jesus. For Jesus, "family" are those connected by faith who share a willingness to do the will of God. If you do "the will" of God, then you are related to others who do God's will. They become your family. Obedience to God, according to Jesus, overrides blood ties.

Jesus' other statements in the Gospels about family reinforce what Matthew records. In Luke 14:26 Jesus uses strong words when he claims that "If anyone comes to me and does not hate his father and mother, his wife and children, his brothers and sisters—yes, even his own life—he cannot be my disciple." Jesus speaks these words in relation to a life of discipleship. According to Jesus, family can never stand in the way of a life of discipleship. With this in mind, Christians—especially students in the college years—must begin to rethink allegiances. If a mother or father is acting as a barrier to doing the will of God, to living out a life of discipleship, then Christian students must look to a new family for those important relationships. Our call as Christians is to obey God, not necessarily our biological parents. When Peter tried to stand in the way of Jesus' journey to the cross and Jesus rebuked him by saying, "Get behind me,

Satan," Jesus reminded us that there may come a time when we must say the same to our parents. It may be painful. It may be the most difficult thing we ever do. But God honors those who "seek first the kingdom."

A Good Illustration

This idea of prioritizing our relational allegiances is vividly illustrated in C. S. Lewis's classic book about hell, *The Great Divorce*. Lewis emphasizes that humans must get their priorities right. Absolute devotion to God must come first; devotion to human relationships is secondary. In *The Great Divorce* the reader meets a number of interesting characters who cannot enter heaven because they cannot let go of their earthly matters and earthly relationships. Their earthly relationships stand in the way of developing a relationship with God. In one particularly powerful scene, a messenger from heaven is in dialogue with a mother about her son. The son is in heaven, but the mother is still in hell because her relationship with her son stands in the way of her relationship with God. Her love for her son (which can be a good thing) has become destructive because it keeps her from loving God. At one point God's messenger claims:

> Human beings can't make one another really happy for long. And secondly for your sake, He [God] wanted your merely instinctive love for your child (tigresses share that, you know!) to turn into something better. He [God] wanted something better. He [God] wanted you to love Michael [her son] as He understands love. You cannot love a fellow-creature fully till you love God. . . . What she calls her love for her son has turned into a poor, prickly, astringent sort of thing.

What Lewis so brilliantly illustrates is that even the most intense familial love cannot replace the love that occurs when we prioritize our love relationships and put God first. It is our devotion to God first that enables us to truly love others in ways that are healthy and enduring. Parents who stand in the way of their children truly obeying and following God are not demonstrating real love and will never receive real love back from their children. Only in letting their children go into the hands of God will parents experience real love. Conversely, only by obeying God first will the child truly have the ability to love the parents in return.

The Surprising Fruit of Faithfulness

If parents resist and discourage your calling, pray and believe that your obedience may be a testimony and witness that could radically change their faith. Initial painful separations between parents and students can become the very instrument that ultimately deepens the relationship. Through letters, updates, phone calls, and conversations with friends of your parents, initial resistance often melts away and the faith of parents can begin to increase. As in the case of Stu, after two additional mission trips and much prayer, Stu found that his father's heart began to soften. After three years Stu was embraced by his family again. His father's attitude toward faith and ministry was expanded. The very act of "defiance" that had caused father and son to initially split became the very instrument that brought their relationship to a whole new level of understanding.

It is important to remember that parental resistance to lives of radical discipleship can often stem from concern and love. Parents have invested many years of emotional energy, time, and resources in their kids. To underestimate this intense love and concern is naive on the part of the student. The idea of a son or daughter doing something potentially risky can be very threatening and difficult. And yet, it is important to remember that your act of obedience to God may become the very act that brings about the ultimate redemption and salvation of the ones you love. I have heard parents say, "I never really prayed before my daughter went on a mission. For the first time in my life I really had to trust God." Or, "I didn't think he could raise the money for the trip. Now I have seen God provide in unbelievable ways." When children provoke these kinds of responses, it is a sure sign that God is teaching the older generation through the faithful acts of the younger generation.

If Jesus Were a Sophomore

I can only speculate, but I imagine there was continual tension in Jesus' relationship with his parents—tension surrounding his very radical view of family.

Can you imagine worried parents being told by their twelve-year-old son that they are not ultimately in charge of his life? Can you imagine a parent hearing their son say that "there will be five in one family divided against each other, three against two and two against three. They will be divided, father against son and son against father, mother against daughter and daughter against mother . . ." (Luke 12:52–53). So much for family reunions! Can you imagine a mother requesting to see her son, only to hear him say, in effect, "Biology has nothing to do with our relationship. What entitles you to be my mother is your relationship to God. The fact that you gave birth to me has little bearing on your entitlement to see me." Jesus' radical view on the concept of family could leave any parent feeling kind of cold.

I wonder what it was like when Jesus tried to leave the family business at age thirty?

"Dad, can I talk with you for a minute?"

"Sure, what is it, son?" responds Joseph.

"Well, I'm sensing that my real Father is calling me to leave the family carpentry business and become a wandering preacher," begins Jesus.

"But son, I'm just about to retire! I thought you would take over the operations. You know your brother. He's pretty unreliable. You could expand the business . . . make a good living for yourself," says the concerned father. "How will you support yourself?" he continues, ever the practical father. "How will you live? What will you eat?"

Jesus smiles thoughtfully at Joseph.

"I'm gonna have to trust, Dad. Have faith. You know, believe that the One who clothes the lilies of the fields and feeds the birds will also clothe me and feed me."

Joseph, not fully convinced by his son's idealism and faith, gives one last attempt.

"You know this is going to tear your mother up. She's a worrier, Jesus. She's been pondering things in her heart since your birth. Are you sure you want to do this to her?"

"Dad," says Jesus, "I'm not doing 'this' to anyone. I'm not doing this to make life more difficult for you, or to make life more worrisome for Mother. I'm doing it because I have a higher authority to which I am accountable."

Who knows if the discussion went anything like this? The Gospel writers do give us a glimpse that Jesus' idea of what constitutes a familial relationship may have been different from his parents' idea.

Again, Luke's recording of the boy Jesus talking to the elders at the Temple is one example of this new orientation toward looking at the role and authority of parents in our lives. In Luke 2:49 the young parents of Jesus are worried sick about their child's disappearance. Jesus makes it clear, at the age of twelve, that he has an allegiance higher than to his earthly parents. "Didn't you know I had to be in my Father's house?" claims the young Jesus, who had been missing for three days. These words sound a little strange coming from the mouth of a twelve-year-old. But they reveal an important truth. From very early in his life Jesus redefines parenthood by giving God, his heavenly Parent, the ultimate authority in his life. Matthew adds further evidence to this radical view on family when he records, "Someone told him, 'Your mother and brothers are standing outside, wanting to speak to you.'" Jesus goes on and points to his disciples and says, "Here are my mother and my brothers. For whoever does the will of my Father in heaven is my brother and sister and mother" (Matt. 12:47–50). So much for VIP treatment.

To say that this ultimate allegiance to God does not cause conflict would be misleading. To usurp the power and control of earthly parents for complete devotion to God creates all kinds of conflict. It causes pain and, sometimes, rejection by our biological parents, our siblings, relatives, and even the leadership of our church. But Jesus knows there are no earthly substitutes for a relationship with God that puts all other agendas as secondary. Nothing is more important than our obedience to the will of God. This is why Jesus' teaching on the true meaning of family is so revolutionary and cannot be taken lightly.

The college and university years are a critical time to establish patterns of priorities and allegiances. Parents and friends will all have expectations. You will feel their strings pulling you in different directions and pointing you toward careers and vocations that they think will be good for you. But what our parents, relatives, and friends think is best for our lives may be completely opposite of what God wants for our lives. The task of the student trying to live a life of discipleship is to sincerely seek the will of God for their lives. When the will of God is revealed—in whole or in part—to the disciple, the task is then to step out courageously and in faithful obedience, believing that God will provide. All of us would agree that if it came down to our earthly parents deciding what is best for our lives, or our heavenly Parent deciding what is best for our lives, we would ultimately land on the side that suggests that God knows what is best for us.

Holding fast to this truth may create conflict, but in the end we must hold to the Scriptural promise that God, not our parents, will never abandon or forsake us.

Remember:

I was raised Quaker and am grateful to my parents for the moral values impressed upon me throughout my childhood. I understand that everything I do must be done consciously, with attention to the impact it has on other people and the earth. I understand that all human beings deserve to be treated with respect and that I have the responsibility to do what I can to see that other people are not abused or exploited. With these truths in mind, buying clothes has always been an issue for me. If they're made in China, chances are they were made by imprisoned Tibetans. Even in the United States, the National Labor Committee, an independent organization focused on the protection of worker rights in the global economy, has deemed 65 percent of apparel shops in New York and Los Angeles bad enough to receive the title sweatshop. In an effort to be as small a contributor to these abuses as possible, I have spent many hours at the sewing machine with my mother, patching jeans bought secondhand and making drawstring pants.

Anna Roberts, student activist, protesting purchasing practices of collegiate apparel

Questions for Reflection

1. Describe your relationship with your parents. Do your parents have an agenda for your life? If so, identify their agenda. How does this agenda coincide with what you sense God is calling you to do with your life?

2. What do you think of how Jesus seems to redefine the concept of "family" as presented in the Gospels? Is it realistic? Is it a view that you can embrace?

3. Have you ever made a decision for God that your family did not support? What were the long-term repercussions of the decision? Do you have any regrets about making this decision?

4. What have your parents given you? How can you demonstrate love and appreciation for the gifts they have given to you? How can you challenge them to deepen their faith through how you model Christian discipleship?

For the Leader

Ask the members of your group to break into groups of two. Have each of the groups put together a short role-play depicting a dialogue between themselves and a parent. The issue at the center of the role-play should have something to do with an aspect of the student's faith and a parental reaction to that particular aspect of faith.

Prayer and Meditation

Lord,

Thanks for the gift of parents.
Show me how I can more visibly demonstrate my appreciation
    for their care.
And Lord, where they have hurt me,
Help me to forgive and let go of things that are inhibiting me
    from growing into the person
You desire me to become.

I pray for wisdom as I navigate this transitional period in my life.
I pray for courage as I begin to embrace life and faith more fully
    for myself.
I pray for strength when I will need to make choices that my
    parents do not fully understand, nor fully accept.

Most important, help me to hear Your voice and Your call for my
    life,
Clear away all the voices that want to direct me and tell me how
    to live,
So I can hear and understand You more completely.

Amen

Chapter 7

Wise Behaviors:
Whatever Happened to Wisdom?

When I was a boy of fourteen, my father was so ignorant I could hardly stand to have him around. But when I got to be twenty-one I was astonished at how much the old man had learned.

Mark Twain

Religious instruction, however sound, is not enough by itself. It brings light, but it cannot impart sight. The assumption that light and sight are synonymous has brought spiritual tragedy to millions. The Pharisees looked straight at the Light of the World for three years, but not one ray of light reached their inner beings. Light is not enough. The inward operation of the Holy Spirit is necessary to saving faith. The Gospel is light but only the Spirit can give sight.

A. W. Tozer

If You Could Have Anything . . .

A recent best-selling book was titled *Ten Stupid Things Women Do to Mess Up Their Lives*. In her book, radio psychologist Laura Schlesinger bluntly outlines an assortment of ways bright, intelligent women destroy their lives. Because this problem is not unique to women, a sequel has been written for men. It promises to be even more successful. Dr. Laura is on target when she asserts that people who have tremendous intelligence, "successful" careers, and competence still have the capacity to send their lives into a tailspin because they make really stupid choices. Chapter titles like "Stupid Chivalry" and "Stupid Ambition" underscore how both men and women get involved in situations that destroy the fabric of their lives and undermine that which brings about long-term health and wholeness in their relationship.

If one reads the newspaper or watches the television with any regularity, it becomes apparent that intelligent people who seem to have their lives on track do not necessarily make good decisions. Successful CEOs with stable families are caught embezzling funds. Men and women in top government positions with all kinds of influence are seduced into absurd sexual acts and subsequent cover-up scandals. Successful college athletes accept short-term monetary bribes only to find themselves kicked out of school. One begins to understand that intelligence and talent do not protect people from making destructive life decisions. That is why Harvard psychologist Robert Coles can say with a twist of irony, "You can get all A's and still flunk life!"

Unfortunately we live in a culture that makes intelligence—rather than common sense, character, and wisdom—the preeminent mark of success. Good grades, rather than understanding and comprehension, are rewarded. Too often grades and SAT test scores are the factors that determine the college a student attends. Grades and LSAT or GRE scores ultimately become the mark by which graduate schools measure the potential of a student. As a society we have become convinced that test scores determine how much a person knows. It is interesting to note that prior to the 1950s, post-college degrees like Ph.D.s were looked upon as a detriment when one searched for employment. Corporations preferred to hire individuals with real work experience, not MBAs from prestigious colleges.

Unfortunately, today our institutions of higher learning have all but forgotten that life is more than simply taking tests and writing research papers. True education is about giving people the skills to live life well and effectively. True education is about helping people make connections between knowledge and action. In our degree-infatuated culture, it is easy to forget the importance of words like *wisdom*—words that place importance not on how much people know, but rather on what they do with their knowledge. It is too bad that educators do not spend more time studying the truths of past cultures and bring these lessons back into the classroom. In ancient Jewish culture, for example, people placed the concept of wisdom above intelligence. Wisdom, not intelligence, was desired. The reason for this distinction is that wisdom had to do with how individuals would live their life. Wisdom, when translated from the Hebrew, actually means "skill for living." According to the biblical tradition, a wise person lived life with a certain skill that differentiated him or her from other people. Ultimately the wise were people who would make good choices that would help themselves, their families, and their communities. A wise person was someone who had the ability to integrate knowledge with real life.

He Could Have Had Anything!

One of the most remarkable Old Testament stories is about young King Solomon. Solomon was thrust into a position of leadership in his late teens or early twenties and was given tremendous responsibility. He was called to govern a country! For many people his age, a position of power and prestige would puff up a person's ego. The privilege and power would be used to live life more selfishly. After all, the king of a country could have anything he desired. Like other kings, Solomon could have used his new position to build his wealth and expand his reputation both in the eyes of his people and in the surrounding countries. Instead, Solomon acted in the best interest of his people.

One night Solomon had an encounter with God. The Bible tells the story: "At Gibeon the LORD appeared to Solomon during the night in a dream, and God said 'Ask for whatever you want me to give you'" (1 Kings 3:5).

For many of us, this is the question we have dreamed of being asked all our lives. It is like Aladdin finding the genie in the bottle and being given the opportunity to make three wishes. Yet when the question was asked of a young king who had a heart after God and desired to be a good leader, Solomon had the humility to realize that he did not have the tools necessary to perform his job with skill. Solomon needed supernatural intervention to assist him in his role as a politician, a leader, and a spiritual guide of his people.

In his prayer to God Solomon made his requests known: "give your servant a discerning heart to govern your people and to distinguish between right and wrong" (1 Kings 3:9). The Scriptures tell us that his request is met by God with great pleasure. Since Solomon does not ask for long life, wealth, or death of enemies, but rather asks for discernment in administering justice, God grants him wisdom and additional blessings that he does not request. As a result of his unselfish request, Solomon begins the journey of becoming a great king because he asked for wisdom.

Put to the Test

Immediately upon requesting wisdom, Solomon is placed in a very difficult situation. His leadership abilities are put to the test. All eyes are watching how this young king will handle a difficult test of judgment and justice. The Scripture says, "Then two women who were harlots came to the king and stood before him" (1 Kings 3:16). Two women each claimed that the baby held before them was their birth child. One of the women said to Solomon,

> "Oh, my lord, this woman and I live in the same house; and I gave birth to a child while she was in the house. And it happened on the third day after I gave birth, that this woman also gave birth to a child, and we were together. There was no stranger with us in the house . . . and this woman's son died in the night, because she lay on it. So she rose in the middle of the night and took my son from beside me while your maidservant slept, and laid him in her bosom, and laid her dead son in my bosom."
>
> 1 Kings 3:17

Solomon needs to discern who is telling the truth and give the living child to the proper mother. At stake is the life of a child and the pain that the true mother may lose her child. It is a difficult situation. This is not the kind of decision one makes by reading a manual on leadership. There was no formula for him to follow. What Solomon faced was a real-life test of his ability to make a delicate, well-grounded decision. The decision required knowledge and understanding beyond Solomon's years. The decision required Solomon to block out the emotions and chaos of the moment and focus his mental capacities on making a choice that would not only solve the present crisis, but would send a message to his country that he was a king who could govern with wisdom.

Amazingly Solomon settles the situation between the two mothers with a tremendous sense of insight and maturity. Knowing that the true mother will step forward and give up her child when Solomon threatens to have it killed, Solomon learns the identity of the child's true mother and returns the child to the rightful parent. Displaying wisdom and an impeccable sense of justice, Solomon passes his first test as a new leader. The people of Israel begin to look to him with a sense of trust and respect.

The writer of 1 Kings in the Old Testament does a masterful job of tying Solomon's request for wisdom with a real-life situation of decision making in which true wisdom is needed. In reading about the early stages of Solomon's kingship, the reader is struck by the significance and importance of wisdom and the relationship between wisdom and good, God-inspired leadership. Wisdom is needed if leadership is to be exercised in a way that brings glory to God and creates an environment of justice.

What Is This Wisdom?

The concept of *wisdom* is key throughout the Old Testament, especially in the books scholars have called the Wisdom literature—Proverbs, Ecclesiastes, and the Song of Solomon. It is in these biblical books that the value and importance of wisdom is upheld. In our world where so much emphasis is placed on academic degrees and accumulated facts, the idea of a deeper knowledge that cannot be bought or earned and that transcends conventional intelligence has been lost. For the ancient Jew, wisdom was held in high esteem because wisdom determined how individuals would live out their lives on a day-to-day basis.

Wisdom (*hokma* in Hebrew) was a term derived from Exodus 31:3 where a worker was endowed with skill in textiles and metal craftsmanship. A skilled worker was a person who performed his or her trade with a high level of artistry and professionalism. A worker who possessed a high level of *hokma* was an individual who did the job with skill. The worker's talents were admired by others. Hence, a wise person is a person who lives life skillfully.

How then does this skill translate into real-life activity? True wisdom, when exercised in the day-to-day grind, demonstrates itself in acts of prudence and insight (Prov. 8:12). Wise people shed light on situations and see beyond the surface. Furthermore, people of wisdom possess knowledge and discretion; they hate pride and arrogance, evil behavior, and perverse speech. Counsel and sound judgment and deep understanding of situations are also the fruit of a life of wisdom (Prov. 8:14). These are a few examples of how wisdom is portrayed in the book of Proverbs. It becomes very evident that those who possessed wisdom in ancient Hebraic culture were the kinds of people who brought stability and leadership to their community. They were people who were respected because they did not make stupid decisions. They were the kinds of people who lived life fully and vibrantly because life decisions were made with skill.

This connection between wisdom and the fullness of life cannot be overlooked. Proverbs makes clear that:

> For whoever finds me [wisdom] finds life
> and receives favor from the LORD.
> But whoever fails to find me [wisdom] harms himself;
> All who hate me [wisdom] love death.
>
> Prov. 8:35

The promise of the passage is that those who seek and find wisdom find life. Wisdom and life are intertwined. They cannot be separated. The quality and fullness of a person's life is directly related to the kind of "skill" with which that person lives his or her life. Without wisdom, without *hokma*, life is lived out on a lower level of existence. Perhaps that is why, throughout the entire book of Proverbs, the reader is instructed to "get wisdom" (4:5), "esteem" wisdom (4:8), and not to "forsake" wisdom (4:2). Again, it is wisdom—not knowledge, not information, not technical skill, not diplomas, not intelligence—that God's people are instructed to seek. God's people are challenged to pursue wisdom because if they possess wisdom they bring a quality of life to their community and to their families that helps create a place of shalom—a place of wholeness, health, and justice. Whether wisdom is reflected in how a domestic political crisis is managed (Esth. 1:13–22), or in the efficient management of a domicile (Prov. 14:1; 31:10–31), or in the construction of the tabernacle (Exod. 28:3), *hokma* offers success to those who possess it. To possess this skill of living in Old Testament times meant that life would be richer and the community and workplace would be healthier. People who seek wisdom help create a God-like place.

Jesus Was Wise

It is obvious from the Gospel accounts that Jesus handled himself and situations with tremendous wisdom. Without degrees from the major rabbinical schools of his day, Jesus dealt with difficult situations and difficult people with remarkable insight. When the woman caught in adultery was about to be stoned, Jesus shared wise words that defused the situation and set her free. When Jesus was asked about taxes and issues of loyalty to the government, he silenced the critics with a simple, yet wise, illustration and words. When performing miracles he used wisdom in instructing the individuals who were healed to remain quiet, lest his mission be distracted. Wisdom was also manifested in Jesus' life in how he balanced solitude with public interaction. Frequently the Gospel writer Mark records that Jesus went off by himself to get away from the busy distractions of the crowds. Jesus managed his life, his prayer time, and his public time with wisdom.

As Jesus displays a sense of skill and wisdom in the way he managed his life, the question begs to be asked: Did Jesus have to learn wisdom? Or was wisdom just supernaturally deposited into the psyche of Jesus one day? It is important for the disciple of Jesus to grapple with and process this question. Whether we believe Jesus received wisdom supernaturally, or whether we believe Jesus had to learn and grow in his wisdom, has tremendous implications for discipleship. Although many would like to think that Jesus was supernaturally given this gift of wisdom, evidence leads the orthodox student to uphold that Jesus fully interfaced with his culture: He learned from the old and aged, he studied people and personalities, and he digested the wisdom sayings of the Old Testament. Luke's Gospel strongly supports this idea that Jesus did not grow in wisdom outside his culture. In an important scene portraying a young Jesus asking questions to teachers and religious leaders, Luke claims that Jesus "grew in wisdom and stature" (Luke 2:52). The Bible supports the position that Jesus, like all of us, grew as a human within a specific historical situation. Through pain, prayer, study, and through the Spirit, Jesus became wise. Therefore, if we, like Jesus, are to become wise we must engage in a *real* world, learn *real* life lessons, and observe *real* people. By becoming students of our culture and sincerely seeking the enlightenment of the Spirit, we will grow in wisdom.

Finding Wisdom on a College Campus

Scripture provides a few suggestions that might help us understand how wisdom may be acquired. The first is found in Luke 2:46. The Scripture reads, "After three days they found him in the temple courts, sitting among the teachers, listening to them and asking them questions." This verse lays out three important principles of how to find wisdom.

1. Good teachers—Associating with wise, mature people is one way to grow in wisdom. At an early age Jesus sought out learned people of whom he could ask questions, teachers who could help him understand things about God and about life. The rabbinical tradition of Jesus' day allowed children to ask questions to their elders and answer questions posed by the older generation. Interestingly, it was the youngest in the group who was allowed to answer the rabbi's question first. This not only affirmed the importance of learning for children, but also gave those within the group the opportunity to build on the youngest one's response. Answers were built upon. Rather than telling the child he or she had the wrong answer, the good was extracted from the child's answer and then developed by those older and wiser in the group. Consequently, children were part

of the learning circle. They were included in discussion and dialogue. What the ancient culture realized is that truth and learning is best passed on through people. The old, aged, and wise were not carted off to retirement communities, but they were part of the community structure and were obligated to pass on what they knew to the up-and-coming generation. Jesus grew and developed within this type of community structure. He learned from the knowledge and wisdom of the aged in the community. God used people to help Jesus grow in wisdom.

Evangelist Leighton Ford sheds light on how young people can grow in wisdom from the elders in a community. Ford wrote in *Christianity Today* that, besides seeking the learned, "if you are looking for wisdom, look for someone who has been hurt deeply and yet their faith has remained unshaken." Ford argues that wise people are those who have experienced suffering. Wise people are those who have gone through significant trials and difficulties in their lives and have not abandoned God. These are the individuals whom young people need to seek out and learn from. Wisdom, according to Ford, is not learned from those with shiny academic credentials and diplomas from prestigious universities and graduate schools. Wise teachers are not necessarily pastors who run big churches. Wise teachers are those individuals who have weathered the storms of life, yet have maintained their commitment to God.

2. Become a listener—Jesus did not simply seek out teachers. The Scripture says that Jesus listened (Luke 2:46c) to these teachers. It was through "listening" that Jesus acquired the kind of information that he needed to grow. Listening was vital to Jesus growing in wisdom.

Although this verse in the beginning of Luke focuses specifically on Jesus listening to teachers and elders, Jesus does provide teaching later in the sixth chapter of Luke as to the kinds of people we should be listening to and learning from. In this chapter Jesus clearly states that there are people from which both good and bad information flows. Jesus gives his disciples a heads-up on the kinds of people from whom the disciples should learn. To make sure that we are drawing wisdom from the right people, Jesus calls us to look at the by-products—or "fruit"—of these people's lives.

> "No good tree bears bad fruit, nor again does a bad tree bear good fruit; for each tree is known by its own fruit. Figs are not gathered from thorns, nor are grapes picked from a bramble bush. The good person out of the good

> treasure of the heart produces good, and the evil person
> out of evil treasure produces evil; for it is out of the abun-
> dance of the heart that the mouth speaks."
>
> Luke 6:43–45 (NRSV)

It is important to note that Jesus asks his followers to look at the fruit of a person's life. Good people, says Jesus, will lead lives that produce an abundance of good and healthy fruit. The rela-tionships of good people will be stamped with the seal of love, peace, and reconciliation. People who produce good fruit with their lives will conduct their business and respond to difficult situations in ways that build other people up and bring honor to God. Fruitful people will conduct their affairs with integrity and carry a reputation that is upright and good. Fruitful people will bring their friends, family, and associates closer to God—rather than leaving them bitter, angry, and resentful. Jesus says that these are the kinds of people we should learn from and listen to, people whose words overflow from a good heart.

A college classmate of mine had difficulty picking a major. He arrived at our college with a declared major in business. He soon changed to a history major. After a few classes in history he decided to be an English major. Finally in his junior year he decided to settle on a major in theology. He shared some very profound words with me. "One day I was sitting in a staff meet-ing with a campus ministry group. There were eight of us sit-ting in a circle planning how we were going to reach out to students at a local high school. In the course of the planning a question came up: 'How did we all end up volunteering for this ministry?'" Everyone in the circle shared. Each of them remarked that it was a certain professor—Professor Baloian—who had encouraged and mentored them to get involved in the ministry. "When I heard all the testimonies of these students," continued my friend, "I realized that this was someone with whom I wanted to study. This professor was obviously making an impact on lives. It wasn't just academics."

The apostle Paul picks up this same idea of finding good teachers when he encourages the people in Corinth to make a judgment about the sincerity and authenticity of his life and ministry—as opposed to the lives of the false prophet "who enslaves you or exploits you or takes advantage of you or pushes himself forward or slaps you in the face" (2 Cor. 11:20). Paul clarifies his authenticity and sincerity by upholding his life, his suffering, and his ministry to the church of Corinth. Paul asks the church to notice the fruit his life has birthed. Based on the authenticity of his life, as opposed to the fraudulent lives of the false prophets, Paul calls the church to learn and grow from his teachings. Wisdom will come to the believers at Corinth if they listen to the teacher who teaches truth. Paul makes it clear that wisdom cannot be passed on from just anyone.

Both Paul and Jesus called followers to use discernment and judgment when selecting people to be their teachers. Their wisdom is excellent for us today. How many of us have been inclined to follow promising teachers or articulate contemporary writers or eloquent preachers only to have them later disappoint us when the spiritual and moral bankruptcy of their lives is exposed? When looking for people from whom we can learn wisdom, we are called by both Jesus and Paul to examine their lives closely and discern whether the fruit of their lives is consistent with their testimony and teaching. C. S. Lewis used the test of time as a good indicator as to whether a voice should be considered as wise. Lewis seldom read a book that was less than a hundred years old. The reason: Books and authors that can survive a hundred years of scrutiny are usually books that have a certain enduring truth and contribute to the development of wisdom. Lewis cautioned against getting caught up in passing fads and new ideas. He believed that letting numerous generations judge a potential "mentor" was the best way to sniff out the good and bad teachers.

3. Ask! Jesus sought out teachers, Jesus listened, and Jesus asked questions. Luke writes that Jesus was both "listening to them and asking them questions" (Luke 2:46). The emphasis of asking questions is very important to note. Jesus was not a radio receiver plugged into God, spewing out divinely written scripts. Despite Jesus' infinite knowledge, his infinite power, and his deity, Jesus asked questions of other mortals! Jesus drew wisdom from people who embodied knowledge and wisdom. To Christians who think they "know the truth" and have an exclusive 1-800 number to God, the fact that Jesus asked questions from human sources should come as an important insight. People who say, "I just go to the Lord for all my knowledge" should look at the life of their Lord—Jesus—and realize that despite his special relationship with God, Jesus was not above learning from other people.

A professor in seminary once gave his students a significant portion of their grade based on how well they could craft questions. At the beginning of each class, each student would have to turn in five questions written on index cards pertaining to the material they had studied. The professor would pick the best questions and build his next lecture around those questions. His objective was twofold. He wanted to be relevant with the material he covered in class. But more important, he wanted to help his students develop the skill of creating and asking good questions. Poor questions, believed this professor, lead to poor learning. Good questions can lead to good learning. According to Luke's account of Jesus' life, part of acquiring wisdom is asking good questions.

Knowledge vs. Wisdom

Robert Coles of Harvard University has made a career of challenging Kolberg's theory of moral development—a theory that suggests that morality and moral courage are somehow linked to our ability to reason and think critically. Coles suggests that if Kolberg's theory is correct, then places like Harvard University should be filled with beautiful, moral people who are an example to the world of goodness and love. Coles says that places like Harvard, full of those who have high abilities to reason and think critically, are far from being moral places. In fact, places like Harvard can be some of the cruelest places in the world. Conversely, claims Coles, some of the most morally courageous people are individuals who have had limited education and have come from poor backgrounds. Coles believes that education has little to do with a person's moral courage and wisdom.

In his book *Medicine and Literature*, Coles tells a gripping story of a sixteen-year-old boy who was born to a poor sharecropper's family in the Mississippi Delta. Coles met this eleventh-grader in 1964 during a research project. The young man had not received the best education due to the community in which he lived. It was evident, however, that the youth was extremely intelligent and could compete with the best and brightest minds. By pulling a few strings, Coles got the young man a scholarship to Harvard. In the words of Tolstoy, the young man represented "uncorrupted peasant wisdom."

The boy made it through his freshman year. In his sophomore year he took biology, inorganic chemistry, and numerous English and history courses. He studied Flannery O'Connor, William Faulkner, Eudora Welty, Walker Percy, and other great fiction writers. He seemed to be on top of everything. As a broadly educated student, he was on his way to being accepted into a top medical school. But then something happened during the middle of the fateful second year. "I was doing fine, I guess, until one day in lab, the organic chem lab, I saw a kid take out something from a bag. He winked at his partner at the next bench and then, seeing me looking at them, they turned their backs on me. Suddenly I woke up from a long sleep. This wasn't the first time I'd seen kids cheating, but I guess I hadn't noticed, not really noticed." The young man continued to debrief his classroom experience to Coles. He claimed that this event caused him to remember other things like slips of paper students would sneak into class to use on their tests and sugar and salt that would help make bigger yields in their experiments.

Once this young man's eyes were opened to the commonplace reality of what was going on, his integrity would not let him continue to participate in the class. He realized that the majority of students were trying to outdo their fellow students. There was no willingness to help one another. Students were not in school to learn and grow. It was dog-eat-dog, with everybody fighting for his or her place on the grading curve. When the young man sought counsel from a local psychologist, he was told that he was afraid of competition and that other students were not "his problem." Steeped in a Baptist tradition with a deep love for God, the young man decided that he could not continue down the medical track. Rather, he graduated with a degree in literature and moved back to the Delta to teach kids English.

The story illustrates a strong contrast of two worlds. One was a world of power, privilege, and academic opportunity. The other was a world of poverty and weakness, and a deep sense of what was right and what was wrong. The young man knew what it meant to be true to oneself. But he could not operate within a system that rewarded deceit, lies, and cruelty toward fellow students. The account of this young man's struggle demonstrates that there is a significant difference between intellect and wisdom. Many students within his class went on to become doctors and researchers. Their knowledge of the subject of medicine got them their credentials and landed them high-paying jobs. But do they have the *hokma*? Do they have the skill to live well and integrate faith, morality, and knowledge in a way that builds up their families and their community? Probably not. Some may grow in wisdom, but others will simply use their education to live selfishly and promote their own advancement.

The apostle Paul said it well when he wrote to the church of

Corinth, "Knowledge puffs up, but love builds up" (1 Cor. 8:1). To "puff up" means to be arrogant and to be proud. Paul knew that when people are given knowledge, one of the tendencies is to look down on those who do not have the same knowledge and judge them as ignorant. The great temptation—or occupational hazard—for students in university settings is to believe that the knowledge they are attaining somehow makes them better than those who do not have the same opportunities. Our desire to learn, to gather knowledge, must be coupled with a sincere desire to be loving and humble people. This ability to love and remain humble—even as one gains knowledge, gains diplomas, and gains degrees—is part of what it means to approach our education with the intent of becoming wise people . . . not just smart people.

If Jesus Were a Sophomore

I can imagine sitting down for a coffee with Jesus to discuss my academic progress. It is the end of my first semester of my sophomore year. The freshman jitters are out of my system. I've managed to pull my G.P.A. up from a 2.8 to a 3.2. I am feeling pretty good about myself. I am finally getting the hang of this college stuff.

I have learned how to study for tests—how to do minimum effort and achieve maximum results. I've kept my campus antennas up and now have a pretty good grasp of which professors should be avoided and which professors can help position me for entrance into a good grad school. After all, why take classes outside my major that might hurt my G.P.A.? Why travel a road that might call me to read more, think more thoroughly, and express myself more clearly? I'm in a groove. I've learned how to work within the system and succeed.

"What have you learned?" asks Jesus as he swigs down another gulp of the Colombian Blend.

"Have you seen my grades? I've really pulled them up," I respond with a degree of self-satisfaction.

"I'm not really interested in your grades," he responds. "What have you learned about life, about yourself, about other people?"

I ponder as he stares at me.

"How are you connecting your learning to your faith? How is your

learning preparing you to be a more informed disciple of mine?" adds Jesus.

By this time I am feeling a little uneasy. I had memorized a bunch of facts. I can recite a bunch of names and dates from the Revolutionary War. I can summarize the major ideas of the influential social scientists of the nineteenth and twentieth centuries. I had crammed for some major tests and scored really well. I had written papers that had received few red markings.

But I never really developed the arguments. I never really pushed my mind to connect the ideas and themes to real-life issues. I never really integrated my faith and worldview into my writings for fear that the professor might lower my grade. My company was calling me to account for my learning, yet I began to wonder what I had really learned. Academically I had improved. How my learning was affecting me as a person and as a thoughtful, reflective Christian, I knew I was falling short. I might be in a better place to keep my scholarship, but I doubted if I was in a better place to reenter the world in a few years as a person who knew how to integrate faith into all aspects of my life. I was taking shortcuts. I was not becoming a wiser person. I was not cultivating the kind of learning behaviors that would help me become a lifetime learner and wise person.

Jesus took full advantage of opportunities to grow and learn. It is obvious from the Bible that Jesus knew his Scriptures. It is also obvious that Jesus knew about the different political and religious groups in his community. He had a keen insight into people's hearts and motives. He was a student of people. Jesus also displayed a great deal of cultural sensitivity in his teaching. It took a wise and knowledgeable person—certainly compassionate—to acquire the ability to speak in symbols and metaphors that average people could understand. All of what is written about Jesus points to a man who did grow in wisdom over his lifetime and who used the wisdom he acquired to fulfill his calling. As disciples of Jesus, we must put forth the same kind of effort to grow in wisdom from the resources that our community offers.

Currently we have access to information like during no other period in the history of the world. Yet we live in a world that lacks wisdom. Unlimited Internet availability, Palm computers, and e-mail give us access to materials and information that one could only dream about a decade ago. As a matter of fact, a person receives more information in a daily copy of the *New York*

Times today than people received in a lifetime only a century ago. But despite our access to all kinds of wonderful knowledge and data, one has to wonder if the world has become a better place in which to live? Bright, intelligent people continue to fail at living. Sexually transmitted diseases, world famine, environmental crises, racism, ethnic cleansing, failed marriages, and overcrowded jails continue to grow at alarming rates, despite our technological advances.

If Jesus were on a college campus today, he would challenge young people not to be seduced by degrees and G.P.A.s and LSAT scores. He would remind us all not to "conform any longer to the pattern of this world" but to "be transformed by the renewing" of our minds (Rom. 12:2–3). This renewing of the mind would include the pursuit of wisdom and not simply knowledge. Like Solomon of old, Jesus would challenge us all to ask for wisdom so that we could become people who administer justice, exercise discernment, and lead people down the right path with integrity. Jesus would want us to use these critical years of our lives to establish patterns of seeking wisdom so that his church could become a more effective and faithful witness in the new millennium.

Remember:

Wisdom is thus not a belief, a value, a set of facts, a corpus of knowledge or information in some specialized area, or set of special abilities or skills. Wisdom is an attitude taken by persons toward the beliefs, values, knowledge, information, abilities, and skills that are held, a tendency to doubt that these are necessary true or valid and to doubt that they are an exhaustive set of those things that could be known.

John Meacham

Questions for Reflection

1. What is a "stupid" decision you have made? What would a person of greater wisdom do in a similar situation? What are some "stupid" decisions you see people making on campus? What are some "stupid" decisions you have seen adults make? Again, what do you think wise people would do in these situations?

2. Who is the wisest person you know? What makes this person wise? How do you think he or she acquired that wisdom?

3. What are sources from which you can draw wisdom? Who are teachers who have birthed "good" fruit and are worth studying under? Are there certain classes you need to take? What might be some important books to read? Discuss your answers with others. Make some commitments.

4. What idea did you find most helpful in this chapter?

5. What are some behaviors or goals you need to establish to acquire more wisdom? Be specific. Make a list.

For the Leader

Ask the group to discuss the following: If Jesus were a student on your campus, how would he go about the process of growing in wisdom?

Prayer and Meditation

Lord,

I confess
   from the early days of my schooling
I have been programmed to succeed within a system that rewards
   achievement over learning and true understanding.
I confess that I have been deeply influenced by a culture
    That confuses speed with competence,
    That confuses acquisition of information with wisdom,
    That confuses good test taking with true intelligence.
Free me from this lie,
Free me from the bondage that calls me to sacrifice learning and
   personal growth for the sake of "scoring well."

Replace these old behaviors with a hunger and thirst to grow in
   wisdom.
Grant me the courage to walk the difficult road of becoming
   wise.
Give me the strength to pay the price of not taking shortcuts.
Please bring people and circumstances into my life that will lead
   me in this direction.

Amen

Chapter 8

Visionary Behaviors:
Without Vision, People Perish

"You will be ever hearing but never understanding; you will be ever seeing but never perceiving."

Mark 4:12

The greatest tragedy is having sight but no vision.

Helen Keller

Aren't We Supposed to Have Vision?

"Would you like to buy a church?"

I was caught off guard. This was one of the biggest and most active churches in our community. But here was the pastor trying to sell it to me! Despite my incredulity, visions began to dance in my head. For the past eight years our youth ministry—desperate for space—had been running summer camps, Bible clubs, and teen programs out of parking lots, musty church basements, and empty, abandoned neighborhood properties in one of America's poorest cities. I began salivating at the thought of this church's full-sized gym filled with kids; the numerous, beautiful classrooms used for teaching Bible stories. The facility would be perfect! It would easily become a beehive of activity for the kids in the community. But I was cautious.

"Umm . . . By the way, why are you leaving the city?"

"Well," stammered the pastor, "we're losing one or two families each year because of the deteriorating neighborhood. My people don't think there's any reason to stay."

Curious. Two earnest Christians standing on the same street corner having two completely different visions. One seeing a declining neighborhood, youth to be feared, no challenge, a shrinking weekly offering. The other seeing teens with tremendous potential, a field ready for harvest, and an opportunity to watch God providentially provide.

Why do people—good people—see things so differently? We sing the same songs, we read the same translations of the Bible, and yet what we see is so radically different. One group wants to run and take shelter. The other group wants to dive in and watch God work in miraculous ways.

The answer, I believe, is *vision*. How we view the world and how we see the people around us is all tied to vision. George Barna contends that the issue of vision is *the* issue facing the church in the new millennium. Churches are dying because there is no vision—no vision to create new ways of doing ministry, no vision to take risks and make changes, and no vision for a world that changes every five years. Barna believes the church needs a new generation of visionary leaders.

How is vision created? How do students of today become the visionary leaders of God's people tomorrow? How does the up-and-coming generation develop the eyes and heart needed to reach a lost world? Part of the answer to these questions is found in how the disciple of Jesus relates to those we might call "strangers." Strangers are those who are different from us—those who find themselves outside our social circles. Strangers may look different, eat different, talk different, and think different. Visionary leadership has the capability of identifying the stranger, the passion to reach out to the stranger, and the creativity to connect with the stranger. Sadly, we have churches full of people who have never allowed the Spirit of God to touch their eyes and give them vision. How then does a student begin to cultivate a lifestyle that fosters vision so that tomorrow's church will be full of people who see the world as Jesus would want us to see it? Let me suggest a few ideas.

Road to Emmaus

In the twenty-fourth chapter of the book of Luke, a remarkable encounter takes place between two of the disciples and Jesus. Prior to chapter 24 we learn that Jesus has been crucified. The disciples were confused and without a leader. For the past three years their lives had had direction, meaning, and focus. For the past three years they had put their faith and trust in a Jesus who was going to create a new kingdom on earth. The death of Jesus had shattered all their dreams.

Two of the disciples were on the road to Emmaus. They were about seven miles outside of Jerusalem when they were approached by a stranger. When the stranger asked what they were discussing, the two disciples proceeded to question the stranger and inform him that he had just missed out on the biggest event to take place in years. The disciples continued to tell their sad story about how Jesus was crucified. The stranger replied, "How foolish you are, and how slow of heart to believe all that the prophets have spoken! Did not the Christ have to suffer these things and then enter his glory?" (Luke 24:25–26).

The disciples still did not recognize that this stranger was Jesus. The disciples still could not see the true identity of this man. He was just a stranger. For some reason—and the Scripture does not specify—their vision was jaded. These disciples were carrying on a conversation with the living, resurrected Christ, but they could not recognize their former teacher and rabbi.

The story then takes an interesting and significant turn. As the three continue to walk together, Jesus infers that he will not be staying with the disciples for the night. Rather than saying good-bye to the stranger, the disciples begged the man to stay with them. The text says that they "urged him strongly." The urging works and this stranger decides to stay with the disciples.

In verse 30 a very significant moment occurs. Luke records that "When he was at the table with them, he took bread, gave thanks, broke it, and began to give it to them. Then their eyes were opened and they recognized him, and he disappeared from their sight." Luke tells his readers that something extraordinary happens when Jesus and his disciples sit down at the table.

The tendency of some interpreters might be to spiritualize the passage and say that the reason they could not see Jesus was that God had mysteriously draped a veil over their eyes. At the right moment the Holy Spirit is released and the disciples are zapped with the spirit of discernment. But the text makes no mention of this occurrence. Luke's emphasis is that the disciples and the stranger sit down, eat a meal, and break bread together. It is in the act of breaking bread that the truth is revealed and the disciples see the true identity of this stranger—they see Jesus. In the breaking of the bread the disciples acquire vision.

Becoming disciples, who see with the eyes of Jesus, means allowing ourselves to get close enough to people so we can see beyond the outward appearances and see people as God would want us to see them. Seeing with the eyes of Jesus also means placing ourselves in situations where we can see the kinds of people Jesus needs us to see. So often Christians stand at a distance and allow their perceptions to be shaped by the media biases and the comments of others. Christians are notorious for putting people in categories and boxes without ever talking to them face to face. Christians are also notorious for putting themselves in situations where they never move beyond their insulated communities. To develop a Jesus vision, disciples must risk and position themselves in places where their eyes can be transformed.

No Longer Strangers

"We better get outta here quick," screamed thirteen-year-old Gooter from the back of the bus. "Who knows what they'll do with a bus fulla *niggas* in this neighborhood."

The bus, packed with fifty city kids—African American, Puerto Rican, and Dominican—had just left a spaghetti dinner at an affluent suburban Baptist church. The church had invited the youth out for dinner and games. Ironically, they arrived at the church, but none of the church youth showed up. The only people there were the Women's Baptist Brigade, a dynamic team of white, seventy-year-old women who cooked great spaghetti.

Rather than canceling the dinner and games, we invited the Women's Brigade to join us. After a hearty dinner, the group sat around, sang songs, and played Win, Lose, or Draw. It was an amazing sight: two completely different groups of people whose paths would never cross. One group suburban, one urban. One rich, one poor. One white, one black. One elderly, one adolescent. The groups were as far apart as planets, but they had a *blast*.

Upon leaving the church, the kids got back on the bus. They had gotten no further than half a block from the church when the bus broke down. There they were, stuck in the middle of an affluent white neighborhood, a busload of inner-city kids.

Within two minutes three police cars circled the bus. Out of one of the cars came a big, burly policeman, two revolvers strapped to his waist, a billy club in hand, and a big, silver badge on his black leather jacket. He came to the side door of the bus.

"Ya got twenty minutes to get this bus outta here," he barked.

"But sir, we've just broken down."

"If you're not outta here in twenty minutes I'm taking you all down to the station!" He pivoted and headed back to his car.

By that time I was beginning to panic. It was one of those "Jesus, come quickly!" moments.

Fortunately, out of the church parking lot came a little white Ford Escort. When it came to the end of the drive, it began to make a turn away from the bus and the flashing lights. Then the car stopped, gradually made a right turn, and slowly inched its way toward the bus.

Out of the car came seventy-two-year-old Gertrude. She grabbed her cane and started walking toward the bus. The police officer intercepted her, told her that she did not want to go near those dangerous kids on the bus, and instructed her to go back to her car. Gertrude would have none of it. She continued her trek toward the bus.

"What's the problem, friends?" she called to me as I sat transfixed in the driver's seat, taking in the unbelievable spectacle.

"I think I need a jump-start," I quickly responded.

Gertrude turned, went back to her car, and pulled it next to the bus's engine. I popped the hood, she clamped on the jumper cables, and in a moment the bus was running again. The kids cheered.

What a contrast. The police officer with all his power and protection responded to our kids out of fear. His response was based on a perception of sensationalized television clips, negative news stories, and maybe some deep-seated racial prejudices. All he saw was black and brown kids from the inner city. All he could think was that these kids could only be dangerous.

If anyone had the right to be afraid, it would have been Gertrude. Gertrude was old and weak. She had no power. She probably would have been afraid had she not "broken bread" with our kids. By having dinner and playing games, Gertrude saw our kids for who they really were—kids. Kids with hearts. Kids who liked to have fun. Kids who laughed. Kids who needed love and attention. Gertrude was able to see beyond the color of skin, beyond the socioeconomic barriers. She saw what was on the inside. Breaking bread provided the transforming moment.

Bread and Vision

As one reads the Gospels, Jesus is often described as having dinner with people whom the religious community would never include. In the Gospel of Mark, Jesus is breaking bread with "many tax collectors and sinners" (2:15). From a distance the religious leaders never allowed themselves to get close enough to those people, for they could not see beyond the stereotypes. The religious leaders judged those people for what they did, and where they lived, and with whom they associated, rather than as individuals who had needs and hurts.

Jesus left his disciples—and us—a model for ministry and a method for developing his eyes. Jesus had compassion for people because he did not see them in the same way other religious leaders did. Jesus saw people differently because he spent time with people. From Jesus we learn that more time is needed eating with people whom the world has judged and stereotyped. By learning to eat with people disciples can begin seeing them in their fullness of humanity and respond with the compassion of God.

With Whose Eyes Do You View the World?

When was the last time you ate a meal with a homeless person? When was the last time you invited a Muslim, a Buddhist, a New Ager, or a nonbeliever to dinner? When was the last time you had coffee with a teenage mom? A gang kid? A prisoner? A poor family? When was the last time you broke bread with someone who was a risk to be around?

So often school, and the insulated lifestyle it can create, fosters a type of detachment from "the world." By isolating ourselves on a campus and surrounding ourselves with certain kinds of people, we can very easily become shut off from the world and from the needs of people different from ourselves. One individual who realized this danger was a significant twentieth-century Christian writer and thinker named Simone Weil. As a student, in order to protect herself from the "Ivory Tower Syndrome," Weil would intentionally drift back and forth between the academic community and the "real world." A year in the university setting would be followed by time spent in a factory doing manual labor. It was in the factory that Weil came shoulder to shoulder with real people who faced real problems. Poor people were not just some abstraction or socioeconomic grouping. For Weil, the working class had names, faces, and children. This real-life experience kept her connected to reality in a profound way. Most scholars agree that Weil could have easily advanced within academic circles. She was intellectually astute and held the admiration of many top thinkers. But Weil intentionally fought against becoming an abstract thinker who was detached from reality.

As a student just out of university, Weil wrote a long autobiographical letter to an influential priest in her life, Father Perrin:

> This contact with affliction had killed my youth. . . . I knew very well that there was a great deal of affliction in

> the world, I was obsessed by it, but I had never become aware of it through prolonged contact. In the factory . . . other people's affliction entered my flesh and my soul. . . . It was there that I was branded forever as a slave.[15]

The experience of working in various factories opened Weil's eyes to the harsh and brutal realities of slave labor. By willingly subjecting herself to the role of a slave, Weil was able to identify closely with those who were treated like animals in the workplace. It was because of these eye-opening experiences that she was able to become a voice and organizer for the rights of factory workers. Because of these lived experiences, Weil developed an uncanny depth of perception into both social and spiritual situations. Weil wanted to see the truth, not just talk or write about it. She broke bread in the truest sense of the phrase with those who were forgotten and abused by society. Because of Weil's willingness to live out her faith in the real world and engage with real people, her writing took on a prophetic quality. Weil took risks. She stepped out of her comfort zone and allowed herself to be changed by what she experienced. Consequently, Weil has opened the eyes of thousands of people over the years through her writings and spiritual insights.

The Happy Prince

Oscar Wilde wrote a wonderful children's book called *The Happy Prince*. It is one of my favorite stories because it is a story about a little prince whose vision is transformed into a Jesus vision. Wilde begins by telling about a statue in the town square. It is a beautiful statue of a happy prince who once ruled the city. People in the town admired the smiling statue. During the course of the story, the reader finds out that the prince was happy because he lived his whole life in the castle and had everything he could ever want. He never saw beyond the castle walls.

Perched above the city the happy prince, now a statue—remember this is a children's story—is exposed to the realities of the world for the first time. He now sees into the highways and byways of his city. Every night and every day he observes the devastation of poverty and sickness. With no castle walls to shield him from the suffering of humanity, the happy prince begins to weep.

The crux of the story centers around a friendship the prince develops with a little bird. The bird becomes the messenger for the prince. When the prince sees need, he asks the bird to deliver the jewels and gold that adorn his body—the statue. To the little match girl, the bird takes a sapphire from the sword of the prince. To the mother nursing her sick little boy, the bird takes some of the gold plate that covers the prince's body. Slowly over time, the statue of the prince is stripped of anything of value. Everything on his body is given to the needy people he sees from the top of his perch. Even the jewels that filled his eyes are taken and disbursed. The statue of the happy prince, which once looked so lavish and beautiful, eventually looks very ordinary and ugly.

The story ends in typical Wilde fashion. Some of the townspeople realize how ugly the statue has become. The mayor orders it to be removed and destroyed. After the statue is taken down from the top of the town square, it is thrown into a furnace. The only thing that does not melt is the prince's heart. Mysteriously it withstands the fiery furnace. Rather than melting, the heart simply breaks in two pieces. In the closing line of the story, God asks an angel to visit Earth and bring back the two most precious things he can find. The angel brings the broken heart of the happy prince and the carcass of the little bird back to heaven.

Wilde's message is profound for those wanting to see with the vision of Jesus. Wilde reminds the reader that our happiness may only exist because we never get out of our castles. Our "castles" may be our circle of friends, our suburban communities, our churches, or our cliques at school. But catching a Jesus vision of the world involves getting out of the castle and seeing what takes place beyond the walls. Wilde also reminds the reader that the cost of really seeing with the eyes of Jesus may be tears, a broken heart, and a depletion of our resources. Vision is costly.

Aching Visionaries

In his powerful book *Lament for a Son*, Nicholas Wolterstorff affirms those who are willing to really look at the world with the eyes of Jesus. Wolterstorff concludes that to have a Jesus vision means to have a broken heart. Those who allow themselves to "break bread" with the world are those who will see the suffering and hardship of humanity. Wolterstorff says that people with a Jesus vision are

> The mourners . . . who have caught a glimpse of God's new day, who ache with all their being for that day's coming,

and who break out into tears when confronted with its absence. They are the ones who realize that in God's realm of peace there is no one blind and who ache whenever they see someone unseeing. They are the ones who realize that in God's realm there is no one hungry and who ache whenever they see someone starving. They are the ones who realize that in God's realm there is no one falsely accused and who ache whenever they see someone imprisoned unjustly. . . . They are the ones who realize that in God's realm there is no one who suffers oppression and who ache whenever they see someone beat down. . . . The mourners are aching visionaries.[16]

Visionary people are those who have caught a glimpse of God's new day and ache whenever they experience and see things that contradict the kind of world God wants for people. Because of this glimpse of God's new day, the visionary's heart is broken and the person mourns. But it is the mourners whom Jesus blesses. Jesus exalts them. Jesus says, "Blessed are those who mourn!" And Jesus promises that this new day, for which they ache, will one day come.

If Jesus Were a Sophomore

"Come on, take my hand," says the Voice.

"Where are you taking me?" I respond with caution.

"I'm taking you out of your palace," continues my Guide.

"But why do I need to leave my palace?" I retort.

"You need a new set of eyes."

"But I see just fine!" I reply in defense.

"You see what's in front of you fine. But you have no vision for what's outside your little world," says my Guide.

I decide to capitulate to the demands of my Guide. We begin to walk throughout the campus—places I have never seen before.

"Why are you taking me behind the cafeteria?" I ask.

"I want you to hear the stories of those who labor to prepare your meals. See the mothers who work all day for minimum wage and then go home to look after their young children? See how hard they work. Look at their eyes. They are tired eyes. As you count your calories, they wonder how they will feed their children. As you complain about the selection in the

salad bar, they wonder how they are going to find a free health clinic for their sick four-year-old."

"I never knew these people were here," I responded with embarrassment.

We move on.

"Why are you taking me to the maintenance buildings?" I ask.

"I want you to hear the stories of those who labor to make this campus look nice," explains the Guide. "You see Miguel. He's here every morning at 4 A.M. to make sure your showers and toilets are cleaned so when you wake up they are ready for you. He brought his parents and family over from Mexico. He supports his sister and her five children. She has not been able to obtain a work visa. Fourteen people live in his small house. Maybe you should tell him how much you appreciate his efforts. Perhaps you should listen to his story one day. It might change your life."

"I've seen him a few times. But I never stopped to talk," I reply.

He leads me on.

"Why are you taking me to this dorm? Don't you know that these students have a reputation for being party people?" I ask.

"I want you to hear the stories of those who live here," responds the Guide. "You see Janice over there. She looks rather striking and confident. She has every guy on campus drooling over her. But look more closely. Look beyond the makeup. Look beyond the pasted-on smile. Don't you see the hurt—the broken heart? The tremendous insecurity? She comes from a broken home. She has never recovered from her parents' divorce. The partying is an attempt to fill an empty void. Behind the pretty exterior there is a shattered person. She is on the way to destruction if someone does not intervene."

"I was always intimidated by her appearance. I never knew she needed a friend. I guess I just saw what everybody else saw. I'm beginning to see."

"Good," says my Guide. "Now let your new vision touch your heart and move you to action. Keep moving beyond your palace and I will begin to show you things."

"Thank you. Thank you for eyes to see," I say.

My Guide disappears.

Jesus wants Christians truly to see the world as he sees the world. We must get out of our palaces and get close enough to people so that barriers and stereotypes can be dismantled. Jesus needs a new generation of young people who will see the world through his eyes—not the eyes of the media and the glitz of Hollywood—and allow their hearts to be broken with the things that break his heart. This opening of the eyes may take place over a cup of coffee, it may take place during a meal in the cafeteria, or it may take place visiting a family in the section of a city to which we would never venture. But usually this transformation takes place only when we are intentional about moving beyond what is secure and comfortable and into areas and relationships that produce a degree of insecurity and self-consciousness. Jesus' life reveals to us that he saw people differently than other religious people did. This is a critical quality for young disciples to strive to emulate. By establishing patterns in our lives now that call us to be intentionally relational and that call us to intentionally suspend judgment on others until we have broken bread with these "strangers," we will begin to cultivate a visionary way of looking at the world. Cultivating the discipline of breaking bread will only enhance our ability to reach across cultural, racial, denominational, and socioeconomic lines with God's abounding love and grace. And by learning to enter into solidarity with the stranger, we will begin to see the world as aching visionaries who pray, mourn, and help create God's new day.

Remember:

You called, you cried, you shattered my deafness. You sparkled, you blazed, you drove away my blindness. You shed your fragrance, and I drew in my breath, and I pant for you. I tasted and now I hunger and thirst. You touched me, and now I burn with longing for your peace.

Saint Augustine

Questions for Reflection

1. Draw a map of your "palace," places where you spend most of your time, people with whom you spend most of your time. What does it tell you about your life? Do you need to expand the "walls"? If so, what might be some new areas into which you should venture?

2. When was the last time you intentionally sat down and had a cup of coffee with someone you had certain preconceived

notions about? What did you learn from the conversation? Did it give you a "new set of eyes" for the person?

3. If you have never sat down with someone who might reflect a significantly different background, way of thinking, theological conviction, or ethnicity, make it a priority to do so. Just listen to that person's story. Make a "bread connection." How does the encounter change you? How does the conversation help you to view people differently?

4. Are you an "aching visionary"? Are you a mourner? If not, begin to pray that God will give you a vision for that "new day" and for those who live short of that new day.

5. List some ways you can begin to develop a new set of eyes—eyes that see the things that break the heart of God.

For the Leader

Ask each member of your group to share based on the following question: If Jesus were to take you on a tour to open your eyes, where would he take you? Describe the places, the situations, and the people.

Prayer and Meditation

Lord,

Peel the scales off my eyes.
Cleanse me of my prejudices.
Purge me of my stereotypes.
Rid me of my preconceived notions of people.

Grant me the courage to move beyond the world of assumptions.
Help me to get out of my palace and see the world you need me
    to see.

And Lord, when I become a mourner,
When I become an aching visionary,
Give me that glimpse of Your new day.
Fill me with with the courage and hope that accompanies
Your vision.

Amen

Chapter 9

Friendship Behaviors: Keeping It Real

Religion and celebrity do not mix. Religion and fame might work well together, but celebrity is a different matter. The distinction? Try this out: Celebrities do not have friends. They are surrounded by people, but are actually isolated....
What are friends for? ... Friends say to people who acquire power and position—and even the pastor of a humble parish has some of that— "Watch it, buddy," or "We knew you when . . ." or "This time you went too far."

Martin E. Marty

Iron sharpens iron,
and one person sharpens the wits of another.
Prov. 27:17 (NRSV)

Visions in Our Coffee

The idea was given birth in one of those late-night study sessions. After a few cups of coffee, a few hours of conversation, a severe deficiency of sleep, and vanishing ego defenses, the conversation reached that magical point when great ideas begin to flow. The small group of college sophomores and juniors began to speak honestly about our relationships with God. There were confessions of struggles with certain doctrines of faith. Some shared struggles of making sense of what an "authentic faith" might look like in a world growing increasingly secular and increasingly hostile to truth and any sense of moral absolute. Others raised questions of social responsibility. What was an appropriate Christian response to AIDS, poverty, and growing environmental disaster? What started as an informal chat in the local coffee bar soon became the most significant experience of our college years.

This late-night discussion group concluded that the content of these conversations needed to be written down and shared with others on campus. After logging some initial thoughts and formatting them into brief articles, our group began to create a small, underground campus newspaper with a bend toward connecting Christian faith to a world much bigger than our campus. Early on it was decided that the paper would stay away from critiquing the administration for increasing our tuition or venting frustration toward various professors on campus. Rather, the paper would focus entirely on challenging students to become more reflective of their faith, to raise questions about the role of Christians in issues of the world, and to ponder how their faith commitments might influence their study and career choices.

The college already had a weekly student newspaper. Even though we were attending a Christian college, the weekly tabloid spent little time writing about issues of Christian discipleship. Between the reports on the successes and failures of the athletic teams and current movie reviews, the articles discussing issues of faith and Christian vocation were rare. Our small group of late-night coffee drinkers decided that there were probably other students who would want to move beyond the weekly drivel of campus life and participate in a broader discussion of faith and discipleship. Our group wanted to challenge students to think about the world, to discover what it meant to live radically for Jesus, and to create a safe forum where students could openly exchange ideas and struggles without being labeled "liberals" or "doubters," "saved" or "unsaved."

Our group ended up calling the paper *Lama. Lama* in Hebrew means *why*. The title was appropriate because most of the questions and issues discussed in the articles and editorials somehow related to the question of why. *Why* was there poverty in the world? *Why* did Jesus really die? *Why* did university students act so apathetic toward issues concerning people? *Why* were students spending money on proms and football games, while others in the world could not feed their babies? *Why* did Jesus seem so radical while American Christianity often seemed so culturally adapted and status quo? Trying to find answers to the questions of "why" was the driving motivator for our group. It was the why questions that gnawed at our souls. It was the why questions that we wanted to build a campus dialogue around. Wanting answers and direction, we launched our first publishing venture.

Our small group of novice writers and thinkers named itself the Inkblots. Since a number of us were enamored with an English writing group called the Inklings, which included authors like C. S. Lewis, Charles Williams, Dorothy Sayers, J. R. R.

Tolkien, and G. K. Chesterton, we thought the Inkblots would be rather appropriate for a group of unpublished sophomore and junior hacks who had problems passing English Literature 101, let alone taking on a printing enterprise. So, under the guise of character names from Lewis's *Chronicles of Narnia*, our newly formed group of novice theologians/writers took the pseudonyms of Puddleglum, Aslan, Reepicheep, and Caspian. Thus the Inkblots began their infamous weekly publication of *Lama*.

Lama soon became the talk of the campus. To a specifically designated mailbox, students and professors sent notes of encouragement and responses to articles. Professors expressed their enthusiasm in seeing students thinking and engaging in dialogue over relevant issues. They encouraged us to keep printing. Students mailed in articles and letters to the editor in hopes of getting published. What emerged on campus was an ongoing dialogue between students and faculty about the meaning of Christian faith and discipleship. For the first time, students were thinking and talking about relevant issues. The interest in matters of spirituality increased significantly on the campus. People were writing letters, submitting poems, and sending us questions. The paper became the rallying point for a growing number of students on campus, and each day more entered this spiritual pilgrimage together. In the student lounges people were reading *Lama*. In the snack bar, people were discussing the new underground newspaper. The paper woke a sleepy Christian college campus from the routinization of Christian faith. For the first time, some students were given the opportunity to get their questions out of the closet and enter into a larger, more honest dialogue about faith and personal spirituality.

With the enthusiastic response of those on campus, the Inkblot editors worked harder, wrote more, and discussed with frequency the ideas that were being put forth in the paper. As we wrote and discussed and interacted with criticism and affirmation, our beliefs became clearer. As the *Lama* staff was forced to grapple with questions and comments, our own faith was inspired and transformed. Late-night discussions became question-answering sessions. How should we answer a question from a student who struggled to understand biblical views on materialism? Or how would we respond to students concerned about the destruction of the rain forest in South America? Or how would we counsel a student who could no longer believe in

God? As students sent in their questions, the group bounced ideas and responses off one another. With each discussion, with each article, and with each published edition, our values became clearer, our convictions deepened, and our life's mission became more evident. We prayed together, we supported one another, and we ultimately became a community who could speak honestly to one another about issues that really mattered.

It is interesting to look back on those days. Many of the Inkblots continue to be involved in some kind of Christian service or ministry. One works with juvenile offenders, one is a missionary, one pastors a church, and one heads up an inner-city mission. Most of the group are still actively involved in trying to live out faith in a practical way—faith that engages the daily reality of meeting real needs. This continued commitment to service and the integration of faith and life on the part of the *Lama* staff still finds its roots in those late nights of drinking coffee, editing articles, and trying to answer the question *why*. Being around people who wanted to grow in faith raised our personal level of commitment. The dreams and visions of friends inspired each of us to keep growing and learning. We learned that our personal commitment to Jesus was profoundly influenced by those with whom we spent our time.

Vision Fosters Vision

One way to put a damper on an inquiring mind or squelch someone who is eager to live radically for the sake of the gospel is to hang around people who are comfortable, close-minded, and content to live out their faith without ever taking a risk. The kinds of friends with whom we spend our time have a direct impact on how we exercise our faith. If we surround ourselves with brothers and sisters who are earnestly growing and stretching themselves, we will inevitably grow and be stretched. If we surround ourselves with those who do not ask tough questions, who do not seek to put their faith in action, and who just enjoy the status quo, we will become status quo–type people.

Over the years I have known students who have had a sincere desire to step out of their comfort zone, take risks for God's kingdom, and learn to share God's love in situations that are challenging and potentially dangerous. What ultimately makes the difference as to whether these desires are pursued is the kind of people with whom these students spend their time. When surrounded by peers who do not share similar goals, passions, and desires, one finds it extremely difficult to put this kind of radical faith into practice. Frequently the spiritual spark, calling, or prompting that has been ignited by God's Spirit through a preacher or book will not grow into a blazing flame because the surrounding company does not add fuel.

Blazing flames of conviction and passion will grow and be sustained over the long haul if there is a small group of people surrounding you who share similar beliefs and values. Commitment breeds commitment. Growing people inspire other people to grow. Finding others who share a similar heartbeat and thirst for growth influences our spiritual lives in powerful ways. A college campus can be a tremendous resource for finding these like-hearted people. Special interest groups, Bible studies, informal discussion groups, short-term mission teams, weekend volunteer groups, or Internet chatrooms can all be places to find people who will inspire personal growth and commitment. Taking advantage of these resources for growth is an opportunity of a lifetime.

When you find others who share similar convictions, make it a priority to pray together, to hold one another accountable, and to challenge one another to pursue his or her calling from God. I believe that one of the primary reasons why the vast majority of college students lose their youthful idealism for God's kingdom is because they never create a support system that will help them sustain their ideals. Without this support system, ideals slowly fade away.

Over the past decade a community of Christians who have a passion for doing urban youth work have gathered in our city. Since the work is difficult—disappointments often outweighing victories—and progress is painfully slow and almost invisible, discouragement is a very real occupational hazard. Staff who faithfully commit themselves to helping kids and then see those same kids get shot, become pregnant, go to jail, drop out of school, or return to selling drugs find it critical to be surrounded by a group of people who keep the vision alive and provide encouragement during difficult times.

No Lone Rangers

Jesus picked men and women who were willing to make a commitment to follow him. Although they had no idea what they were getting themselves into, Jesus picked a group of disciples who were willing to put their vocations and careers on hold and commit to his kingdom vision. The fact that Jesus called his disciples his friends is an amazing testimony that Jesus needed people around him who would support him, encourage him, talk to him, and learn from him. Jesus claims, "You are my friends if you do what I command. I no longer call you servants, because a servant does not know his master's business" (John 15:14–15). It is important to note that the most complete, fully human, secure, powerful person to ever walk the face of the earth needed other humans in his life for support. Jesus could have been a loner. He could have been a one-man show. Jesus could have distanced himself from his followers, only allowing them access during times of teaching. But Jesus chose to live and share his entire life with twelve men and let these disciples see all aspects of his life. Jesus did not use his power and privilege to isolate himself.

When Jesus entered public ministry he took a team with him wherever he traveled. The Gospels tell us that almost the entire tenure of Jesus' three-year ministry was spent with a group called the disciples. Those twelve men ministered together, ate food together, prayed together, and learned together. From the beginning Jesus set the Christian agenda: Faith would be lived out in groups of people living in relationship with one another. Throughout the life of Jesus it became apparent why this principle was so critical. When crowds surrounded him, it was important to have friends who could act as a buffer. When the mission needed to be expanded, it was important to have people whom he could send out. When certain events took place, it was important to have others around who could experience the event with him. When it was time for Jesus to leave this world, it was important that relationships were established between the disciples so that the whole movement would not collapse. Friendships, not celebrity isolation, defined Jesus' life and mission.

It may have been easier for Jesus to work alone. After all, he was perfect. Jesus may have even been more "efficient" without twelve sometimes very stupid men tripping over his heels. Think about it: Jesus would not have had to put up with Peter's arrogance and impulsive activity. The childish egos of James and John would not have consumed his time. He would not have had to deal with the frustration of the disciples who never really understood his message or purpose. But Jesus committed to living his life out within the context of a group of friends. The son of God willingly became vulnerable to other humans.

The Discipline of Vulnerability

It's hard to be vulnerable. It is difficult to place ourselves in a position where we are accountable to another human being. Few of us like appearing weak. Few of us like to admit that we need other people in our lives. And yet when Christians fall—especially Christian leaders—it is usually because they do not have others to hold them accountable. They do not have the kinds of friendships in which they can really share. No one really knows what is going on in their life. In his book *In the Name of Jesus*, the late Catholic writer Henri Nouwen reminds us that Jesus sends the twelve out in pairs (Mark 6:7) and that "if two of you on earth agree about anything you ask for, it will be done for you by my Father in heaven. For where two or three come together in my name, there am I with them" (Matt. 18:19–20). Nouwen's point is that the Gospel is proclaimed most powerfully and authentically when we are in some kind of community that challenges us to be vulnerable. According to Nouwen, the way in which Christians resist this Lone Ranger mentality is by committing to intimate relationships where confession and forgiveness take place. "How can priests or ministers (or students) feel really loved and cared for when they have to hide their own sins and failings? . . . I am not at all surprised that so many ministers and priests suffer immensely from deep emotional loneliness."[17] Toward the end of Nouwen's life, he would not travel alone to do lectures and retreats. Nouwen found that he was more effective when he traveled with someone who knew him. For Nouwen, having a brother with him on the road helped him to pray more regularly, protected him from loneliness, and helped him to avoid various forms of temptation. Having someone to pray with and talk to before and after ministry events ultimately made his ministry more powerful and enjoyable.

Unfortunately, contemporary church culture has created a kind of Christianity that places little importance on building true fellowship and accountability. It is easy for people to just show up to church on Sunday morning without ever engaging in the lives of other Christian brothers and sisters. Students can anonymously drift in and out of church without anybody in the congregation knowing what is taking place in their life. Students can be struggling with troublesome issues, significant life questions, personal sin—and nobody knows. Students can be dreaming dreams for the kingdom, searching for God's will, or looking for opportunities to put their faith into action, yet no one around them will understand the depth of their struggle. The sooner a young disciple can understand the symbiotic relationship between a vibrant personal faith and the intimate, confessional-type relationships with other believers, the healthier and stronger the young disciple will become. In the words of Bonhoeffer, "only in the fellowship do we learn to be rightly alone . . . and one who seeks solitude without fellowship perishes in the abyss of vanity, self-infatuation, and despair."[18] Bonheffer believed that one could not be a disciple of Jesus without being in fellowship (relationships) with other Christians.

Building Rituals of Vulnerability and Accountability

Every other Thursday morning at around 5:30 A.M. I grudgingly run across my bedroom to hit the off button on my alarm clock. If it were not for the fact that I would be meeting three other guys in less than an hour, I would surely succumb to the temptation of hitting the snooze button—or dream bar—and crawl back into my warm bed. There is something motivating about knowing three other guys sacrificed their sleep and are waiting for me. I need this kind of accountability in my life.

For a couple of hours, the four of us drink coffee, talk about our week, and listen to the struggles and joys of one another's lives. If somebody needs advice, we counsel. If someone needs to be uplifted, we encourage and build up. If one of us needs prayer, we pray. If one in the group needs to confess sin, he is given the opportunity to share in confidence. The group is a safe and challenging place to go each week for accountability and encouragement. It is instrumental in helping me keep my faith real and active.

It is fair to say that the four of us struggle to lead disciplined spiritual lives. We struggle to meet goals. We struggle to be faithful in prayer and reading. We struggle to be intentional about building better relationships. We struggle with keeping our faith sharp and alive. What our small accountability group provides is a place where we can attempt the very difficult task of "working out our salvation" in a world hostile to Christian faith. In being priests to one another, we grow as people and as Christians.

How many of us can attest to having weeks and months pass without ever really praying or studying Scripture? Our intentions are good. We want to do it. But for some reason it gets

pushed to the back of the priority list. Interruptions are contin-
uous, and we fail to do what we have set out to do. Having real
friends who hold us accountable keeps us from falling into these
ruts and patterns. The earlier in our lives and spiritual journeys
we realize that a vibrant, alive, growing faith is best lived out in
a small communal setting, the better. In the long run, intimate
and godly friendships with people who are committed to growing as disciples will contribute more to our spiritual health than
memorizing Scripture, going to every spiritual growth confer-
ence that comes to town, or even religiously attending church.
Real fellowship is critical.

Early in his career, Billy Graham realized that if he were to
establish a long, enduring ministry, he would need to avoid some
of the pitfalls faced by other evangelists. One rule that he established for his life was that he would never be alone. While trav-
eling and preaching on the road, Graham would always have
someone by his side. At his hotel after the big crusades, there was
someone with him. When he counseled other people, someone
was always within arm's length. Graham believed that if he were
alone he would be susceptible to temptation, which could ruin
his ministry. Graham also had people looking out for his spiritual health. He submitted himself to others in an effort to hold
himself accountable in the areas of prayer and personal devotion.
Each morning someone would give him his Bible and clear space
for him to be quiet.

The structure and accountability was built into Billy Graham's life because he realized that alone he would fail. If it had
been left up to Graham to decide whether to pray or watch television, he would probably have chosen the television. If it had
been left up to Graham to go home to an empty hotel room, he
might have found himself going home with someone other than
his wife. At an early age, Graham made a very wise decision that
has helped mark his decades of ministry with integrity. He had
seen the demise of other men of God, and he was determined
that it would not happen to him. At the very early stages of his
career, he created a small accountability group and built certain
structures into his life because Graham wanted his ministry to
endure. His guiding ideals and standards were created early in
his career as opposed to later. As a man in his early twenties,
Graham and a few of his closest friends met in a hotel room in
Modesto, California, and laid out "The Modesto Manifesto,"
which would become the blueprint for the rest of his life.

If Jesus Were a Sophomore

Picture this scene.

It is early in the morning. The dew covers the sprawling lawns in front of the dorms. Birds are chirping, sounding like a choir warming up for an important concert. The first signs of the sun's rays break forth from behind the foothills. It is still too dark to see clearly. Details still find themselves waiting to be identified. In this predawn silence, the campus still enjoys the last few moments before students begin their frantic rush to classes and appointments.

Out of a dormitory door well emerges a couple of silhouettes. Indistinguishable from each another, they slowly walk across the campus toward the football stadium. As they near the front gates they are met by two other figures. The four images quickly disappear through the gates and into the vacuous stadium. Moments later they appear in the stadium, scaling the stairs toward the top like tiny ants climbing a dirt pile. At the top the four figures seat themselves on the dew-covered bleacher seats.

To the outside observer, the meeting would appear fairly uneventful.

Four people sitting still. There is little movement. For the first twenty minutes they appear to be staring at a little book, which they pass from person to person. This is followed by a period of time when the four figures bow their heads. They appear to be praying.

As the sun continues its ascent, the group becomes increasingly visible. Four young men are occupying the seats.

Into the stadium wanders the old groundskeeper, Hank Waters. He immediately spots the cluster of young men on the crest of the stadium. It is a regular occurrence. At least twice a week these four gather. They never cause any kind of disturbance. Hank likes to see the stadium used by someone other than yelling coaches and cursing players.

He knows the boys by name. They call themselves an "accountability" group. Hank has difficulty understanding the concept of accountability. This seems a little odd. Religion is a very private matter to Hank. He has never needed anybody to tell him when he should pray and when he should read his Bible. Faith is between him and God. Why they need one another he does not really understand.

But whatever they are doing seems to be working. Hank hears about this group from other faculty and from other students. Their lives seem to be touching other lives. They have a certain vitality and presence that is spilling over into the life of the campus.

Hank doesn't understand why, but he knows one thing. He will make sure that the gates are opened every Monday and Wednesday morning.

Jesus needed friends. Unlike other significant spiritual leaders, Jesus did not live in isolation. Whereas other spiritual gurus headed to the desert or mountains to live out their spiritual quest away from the distractions of people and life, Jesus chose to connect himself with ordinary people. This is a profound and important truth about the person of Jesus. It is a truth that should guide us as we seek to establish behaviors that will help in our quest to become more like Jesus. Our spiritual journey is to be lived out in the presence of other believers.

If Jesus were advising college students today, I believe he would strongly encourage young disciples to develop the behavior of finding friends who were intent on growing in their faith and serious about acting out their faith in the real world. Jesus would also encourage students to develop the capacity to cut out of their lives relationships that would detract them from their growth as disciples and inhibit them from fulfilling their life mission. Jesus would also encourage students to begin the task of learning how to live out their faith in community with other people who are committed to true vulnerability and real accountability.

Our "me" centered culture—which calls its citizens to become self-sufficient, strong, and independent superstars—is a detriment to the kinds of behaviors Jesus needs us to develop. Jesus needs young disciples to learn the agonizing process of exposing our weakness by inviting others into our lives who can point out our shortcomings, celebrate our triumphs, and move us beyond our failures and sorrow. Establishing these kinds of behaviors during our young adult years will ultimately produce healthier, stronger, and more enduring servants of God.

Remember:

This hour of history needs a dedicated circle of transformed nonconformists. The saving of our world from pending doom will come not from the action of a conforming majority but from the creative maladjustment of a dedicated minority.

Martin Luther King Jr.

Questions for Reflection

1. List your five closest friends. How do these friends contribute to your spiritual growth? In what ways do they hold you accountable?

2. Do you have a support group? If so, are there things you can do to create a greater sense of vulnerability and trust? If not, who are some potential people you could meet with on a regular basis?

3. Who are some people who model a commitment and faith that resembles the kind of disciple you desire to become? List them. Have you thought about asking them to form a small group?

4. Identify a Christian pastor and/or missionary whom you admire. Call, meet, or e-mail them and ask about the importance relationships have played in their lives. Ask them to give you some advice in this area of your life.

5. What are some ideas from this chapter that you found helpful? Discuss.

For the Leader

Ask your group to discuss the following question: If Jesus were a student on your campus, what might he do to build significant, spiritually enriching relationships? What kind of people would he find to meet with? What kinds of activities would they do together?

Prayer and Meditation

Lord,

Thank you for your promise that wherever two or three are gathered in Your name, You are present.
Thank You for how You modeled accountability with other people in Your own life.

Help me to find some good friends.
Help me to find friends who will challenge me to grow and keep me on the right path.
Bring into my life people who model discipleship and commitment.

Protect me, Lord, from relationships that will distract me from my pursuit of You.
Make me allergic to such relationships.

I do not want to travel this road alone.
I pray for Your help.

Amen

Chapter 10

Risky Behaviors:
Stepping Out in Faith

Most people tiptoe through life, only to arrive at death safely.

Woody Allen

Be daring, be different, be impractical; be anything that will assert integrity of purpose and imaginative vision against the play-it-safers, the creatures of the commonplace, the slaves of the ordinary.

Cecil Beaton

A Jump into the Abyss

I stood at the pay phone outside my dorm room and tried to draw the courage to make the call. I knew it would be difficult. Time after time I picked up the receiver only to hang it back up. Like an insecure adolescent trying to ask out his first prom date, anticipating potential rejection and embarrassment, I too wondered what kind of reception I would receive.

I anticipated my dad's questions. They would be questions of practicality. He was the family pragmatist—a professional accountant. I could foresee his reaction to the news that I was not going to get a job for the summer. Questions couched in parental concern: "How are you going to pay for school next fall? Do you know how much money you could earn this summer? Why do you want to throw away your education?" Fair questions. I had no answers. Logically it made no sense to give up a summer of work and serve as a volunteer in the inner city. With a depleted savings account, I would not have money for fall classes. For my father, who dealt in a world of bottom lines and balanced budgets, my decision would be interpreted as career suicide.

From my mother would come questions about safety. As the perpetual worrier, protector, and mother hen—who carefully raised her children in the safety of suburbia—my spending a summer in a community known for violence, gangs, and guns would undermine all that she had done to protect me from the harsh realities of the world. My mother was a homemaker, and her only encounter with the city was through sensationalized reports from news specials and *Time* magazine. The images she associated with the inner city were gangs, drugs, homelessness, and delinquent youth. Hearing that her only son was going to spend a summer in this kind of environment would be something to keep her awake nights. Her soft-spoken, indirect questions were already forming in my mind. "Where will you live?" "Will it be safe?"

Ring . . . ring . . . ring . . .

"Hello?"

"Hi, Dad."

"Hi, son. What prompts you to call at this time of day?"

"Well . . . I need to talk to you and Mom about something."

"What is it, son?"

"I . . . I won't be coming home this summer to work."

"Oh? Where are you going?" asked the concerned voice.

"I've decided to work in the inner city of Los Angeles," I stuttered. (There was a long pause.) By this time my mother was on the other extension.

"Will you get paid?"

"Well, not really," I responded.

"I thought you were going to work this summer? I thought you wanted to go back to school this fall?" continued my father, his voice laced with parental pragmatism.

The questions of what, how, and where lasted for the next half hour. As anticipated, I had no substantial, well-thought-out, logical answers to any of their questions. All I could really say was that I felt called by God to go and serve. Beyond this sense of calling, I hadn't really figured anything out. All I knew was that I was *supposed to go*. Yes, I wanted to return for my junior year of college. My grades were good, I was having the time of my life, and I was hoping to graduate with my class. I knew my parents did not have the financial means to make up the shortfall for what I would not make by volunteering during the summer months. I would be on my own. Returning to college in September would take a miracle.

The spring semester had been a tumultuous time. Reading Dietrich Bonhoeffer's *Cost of Discipleship* and taking a course on the life and teachings of Jesus had really challenged me to consider following in the footsteps of Jesus. Bonhoeffer wrote about the cost of what it meant to be a disciple. Not only did he write about it, he was executed by Hitler because his faith called him to act out against the evil Nazi regime. Even though Bonhoeffer had the opportunity to live comfortably in the United States and accept a teaching post at Union Theological Seminary, he chose to go back to Germany and begin an underground seminary. Bonhoeffer truly lived out his claim that "when Christ calls a person, he bids that person to come and die." Bonhoeffer was willing to die for his convictions and faith. He listened to God's Spirit, rather than the compelling voices of family and friends. Bonhoeffer made a decision that looked stupid in the eyes of those who did not understand the kingdom. He had risked everything because of his compelling urge to live obediently to Jesus. This Bonhoeffer fellow had gotten under my skin.

To follow God's prompting and give up a summer without income was, without a doubt, educational suicide. My parents still thought I was throwing away my education, and my college buddies did not expect to see me back in school in September. But at a certain point I had to ask the question: If God calls a person to serve, does not God also have the capacity to provide for that person? I knew I could do the safe, rational, and practical thing and have the full support of everyone. Friends, parents, pastors, and professors would all back the practical decision. Or I could choose this other road that did not make any practical sense, did not have a predictable ending, and would take every ounce of faith I could muster. Deep down I had a sense that if I chose to play it safe I was denying God's power and ability to provide. To not risk and pursue this call would be an act of disobedience. Of course, most of those around me would not look at the decision to get a good-paying job for the summer as some great sin. Publicly I could still maintain my image as a good Christian kid. But to be true to myself and true to the call of God, I knew that to choose against God's call would be like saying, "I can sing songs about your providence, Lord. I can read Scripture about your miraculous provision, teach lessons on the biblical heroes of faith, but Lord, I am not willing to act on these promises—I claim one thing with my mouth, yet I don't *really* believe it true for me!" This was the ultimate test of real faith. If I wanted to move to a new level of faith and spiritual awareness, I would need to take a leap of faith and begin establishing patterns of risk-taking in my life. I would need to embrace a new definition of faith. In the words of Greg Ogden, I needed to believe that faith "is putting ourselves in situations where if God does not show up, we're in trouble." I took the jump.

A summer in the city changed my life dramatically. Being exposed to urban issues, multiple cultures, differing races, and problems that I had never encountered opened my eyes to a much bigger reality than I was used to. I learned from single moms the struggle of raising kids with few resources and little community support. I talked with teens about their involvement in gangs, and lived in a rehab house with men trying to recover from drug addiction. I befriended homeless people who would show up on the doorstep of the church asking for food. I visited mosques and temples and met people who believed differently. I met faithful servants and ministers of Christ who had labored in the city for many years. These experiences stretched my new-forming faith. God used the summer to develop in me a lifelong passion for the city.

But the greatest lesson learned was watching the miracle of God's provision unfold before my eyes. By the third week of August things were still looking a little bleak. The college wanted a down payment for classes. At this point I was convinced that I would not return to school in the fall. But God had different plans. Just before the deadline for re-enrollment passed, I received an unexpected scholarship. Then a few anonymous gifts arrived. And finally, I secured a job on campus. I was back in school. God's involvement was evident. My decision to throw it all away by following God's prompting had been honored. I had taken the first major risk of my life, and God had demonstrated incredible provision and faithfulness. The provision of tuition was beyond coincidence. God had moved. My faith had grown. I was ready to risk again.

Limiting God

Over the years I have heard many college students talk about wanting to do ministry in communities and countries where there is great need. Their hearts have been broken by a compelling sermon, a moving documentary, or a book. They sense a call to serve and reach out. But when the financial vulnerability of the situation becomes real, these same students slowly change their decisions. The initial zeal is lost. Either they walk away from the opportunity or they choose to serve in ministries where they could make money. These wonderful, eager students usually end up ministering in more affluent, upper-middle-class communities—communities where there may already be an abundance of ministries.

Repeatedly I talk to college students who want to come to the inner city or go on foreign mission to impoverished countries. At the risk of not knowing how they will meet their financial obligations, they become paralyzed by the potential obstacles. "I would love to work with these kids one day. But I need to get a job and save some money," becomes the all-too-frequent mantra. Sadly the promise of money holds more power over these students' lives than the promises of God. God is never even given the opportunity to fulfill their need. These students make their decisions based on what seems practical, responsible, and prudent. Before God is even given a chance, the voice of logic kicks in and dissuades any step of faith. The journey of faith, which often sends us to places and in directions that seem completely illogical, is ended before it can really begin.

Habits of Faith

Faith often defies logical sense. Consider the disciples. They were a group of working men. The Scriptures make it clear that they were not a bunch of loafers. They had jobs. Despite the unpredictable nature of the fishing industry, it seems that they had some security. They owned their boats. They had nets. They had a future. Their livelihood and daily sustenance revolved around their occupation as fishermen. Despite the bad reputation, Matthew probably did all right as a tax collector. Luke probably paid his bills by providing medical services. Enter Jesus.

When Jesus called this group to follow him, they gave it all up. Guarantees of compensation were not part of the recruitment package. With no knowledge of what the future would hold, these men threw their entire lives at the feet of Jesus. They had to trust. They had to travel around the Judean basin with only the clothes on their backs (Matt. 10:10). They had to rely on this Jesus character to meet their physical needs. But it was in this act of abandonment that these men learned the secrets of the kingdom. They watched the Master turn a sack lunch into a feast for thousands (Matt. 14:13–21). They watched him raise people from the dead (Matt. 9:18). They experienced healings and miracles beyond their wildest imaginations. Through this trust-walk, the disciples began to see not only that Jesus spoke words of promise but that those words of promise became reality. By experiencing daily miracles, these men of little faith became believers who would shape the entire history of the world because they began to act on the promises of God. But it is important not to overlook the fact that this personal transformation of the twelve disciples all began with an initial willingness to risk. These normal men began to transform into disciples when they began to abandon their personal security—that which made practical sense—and follow Jesus. Oswald Chambers, the great devotional writer, powerfully wrote about risk-taking and the call of God when he said,

> If you debate for a second when God has spoken, it is all up. Never begin to say—"Well, I wonder if God did speak?" Be reckless immediately, fling it all out on God. You do not know when God's voice will come, but whenever the realization of God comes in the faintest way imaginable, recklessly abandon. It is only by abandonment that you recognize God. You will only realize God's voice more clearly by recklessness.[19]

The way Oswald lived his own life was a consistent reflection of his words. As a talented art student, he gave up his artistic ambitions because God was calling him in another direction. He obeyed the voice of God, started a missionary-training school, and eventually served as a military chaplain for men and women serving in the Egyptian desert. He died at a relatively young age at this post because of the lack of medical care. Ironically it has been his sermons (he never wrote a book) that have lived on, inspiring thousands of readers over the years. Chambers did not just write about risk, he took risks and displayed "reckless abandonment" in his own life for the cause of Christ.

It is critical to understand that this ability to totally trust—to throw one's whole self and one's whole life into the arms of God—does not appear overnight. Becoming a person of faith takes time. Faith evolves and grows. True faith is not the by-product of a terrific worship service. Faith does not become part of our lives because of a great book we read. Faith is not simply memorizing all the wonderful Scriptures that talk about the promises of God. Real faith, the kind that provides a person with the confidence to engage in radical acts of discipleship and to place ourselves in situations that are way beyond our control, takes time to cultivate. It is like a plant that grows with each watering. It is like a muscle that gets stronger each time it is used. When we take a step of faith and watch God meet us, it provides us with another event in our lives on which we can look back and say, "God provided. God met me." As more and more of these God-events occur, a disciple of Jesus can walk more and more confidently by faith.

From Bookworm to Martyr

The life of the archbishop of San Salvador, Oscar Romero, who was assassinated on March 24, 1980, is a powerful example of how true faith develops in people as they take bigger and bigger steps of faith. Selected as the archbishop because he was a "bookish," institutional guy, the higher authorities within the Catholic Church and government thought they had the perfect candidate to maintain the status quo. After his selection, the faith of Romero began to change. From someone whose faith was rooted in the exposition of pleasant sermons and homilies, Romero was slowly jilted out of his protected life. Over a three-year period, Romero was transformed from a timid religious bureaucrat to a powerful prophet who was willing to confront political and military leaders about the conditions of the poor. How did it happen?

One faith-defining moment in Romero's life was when he sought to reclaim a church that had been taken over by military personnel for a barracks. Romero, returning to the church to collect the Eucharist supplies at the altar, was greeted by guards armed with machine guns and totally unsympathetic to his plea. With the guards pointing their guns and ready to shoot him, Romero boldly walked to the front of the church to collect the holy wafers and wine. Just as he was about to gather the elements, the altar was riddled with gunfire. Scared, sweating profusely, and on his knees, Romero continued to fulfill his mission by gathering up the fragmented symbols of Christ's body. He then carried the wafers and wine outside to the people. Romero did not capitulate to the intimidation of the guards. He confronted the aggression head on with courage and faith. God protected him.

From this point on in his life, Romero was no longer controlled by fear. He became bolder. He became more outspoken. He became increasingly confident in the power of God. Romero began to act like a man who could truly move mountains. Although his bold acts of faith eventually led to his assassination, Romero's legacy and life continue to inspire those who are oppressed and those who desire to live out their faith more authentically.

A Habit of Risk

The group sitting around the table at the board meeting was an interesting assortment of personalities. Their backgrounds, their upbringing, their Christian tradition, and their theology were all extremely diverse. Otis Johnson, an African-American who grew up in the inner city, was from a conservative Baptist background. He loved the Scriptures and believed in them with all his heart. Jack Smith, on the other hand, was a Methodist elder. He had grown up in affluence and had not spent much time encountering some of the realities of the inner city. Jack was a bit more liberal than Otis. Susan Stand was a Presbyterian, Don Steward a Catholic. All thirteen of the board members sitting around the table had a different story. But they all gathered once a month to provide direction for our ministry.

For over a year our ministry had been dreaming and planning to open a school. It would start small—with just a few classes—but the plan was to add a grade each year until the school reached eighth grade. Since the school was located in an impoverished city with an abysmal public school system that sends fewer than 5 percent of its graduates to college (a 60 percent dropout rate), and since the mission of the school was to provide a quality Christian education for children who normally could not afford such an education, there was a great need to raise a truckload of money to underwrite the cost of each child. Every child to attend our new school would need sponsors. Thousands of dollars had to be raised to get the project off the ground and get the school through the first year.

By our June meeting the fund-raising goals, set by the board of directors six months prior, had not been met. At this particular board meeting a decision needed to be made as to whether the school would move ahead or stay closed for another year. About half the money needed had been raised, but not nearly enough for the school to complete the necessary renovations and pay the teachers for the first six months. Students were signed up. Families were excited. Teachers had been secured. But the board had to decide whether we should step out in faith or spend another year raising the money needed.

"I don't think it's a good idea to start this September," opened the treasurer. "We haven't reached our goal. We don't have the money in the bank. It would be irresponsible to open the school." He was cautious and concerned.

Out of the corner of my eye I noticed Otis reaching for his Bible. While others continued to share their opinions, he thumbed the page of his worn, leather-bound King James Bible. As Otis waited for a break in the increasingly heated discussion, which was now moving in the direction of caution and doing what seemed practical, I could sense that he was getting ready to preach one of his mini-sermons. With the board moving in the direction of not starting the school, I quickly prayed for the Lord's intervention.

"Let me read a Scripture," began Otis, who had been silent to this point. "Faith . . ." he paused, cleared his throat, and raised his voice an octave. "According to the writer of Hebrews, 'faith is the substance of things hoped for and the assurance of things unseen.'" The whispers and chitchat came to an abrupt stop. Everybody knew that old Otis was about to roar. After enthusiastically reading six verses from Hebrews, Otis closed his Bible, took a deep breath, and looked at each person around the table. "Let it be known," he began. By now all the board members were hanging on each word. "Let it be known that I will resign from this board if we do not go ahead with the school. The donations we have received so far send a clear message that there are people out there who believe in this project. Right now I think they have more faith than we do." The room was still. "When and where in the Scriptures have God's people ever had everything in place before they followed the call? My Scripture . . . my Scripture tells me about a God who called a group of slaves in the desert with no guarantees of outrunning the Egyptian army. Did God provide? Was God's promise kept? My Scripture tells me about a boy named Daniel who wouldn't bow down to some idol. Did he have any guarantees? No! Did God provide? Was God's promise kept? Yes! My Scripture tells me about a group of fishermen who left everything they had to follow Jesus. Did they have any guarantees? No! Did God provide? Was God's promise kept? My friends," finished Otis in an almost feverish tone, "let us remember that 'faith is the substance of things hoped for, and the assurance of things unseen!'"

You could have heard a pin drop. Everyone sat stunned. The message had been delivered. Otis had let the Word speak, and everybody knew that God was calling the board members to move beyond their comfort zone and take a risk. The pieces were not all in place. Moving ahead with the project would involve trust and a great deal of faith. If the school failed, it would cause embarrassment. If we moved ahead with the project, the board and staff would have to rely on God in ways that we had never done in the past. Everybody knew that God wanted us to open the school. The issue was whether we would stand in the way or move to the side and let God provide. If the school succeeded, it would be because God allowed it to succeed. Like Gideon of old who went to battle with a mere three hundred soldiers against a mighty army of thousands, any success would be the Lord's doing. A school that succeeded would be God's victory, not ours. The vote was called: eight in favor. One against. One abstained. The project would move ahead. Four months later the CamdenForward School opened.

It was exciting to watch the classrooms come alive. Children were learning. The school quickly became one of the most positive things in the community. On a program level, things were great. Financially, however, the school was struggling. In the third month of operation the money was about to run out. It looked as if Otis had been wrong. Doubts began to seep into my brain. Should we have listened to the treasurer? Had he been right? Did we misread the will of God? The choice to move ahead did not look promising. Did we miss God's leading? Did we act foolishly?

Since the school fell under my jurisdiction, I was getting a little nervous. Payroll was just around the corner and there was no money. What would I tell the teachers? The kids? The parents? What was I to do when we could not meet our financial commitments? I began to pray.

The end was coming. I really doubted if our ministry would survive. We did not need just a few small gifts. We needed big money and there was none coming down the pike.

On a Tuesday morning, four days before payroll, I received a call. A donor wanted to give a gift—a $50,000 gift to the school! All the donor asked me to do was phone a stockbroker to set up a trading account, and he would transfer his stock gift into our account. Prior to that Tuesday morning, our ministry had never received a stock gift. I called the broker and set up an account. I was thrilled and began to feel a little disappointed with my wavering faith. God had given us a stunning new breath of life!

Fifteen minutes later, after wrapping up the first stock transaction, the phone rang again. "Do you accept stock gifts?" said the voice of another donor on the other end of the phone.

"Sure . . . well, ah . . . yes, of course!"

"Do you have a broker?"

"A broker? Oh, *sure*," I said with a silly, confident voice. I didn't reveal my little secret that I had just set up our first account with a broker ten minutes before!

"I'm sending over some stock," he began. "Forty-five hundred shares. They're trading at $21 a share. Can you use them?" I responded with an emphatic, "Yes!" Now smiling uncontrollably I hung up the phone. I couldn't believe it. Two gifts. Close to $150,000! And it wasn't even ten o'clock in the morning yet. Needless to say, I did not want to leave my office for the rest of the day.

How exciting to know that when God is in something, God gives the means to make it happen. Jesus said, "God already knows all your needs and God will give you all you need from day to day if you live for God and make the Kingdom of God your primary concern" (Matt. 6:32–33 NLB).

The Scriptures are clear. God is in the business of providing, of doing miracles, and of moving mountains. But if we want to participate with God in these miracles, we must be willing to take risks ourselves. We must be willing to step out and trust that the impossible will become possible. We must be willing to believe that God loves to meet our acts of outrageous faith with outrageous displays of love and provision.

It is critical for young disciples to begin cultivating a lifestyle of faith early in their faith journey. Waiting for the day "when all your ducks are in a row" is not a formula that stretches a person into a disciple who will "move mountains" and believe that the impossible can happen. We must all come to grips with the fact that if God is God, then God is capable of doing whatever needs doing. We cannot limit God.

Habits of Faith-Filled Acts

I approach life much differently now because of initial faith steps taken during my college years. Although my decisions may be different now, I am still confronted each day with options that demand I act on God's promises—or not act. I still step forward sweating, wondering, doubting, and not knowing where the money will come from, or how the resources will surface, or how things will all fit together. But because God has always provided in unique and miraculous ways, I have a certain underlying confidence that God will provide one more time. Little steps of risk and faith today do help us all prepare for those bigger, more exciting, and truly awesome acts of faith yet to come.

One of the ministries I admire most in the country is directed by a man named Bob Lupton. Years ago, Bob moved into an inner-city neighborhood in Atlanta and began to slowly rebuild the community. His work with youth and community organizations over the years has been admirable. Bob also offers some of the best insights in the country on how Christians should respond to some of the urban problems facing our country.

Bob tells a powerful story of how he started his work in the city. He was finishing his tour in Vietnam when God began to place a burden on his heart for the inner city. At first he did not know what to do with the burden, so he prayed about it, asking God to give him further direction, and then finished out his tour. Upon returning to the United States, Bob began to seek out organizations that worked with young people in the city. The one condition that he laid before God is that he would do anything except raise money to support himself and his young family. God had another idea.

Sure enough, within a few months, Bob landed a job with Youth for Christ in Atlanta. He would be working with children from the inner city. But to his disappointment he would also need to raise personal support. The idea of going out and asking people for money was humiliating for Bob, especially when these funds would be desperately needed to support his family.

Bob began setting up appointments to speak at different churches in the Atlanta area. The head office of Youth for Christ had sent him a slide show and pledge cards to promote his new work. Bob was now a fully bona fide missionary.

The first attempt at raising money was at a little Presbyterian church just outside the city. About eight people showed up one Sunday night for cookies and the presentation. When Bob turned off the lights to show the slides, the slides did not correspond with the manual. He tried to do his best from memory, but the presentation was disjointed and disorganized. When the lights went on, Bob buried his reddened face, packed up his slides, and headed for the back door of the church. He was embarrassed and filled with a total sense of failure.

While Bob was putting the slide projector in the trunk of his car, he noticed two men walking out of the church toward him. As they got closer, he noticed that they were crying. Bob thought, "I know I was bad, but surely I wasn't that bad." The men stopped in front of Bob. One of them asked, "Bob, what will you need to support you and your family this year?" Bob was a little caught off guard. "Why would they be asking?" he thought to himself. Off the top of his head, Bob came up with the salary he still needed to raise. The two men looked at Bob. One finally spoke. "Bob, Sam and I want you to know that we were moved by your presentation tonight and believe in what you're called to do. We want you to know that we'll make up the difference of your salary for the first year."

Bob was speechless. Shell-shocked. He could not believe what he was hearing. The pressure of raising support for him and his family had been lifted. Bob could now concentrate on programs for the youth. God had miraculously provided. Bob's calling was confirmed.

That encounter took place about thirty years ago. Just recently the second of the two men passed away. For the past thirty years they had faithfully sent in donations every month to Bob and his ministry. For the last thirty odd years God has provided for Bob and his family in miraculous and wonderful ways. For the past thirty years Bob has been giving witness to God's kingdom by transforming former "war zones" into livable, healthy communities where inner-city children can grow up in safety and health.

If Bob had not chosen to obey God, step out in faith, defy "common sense," and go against his own instincts, a wonderful life-transforming ministry would have never been birthed in Atlanta. Because Bob was willing to fully put his trust in God and believe wholeheartedly in God's provision, God was able to move powerfully in the life of a human being and establish one more kingdom bulkhead in an area that had been overcome by destruction and chaos. At the risk of looking foolish and appearing naive, Bob stepped out in faith.

If Jesus Were a Sophomore

"What do you think I should do, Jesus?" I ask, directing my question to the bunk above me. It's dark. I see nothing.

"Should do about what?" comes the response.

"Should do about the summer?"

"What are your options?" comes the Voice.

"I sense I am being called to go on a mission trip to the Third World."

No comment comes from the top bunk, so I continue.

"But I've got to raise money. You know, ask people for support. And then I have the tuition question for the fall. Where will the money come from? And then there is the parent factor. They will think I'm nuts."

"So what's stopping you?" asks the Voice.

"Well . . . I'm not sure. It's just that nothing is guaranteed, you know."

"Why do you think you should go on this trip?" probes Jesus.

"I think God wants to stretch me. Make me a person of faith," I answer.

"Perhaps that is why there are no guarantees. If it were all guaranteed there would be no faith. There would be no stretching. There would be no risk," he says.

I ponder the thought. I know he is right. I just do not want to admit it. It is one thing to talk about faith and about "risking it all" for God. It is another thing to actually act on it.

"What is the worst thing that could happen?" adds the voice from above.

"I could get killed, die from malaria, and not get enough tuition to return to school in the fall," I respond.

"I thought you were already 'dead'? You know, taken up your cross? Laid down your life?"

I always hated his poignant reminders.

"What's the best thing that could happen?" he asks.

"I guess I could experience God in a whole new way. I could watch God provide and protect in ways that I have never experienced. I guess I could really discover if God is God."

"You've got to make the choice," concludes my Advisor. "You have to decide how you are to live your life. Can you ever really experience promises of God if you don't put yourself in situations where, if God doesn't show up, you are in trouble?"

Jesus calls his disciples to be risk-takers. Jesus calls those who follow him to become people who put their ultimate trust in the abilities of God. Garreth Higgins, a former student intern, recently sent me some reflections on the topic of risk. He writes,

> I don't think Jesus took risks for the sake of risk; he walked with God, and learned/discerned God's ministry, so he knew exactly what he was supposed to be; so his subversiveness was not cavalier or spontaneous—it was in the service of the kingdom which he was establishing. That is to say, he did not take risks for the adrenaline rush (although, of course, he did know how to have a heaven of a good party!), but his subversion happened because he knew it was right! True risk, and the kind of risk we are

> encouraging here is not necessarily "heroic." . . . It is walk-
> ing closer with Jesus in our everyday lives, lives which
> often consist of the mundane.

Garreth's insight is critical when he draws a corresponding relationship between risk-taking and the pursuit of God's kingdom.
Risk-taking is never an end unto itself. Biblical risk-taking
always corresponds with obedience to God. Consider again
Jesus' admonition to "not worry about your life" (Matt. 6:25) or
about things like clothing and food. It is a pretty risky command, and, if pulled out of context, could imply that we can just
sit back and believe that God will take care of everything. But
Jesus reminds us that the promise of provision is coupled with
the command to seek first God's kingdom and God's righteousness (Matt. 6:33). The risk of trusting God for "all these things"
goes hand in hand with the active verb of seeking to bear witness, and give evidence to, a world of justice, peace, and pros-
perity for *all* people.

The church of the new millennium desperately needs a fresh
generation of young leaders who will make faith-based decisions. If this new generation of risk-takers is to appear, students
need to begin to use their college years to establish behaviors
and lifestyle patterns that include risk-taking and the discipline
of total abandonment for God. I believe that Jesus would encourage collegians to start each day by asking, "How can I take
a risk for God today?" "How can I walk by faith and not by
sight?" "How can I truly seek God's kingdom and trust that the
rest will be added?" "How can I begin to develop patterns of risk
and total trust that will become habit as I prepare myself for
leadership in the new millennium?"

Remember:

It's not the critic that counts, not the man who points out
how the strong man stumbled, or where the doer of deeds
could have done better. The credit belongs to the man
who is actually in the arena, whose face is marked by dust
and sweat and blood, who strives valiantly, who knows the
great enthusiasm, the great devotion, and spends himself
in a worthy cause. Who at best knows in the end the tri-
umph of high achievement and who at worst, if he fails, at
least fails while doing greatly. So that his place shall never
be with those cold and timid souls who know neither victory nor defeat.

                                        Theodore Roosevelt

Questions for Reflection

1. What is the last significant risk you took for God? How did you feel prior to the risk? What was the result? How have you grown through taking risks?

2. What stands in the way of you taking more risks? Identify some obstacles. Be specific.

3. What are some risks God is calling you to take right now? Both small and big.

4. Who are some Christians you know, or whom you have read about, who have taken risks for God? What kind of risks did they take? What were the consequences of their risk-taking?

5. How can you begin to build risk-taking behaviors into your life?

For the Leader

Ask your group to consider and discuss the following: If Jesus was a young adult living in the twenty-first century who wanted to develop risk-taking behaviors, what kinds of things might he do?

Prayer and Meditation

Lord,

My instinct calls me to survive.
My instinct calls me to protect my life.

Yet Lord, I know that to find life I must lose it for Your sake,
Yet it cuts against every fiber of my being to surrender my life.
Spirit, release me from the need to protect,
Spirit, free me from the tendency to just survive.

Give me the courage to risk.
Show me this day,
Show me now what I must do to build the behaviors of risk into
   my life.
Lay those little steps before me.

Protect me from waking one day,
Only to find myself wrapped in a shell that cannot be broken,
The shell of fear, of status-quo living, of self-preservation.

I desire to live by faith, not by sight.
Toward this end I pray.

Amen

Chapter 11

Tolerant Behaviors:
Learning to Work Together

The exclusion of the weak and insignificant, the seemingly useless people, from a Christian community may actually mean the exclusion of Christ; in the poor brother Christ is knocking at the door. We must, therefore, be very careful at this point.

Dietrich Bonhoeffer

The [person] who lives in a small community lives in a much larger world . . .The reason is obvious. In a large community we can choose our companions. In a small community our companions are chosen for us.

G. K. Chesterton

Loving Across Differences

A group of college students arrived at our ministry to work together for the summer. It was a rather eclectic troop. They came from all over the world: Scotland, England, Canada, and an assortment of states. Besides their geographical and historical differences, there were some obvious theological and denominational differences. Within the group were Baptists, Catholics, Pentecostals, Presbyterians, Lutherans, and a number of other denominations.

It was our first morning to have devotions together before we embarked on our mission of providing summer camps for inner-city children. The group was excited about their summer of missionary service. They anticipated challenges, and many wondered whether they were up for the task. Everyone arrived to devotions that morning with expectations of how worship should proceed. They were looking forward to the opportunity of praying and singing together. Everybody loved to sing choruses and praise songs. Others were eager to study the Scriptures and get into God's Word. Favorite verses were underlined with fluorescent-yellow highlighters in the Bibles of those who had arrived early for meditation. It was going to be a great morning.

The worship leader began to strum his guitar and lead us in some praise choruses. The response was interesting and reflected the diversity of the group. Suzie, the Pentecostal sister on my right from Orange County, California, had her hands raised and was mumbling "Hallelujah" with every break in the rhythm. She had obviously found her stride with the worship leader and was finding comfort in the song selection. To my left, however, was a Catholic brother named Garth. With his head reverentially bowed, he was connecting with God by quietly trying to meditate.

Suzie got progressively louder. With each note she let the group know that she was "being filled" with the Holy Spirit. After a time of moaning in agreement with the words of the worship songs, Suzie began to chant, "Lord, take us to your throne! Take us to your throne, Jesus!" With eyes closed and hands raised toward heaven, Suzie was beginning to experience the fullness of the worship experience . . . in her own way.

Garth was a little uncertain as to what he should make of Suzie's activity. It was obvious that the worship he had experienced during his life was a bit more reflective and much more subdued. This was Garth's first exposure to vocal and participatory worship. Each time Suzie would chant "Lord, take us to your throne!" a little louder, Garth's furrowed brow would provide a glimpse of his growing perplexity. At last, when he could not resist any longer, Garth leaned over and whispered in my ear, "Why does Suzie want to leave? We just arrived here!"

Coming Together

Trying to get a group of Catholic, Baptist, Presbyterian, Lutheran, and Pentecostal students to come to a consensus on worship styles is a challenge. Besides the challenges of doing mission work together, sharing limited resources, sleeping in overcrowded conditions, and cohabiting for eight weeks with people who do not embody similar living habits, trying to unify such a group in common mission and service is extremely difficult.

Yet the ability to find common ground is so crucial to the future of the Christian church. More and more the body of Christ is polarizing. On one side we have the conservatives who can sometimes embody intolerance and a sense that "we alone have the truth." On the other end of the spectrum are the more liberal folk who sometimes embody total tolerance and believe that almost anything is okay. The two groups can drive one another crazy. One group may believe that to vote anything but Republican jeopardizes your salvation. The other group may believe that to vote anything but Democrat makes you mean-spirited and cold-hearted. One group may believe that to have a glass of wine with a meal puts you on the fast track to hell. The other group believes that Jesus turned water to wine—not to grape juice—and therefore it is biblical to drink wine. The list goes on and on.

Rather than learning to appreciate and respect diversity, people who believe differently from ourselves are often demonized and treated as though they are lepers. More than ever, a new generation of young church leaders is needed, leaders who are committed to bridging differences and modeling a new church that is multi-ethnic, multi-denominational, bipartisan politically, and welcoming of people who worship differently and implement their faith in different ways.

Sadly, our denominational upbringings often shield us from the rich customs of other Christian traditions. Once we get locked into a particular denomination—this can happen even if we belong to a "nondenominational" church—we isolate ourselves from people who are different. We become comfortable worshiping in certain styles and interpreting Scripture through certain lenses, and we live out our faith only in adherence to the expectations set by those with whom we fellowship. Unfortunately the opportunities to meet other Christians and understand their thinking and actions are very limited.

The former director of our Philadelphia program was a Lutheran clergyperson from Minnesota. Steeped in the traditions of the Lutheran church, John had a passion for Lutheran liturgy. During the corporate gatherings of worship in the summer months, John would weave Lutheran liturgy into the worship experience for all our summer missionaries. It used to drive the young people from Pentecostal churches crazy. "I hate this liturgy stuff!" they would complain. "How can the Spirit move if all we do is liturgy?" John would never capitulate to the voices of discontent. He thought it was important for these young Pentecostals to become exposed to a different side of the Christian tradition. Oddly enough, by the end of the summer some of the students developed a deep love and appreciation for the depth and theological richness of the Lutheran tradition. My friend John used the opportunity to expose collegians to a new way of worship. They became more tolerant and left seeing that even Lutherans could be filled with the Spirit!

One of my students recently returned from Europe with his university gospel choir. He had grown up in a very fundamentalist church. In his church, drinking alcohol was equated with performing one of the seven deadly sins. Alcohol was an instrument of the devil. After three weeks in Europe, my student could not get over the fact that many European Christians went out to a tavern after church, had a drink, and never thought anything of it! For this particular student, encountering people who loved and served God and yet lived out their Christian witness differently than his church did was an eye-opening and liberating experience. He realized that the body of Christ was much bigger than his storefront church. He realized that God's Spirit was alive in people who did not live according to his version of biblical truth.

An Inclusive Jesus

One of the remarkable things about Jesus was the way he interacted with people. As a Jewish man, steeped in the traditions of the Old Testament and bound by some of the historical realities of his day, Jesus did many things that raised the eyebrows of his contemporaries. When Jesus talked to Samaritans and used them as examples in his parables, Jesus cut against the cultural norms of his day. Samaritans were people viewed as half-breeds by the orthodox Jew. They were an embarrassment to the Jewish race. Yet Jesus included these people in his mission of love and sharing God's grace. In the Temple, Jesus honored the traditions of Jewish law but he also shared the message of the kingdom with those who had been excluded from Temple worship. Lepers, bleeding women, and those with physical defects were all excluded from Temple worship. Yet Jesus includes these people in his mission and ministry. As a man who came from a modest socioeconomic background, Jesus was comfortable with both the rich and the poor. He had dinner with Zacchaeus, yet he also ate dinner with the prostitutes. The Gospel accounts make a deliberate attempt to show us that Jesus was not exclusive to one particular group of people. Jesus embodied a life of inclusion. His life was an example of how God's kingdom includes all of God's creation.

Those who had been cut off from the Temple—the Temple was the human vehicle that allowed people to connect with God—were sought out by Jesus and welcomed back into communion. Those who were deemed unacceptable by society, for whatever reason, were not excluded by Jesus. By having dinner with sinners, healing people on the Sabbath, and touching the untouchables, Jesus challenged the social structures of his day. Regardless of the personal cost of ridicule and hardship, Jesus made it very clear that God's kingdom is not a kingdom that excludes people because of race, ethnicity, gender, or socioeconomic status. In the process of including "the outsider," Jesus sent a clear message that the kingdom of God is big and includes people who had been excluded by those who held positions of leadership within the religious community.

Rodney Clapp writes powerfully in *Families at the Crossroads: Beyond Traditional and Modern Options* that

> Jesus spoke in parables honoring such despised ethnic groups as Samaritans, thereby ignoring racial boundaries. He scandalously taught women and conversed with them in public, thereby trespassing sexual borders. He included among his disciples Simon the Zealot and spoke the words of new life to Nicodemus the Pharisee, thereby opening himself to the array of people who were strangers by virtue of their politics. He called the adulteress from the estrangement of the stoning circle back into the circle of community, thereby crossing moral borders. And he invited the ritually "unclean" to his table, thereby breaking religious taboos.[20]

For us Christians, Jesus becomes our example of inclusion and tolerance. Jesus ignored what was acceptable and reached out to people who were risky to be around—especially for a religious leader. As disciples of Jesus, we must move to the place where we can broaden our boundaries of who is "in" and who is "out" and begin to realize that the kingdom Jesus preached was one much larger than the one other religious leaders were preaching.

The questions confronting those of us who want to preach and live the same kingdom message that Jesus preached and lived are: "How do we develop an appreciation for the rich traditions of Christian churches that are different from our own?" "How do we exercise the grace and love that Jesus demonstrated to those who do not behave and think as we behave and think?" "How do we become Christians who, despite differences in politics and worship style, can work together and united around the kingdom mission?"

Answering these questions is critical because the authenticity and impact of God's witness in the world can be tied to the ability of our churches to unite, include, and get along with one another. Unfortunately the history of the church is full of glaring examples of Christians who could not learn to work through differences or display grace and tolerance to those who needed grace and tolerance in their lives. For example, my eyes were opened when I learned that the number one reason Christians leave the mission field is because of conflict with other missionaries. I would have thought that the reason missionaries leave the field was due to culture shock, snake bites, an inability to relate cross-culturally, or the inability to learn the language of a particular people. With all the external adversities of moving and living in a new culture, I never would have guessed that the major hindrance to long-term mission work would be conflict with other people working on the same team. In my short experience of working in missions, however, I have begun to see how these studies concur with what really happens in Christian ministry. The real enemy of God's kingdom work does not come from outside the camp but comes from within. Simply put: Christians have a hard time getting along with one another. Since this is true, how do we become kingdom people who can create unity within the body of Christ rather than division and become people who are dispensers of grace rather than intolerance?

Not Like Me

I appreciate the words of one college student who worked with our ministry. Ming Lee, coming from a Korean Presbyterian background, wrote in her journal, ". . . living and working with people from different Christian traditions has helped me to realize that the way I praise and worship God is not the only or best way. It has helped me to see how big God is—that God is present everywhere! It was easy to think that God only existed in my hometown." Adjusting to different styles of worship with an emphasis on different aspects of the faith stretched Ming to see that the body of Christ is big and that God is at work in traditions other than her own. Entering into relationship with a very diverse group of Christians her age, who love Christ and desire to serve faithfully, broadened Ming's worldview and expanded her understanding of how other Christians live out their faith in the world. Instead of judging people from a distance, Ming's experience of building relationships with others different from herself has helped her to see beyond external behaviors and connect with the hearts of other people. In understanding hearts, as opposed to behaviors and doctrines, Ming learned to be an agent of reconciliation rather than an advocate of divisiveness.

In our ministry there is a commitment to learning and listening to people who are different from us. Because many of our students come from Protestant backgrounds, I will often bring in speakers from the Roman Catholic traditions. My favorite speakers are the Franciscan monks. These brothers share about their vows of poverty and chastity. They share how they try to capture the spirit of joy St. Francis had when he embraced the leper and the poor. For many of our college students this is their first encounter with Catholicism. All they have been told during their lives are the negative aspects of the Catholic faith. Many have been told that Catholicism is bad and that Catholics are not going to heaven when they die. But when our students meet these brothers who are deeply committed to Jesus and embody a spirit of love, peace, and joy in their lives, they begin to realize that these are brothers in Christ who proclaim the good news message of the Gospel. The attitudes of our students change. They begin to see that these brothers are very much a part of the body of Christ.

Look at Your Campus

The beauty of some university and college settings is the diversity of students. Unless it is a very exclusive institution that attracts only certain kinds of students from certain denominations, there are often opportunities to build relationships with students from a variety of backgrounds. Unfortunately one of the first things students do when they get to college is find groups of people who are exactly like themselves. Clubs around campus like the Baptist Student Union, the African American Student Association, the Christian Environmental Association, InterVarsity, or Campus Crusade can potentially cut us off from students who are different from ourselves.

A few years ago I was amazed at the reaction I received to my suggestion of having two significant campus Christian groups partner to sponsor a joint activity. "How could we do that?" responded one of the leaders. "They are too *liberal* for us." Already at the young age of 21 these groups were falling into the trap of playing Christian politics. Rather than looking for common ground and looking together at their campus as a mission field, they were worried about what donors and denominational heads would think if they got together for an event. Ironically, when I asked the leader of the one group whether they had ever actually sat down and openly dialogued about some of their differences, the leader responded that they hadn't tried that. The two groups did not really know how they were different. They just assumed. Despite the fact that they read the same Scripture, sang the same praise songs, and listened to some of the same Christian artists, they never bothered to take the time to reach beyond their preconceived ideas and notions and really get at the truth.

As young Christians and emerging church leaders, we must develop the habit of moving beyond assumptions. We must put ourselves in situations where we are around people who are different than ourselves. We must make every effort to learn the discipline of inclusion and become people who unite, rather than divide, the body of Christ.

The Polarization of America

With the rise of the religious right, religious sectarianism, heightened racial tensions, and the ever-increasing ethnic diversification of our cities, God needs a new breed of Christian young people who are committed to inclusion. More than ever Jesus needs people who are committed to moving beyond their boundaries of comfort and who will open their arms wide and learn to embrace and work with people who are different from them. As the people of God, we must realize that Jesus had a higher calling for his disciples than simply being loud-speakers of correct doctrine and theology. Jesus called his disciples to love. It was a love for one another and for others that was to be the characteristic marking the first-century Christian.

Charles Colson puts it wonderfully when he writes that there is only one way people will genuinely hear the gospel message: by observing how the church itself lives. Colson comments that it is in the thirteenth and seventeenth chapters of the book of John where Jesus identifies how the world will know we are Christians—when the church is visibly united in love. It is when the diversity of opinions, background, experiences, and traditions of the body of Christ can be worked out in love and tolerance. It is then that our testimony to the world will be strongest and unshakable.

Jesus' life was a living testimony of tolerance and love for others. Frequently the Gospel reader meets a Jesus who bends tradition and protocol to uphold the greater value—that of love. Jesus breaks the rules of the Sabbath—to demonstrate love by healing the sick. Jesus breaks an Old Testament law on purity—to demonstrate love through touching and by bringing health to a bleeding woman. Jesus disregards the expectations of his contemporaries—to demonstrate love by eating with the outcasts, prostitutes, and tax collectors. The Gospels record numerous episodes where Jesus lets go of ideology and "legal" correctness for the sake of loving someone who had been disconnected from the community of believers.

Living Diversity

In our mission organization it is always fun to put people from different traditions on the same team. A few weeks into their eight-week summer experience, students realize that they must compromise and bend some of their positions and doctrine to move forward as a community. To hold fast to "their ways" and to maintain the need to "convert" everybody on their team to their way of thinking will eventually divide the staff and thwart their mission. To see students learn to broaden their appreciation for the traditions of others is always encouraging. To see a conservative fundamentalist, who believes that his Catholic brothers and sisters are not "saved" and are going to hell, befriend a Catholic brother or sister and see the evidence of the Spirit's fruit in their lives is truly remarkable. To see a Lutheran who has recited liturgy all her life enjoy the freedom of spontaneous worship and singing is remarkable. To watch a Pentecostal who has never understood the depth and beauty of liturgy come to see the Spirit work through structure is exciting. To watch a young man adamantly opposed to the ordination of women fall in love with a young woman studying to be an ordained Presbyterian clergyperson is exciting and humorous. These are all tremendous moments of growth.

Unfortunately, however, there are not always moments of growth. One of the most remarkable displays of intolerance happened in the summer of 1989. A young man from a conservative Midwestern church background arrived at our ministry. He was placed on a team with twelve other college students from around the country. They were housed in one of the poorest sections of the city. The streets of South Camden look like Berlin after the Second World War, full of abandoned, burned-out buildings. Watching children grow up amongst the violence, drugs, and social decay is enough to make anybody question the justice of our country. To add insult to injury, the long, hot summer days are brutal on the children from the south side since they enjoy none of the benefits of traditional summer vacations—no pools, no trips to the beach, no days at the amusement park; just long, hot, inner-city days with absolutely nothing to do.

At the first staff meeting, our site director, Wendy Smith, showed up with a Bible in her hand. She asked the others on staff to pull out their Bibles to study a passage of Scripture that would have application to their ministry that week. As soon as the request was made the young collegian from the Midwest gathered his belongings, stood up, and walked out of the room.

After the staff meeting, Wendy cornered her new staff worker and asked him why he left the room. His response was simple: "In my tradition, women do not teach men Scripture!" When Wendy continued to share that one of her responsibilities was to guide the team through various portions of Scripture, he replied that he would have to leave the room each time she shared. He would not allow himself to violate the clear biblical principles that a *woman* is not allowed to lead a man in Bible study.

The young man ended up leaving the ministry within the first week. He would not back down on his doctrine that held to the belief that women cannot teach men the Scriptures. Despite the incredible need for youth workers in the community, despite the hundreds of hurting children who could be touched with the Gospel, the young man could not bend his doctrinal convictions and work with a team of committed Christian servants to share God's love with children. The already overloaded team would now have to carry an even greater responsibility. He gave little regard for the increased load that the remaining staff would have to shoulder. The young man's theological convictions were more important than what God was about to do through Wendy and through the team.

To no one's surprise, the same God who, according to our young friend, "disapproved" of women in leadership did bless and use the South Camden team in a powerful way that summer. The remaining students prayed together, argued together, cried together, and laughed together. Despite their differences, children made new commitments to Christ, hungry families were fed, and many children participated in creative programs that affirmed their dignity and made them feel significant. God's presence was evident. All the students left after the summer realizing that God was bigger than their personal differences, that God was bigger than some of their theological differences, and that God was bigger than their denominational doctrines. The students transcended their differences and celebrated their diversity.

If I Had My Choice

Recently, in a *Christianity Today* essay titled "Why I Don't Go to a Megachurch," writer Philip Yancey drew from the insight of G. K. Chesterton to support his resistance in recent trends toward megachurches. Chesterton wrote, "The man who lives in a small community lives in a much larger world . . . The reason is obvious. In a large community we can choose our companions. In a small community our companions are chosen for us." Yancey continues to say that when we move toward megachurches, we are not forced to interact with people different than ourselves. Attending a large church is like visiting a shopping mall with specialized stores. We simply pick and choose where we are most comfortable. The problem with those choices is that we are never forced to interact and work through differences with people unlike ourselves.

One of the statements I continually hear college volunteers say is, "I would never choose to live with those who I have to live with right now!" Or, "If I had my choice I would not work with these people. We have nothing in common!" A few weeks or months later, these same people are usually saying, "This was the toughest but best experience of my life." The same students who were complaining continue by adding, "Living with, working with, and learning from people who have different tastes, different traditions, and different ways of living out their faith only broadens our understanding of God's kingdom, especially when we see God work through us."

Part of being a disciple of Christ in the ever-changing demographics of this century is to realize that there are thousands of Christian brothers and sisters who are sincerely trying to spread the good news throughout the world who may believe and express their faith a little differently than we do. Rather than judging those brothers and sisters from a distance, we can set an example for the church and not cower from difference by showing intolerance. By placing ourselves in uncomfortable situations, building relationships with people whom we find uncomfortable, we learn, as Chesterton so insightfully claims, to "live in a much larger world." As our world becomes larger, so must our understanding of the body of Christ.

Breakthrough Moments

I remember a significant breakthrough moment between one of my feminist staff workers and a conservative male worker. From day one Jan had a particular disdain for one of her male coworkers. Jan did not believe in the traditional roles of women, was a strong advocate of the inclusive language argument, and believed that women should have full participation in all roles within the church. Unfortunately, Jan was assigned to work with a male who believed in the traditional role of females, believed that all the male pronouns in Scripture were inspired by the Holy Spirit, and believed that women should not be ordained. These two staff members did their best to avoid contact with each other. On a small staff of fewer than twenty people, however, it was hard for them not to interact. Staff meetings often became battlegrounds for intense arguments.

Questions about which Bible translations should be used during Bible class for the children or how certain passages about God should be interpreted often fueled the debate fire. Their dislike for each other grew as each of these individuals crusaded for what they thought to be *The Truth*. Neither one of these workers seemed interested in backing down from their position. I did everything I could do to appreciate the two perspectives and help them continue working together.

One day Jan came to me and said, "You know, my attitude toward Bill has changed."

"What do you mean?" I replied, somewhat startled. "He hasn't changed his views. He still believes in things you don't agree with."

"I know," she continued. "But the other day I saw something in Bill that really changed my attitude." By this time I was really curious. This wasn't the Jan I had worked with for two years.

"What did you see?" I asked, trying not to look too intrigued.

"Bill's kid had just vomited all over his car. It was a mess. The child was screaming. His wife's clothes were a soaking mess. She was frustrated and about to lose her cool. D'ya know what Bill did? He gently put his hand on his wife's shoulder, told her not to worry about the mess, and affirmed to her that he would clean it up. Then he gave his caring attention to settling their child down. He rolled up his sleeves, tenderly quieted the baby, and then cleaned her from head to toe. To top it off, Bill washed the entire front seat of the car! I was moved by his humility. I was deeply touched. I was impressed."

The two staff workers never became the best of friends. They continued to disagree over most issues. But the tone of the disagreement changed. Bill's humble act of serving transcended his conservative theological convictions and helped Jan to see that beyond beliefs and doctrines is a heart. For a moment Jan saw that on an ideological level, she and Bill were still miles apart. But on a practical, hands-on level, Jan was touched by the love and tenderness Bill demonstrated to his wife. My feminist friend never did totally agree with her conservative brother, but a new respect began to develop toward Bill as a person, as a father, as a brother in Christ. If given the choice these two would never have chosen to work together. On a university campus these two would never be involved in the same fellowships, political groups, or special interest groups. Because they found themselves in an environment where they had to work together, disagree together, and finally see each other's heart, a bridge was built between two very different schools of Christian thought.

Most the time ideology divides people before they ever get close enough to see the heart of the other. People get locked into their groups, their "camps," and their clubs and never venture into situations where they must really engage with people who hold different beliefs and opinions. Because my young feminist staff worker and my conservative brother worked together long enough to see beyond their ideas, they became a little less judgmental toward each other. Bill came to believe that all feminists were not damned, and that people can argue for inclusive language and still love Jesus. Jan came to realize that ideology is not the only criterion for judging character. Both Jan and Bill began to see that authentic spirituality is not simply a function of correct thinking. Authentic spirituality involves action.

If Jesus Were a Sophomore

"I can't stand that guy. What a self-righteous, arrogant, pious jerk!" I muttered under my breath as I tried to get the key in my door.

It was the third time in less than a week that I had been assaulted by my zealous hall mate. He was the guy who blasted praise music until the early morning hours. Every time a person would pass his doorway, he would be there to distribute another Bible verse. But today he crossed the line. He was circulating a petition and wanted every Christian in the dorm to sign it. The petition was to be taken to the president of the college. The issue: banning non-Christian music from the dorms. Of course the issue was polarizing the dorm. Those with a marginal faith were only further repulsed by another narrow-minded, judgmental Christian. Those from more conservative backgrounds were jumping on board and hoping to make a statement to others on campus. World War III was about to begin—over Christian music!

Since I decided not to sign the petition, he immediately questioned my salvation and told me that I needed to pray that the Holy Spirit should convince me of my wayward thoughts. I was steamed. There was no opportunity to dialogue—no room to discuss what the variable might be that would distinguish "Christian" from "non-Christian" music. Classical, jazz, folk? I assumed that these would not make the cut.

Sure, I agreed that some music should not be played. Many lyrics were denigrating and not consistent with basic Christian principles. But heck, who was going to be the judge of what music had enough of God in it and what music did not?

"Your attitude is a little harsh," came a Voice from the corner of my room.

I knew the Voice. He was back again for another visit.

"Harsh? Harsh? This guy is an embarrassment to the faith. He's alienating people," I retorted, a little grist in my voice.

"So are you going join the bandwagon, crucify the brother, and divide the dorm?" asked my Friend.

"You didn't do much better with these types!" came my reply, forgetting momentarily who I was talking to. "You used a few stern words for those who played pious games in the name of God. Remember?"

"There was a difference," continued the Voice. "Their hearts were in the wrong place. This brother's passion is just a little misguided. Underneath his zeal is a good heart."

"You know I have difficulties with his kind of people." By now I was trying to evoke a little sympathy. He wasn't buying it.

"You will always have difficulties with many kinds of people. The music is not the issue. If it's not music, it'll be something else. The bottom line is this: Will you act in a way that pleases Me? Will you allow your character to be eroded by someone's petty differences? Will you allow your heart to fill with hatred over matters that really aren't important?"

Now I was silenced. What else could I say? I knew He was right. I could not let the circumstances surrounding me dictate my attitude and actions. I could not be governed by the actions of others. The true test of my faith was how I responded to my enemies. The true test of my belief was whether I could rise above the issues at hand and look for ways to bring about reconciliation.

Would I make the effort to try to connect with someone whom I would rather avoid and dislike? Could I be an agent of peace? Could I model tolerance?

"Do what I commanded," came the Voice again. "Love your enemies. Pray for those who persecute you. And be a peacemaker. This is what I desire."

The years of young adulthood are critical for establishing patterns of tolerance. Before people get locked into a career, a family, a denomination, they are given the opportunity to make their world a little larger by meeting people within the larger Christian community who are different from themselves. Take a look at the school cafeteria or snack bar. Likely, you will see young people from Hong Kong sitting in one area, the African American students at another table, and the Latino students at another. I believe that Jesus would want us to take the challenge and move beyond our comfort zone. I believe that Jesus would want us to reach across the lines of ethnicity, socioeconomic status, and denominationalism. I believe Jesus is tired of the old adage, "Birds of a feather flock together."

Jesus wants his disciples to take time to find, learn about, and love people who are different from themselves. Jesus wants his people to search the corners of their campus in an effort to find hurting, broken people who are alienated from others and from God. Jesus would not identify with only one Christian group. He would work to bring about reconciliation among the various Christian factions on his campus. Jesus would make an intentional effort to listen to and understand people from different traditions and try to facilitate their union. Jesus would not give the cynics, the agnostics, and the humanists more fuel for their arguments against God and Christian faith by taking sides in theological debates that are divisive and mean-spirited and attempt to tear down other Christians.

As the Christian church continues to hotly debate differences and things that divide, will the up-and-coming generation of new leaders feed this polarization and division, or will today's collegians be the kind of people who tolerantly strive to bring about peace, unity, and reconciliation? Will today's collegians become the preservationists of long-held differences and theological intolerance? Will today's collegians continue to hold fast to the divisions of the right and left, liberal and conservative, "spirit-filled" and non-charismatic, black church/white church, or the heavenly minded and the socially concerned? Or will this be the generation that has learned the behaviors of tolerance and that becomes intentionally committed to seeing beyond differences of thought and ideology to engage in dialogue and bridge-building? One only has to look at Northern Ireland, Kosovo, Rwanda, Israel, or Somalia to realize that religious differences can become part of the toxin that poisons the prospect of peace. One only has to look at increasing numbers of hate crimes and racially motivated conflicts to realize that the people of God must be modeling and creating opportunities for different groups to come together and set an example for our larger society.

Two thousand years ago, on a hill outside Galilee, Jesus cried out to those following him, "Blessed are the peacemakers, for they shall be called the children of God." Let us live as God's children. Let us live as peacemakers.

Remember:

So, don't look down upon people whose behavior is different or offensive. Love them, honor their dignity as human beings, creations of God, find out why you believe the behavior is wrong, and challenge it when necessary. But do not do this from a position of superiority or distance. We must build relationships with people before we challenge their values! Perhaps we also need to be asking questions about what the CHURCH tolerates—the arms industry, global capitalism, unfair trade with the developing world, idolatrous patriotism, homelessness, etc.

Gareth Higgins, student intern, Northern Ireland

Questions for Reflection

1. What kinds of people are difficult for you to get along with? Why?

2. What do you do when you come into the presence of people whom you do not like?

3. How do you react to Christians who hold different views and theological positions than you do?

4. Who are some people you need to learn to tolerate? What

concrete steps could you take to become more tolerant of these people?

5. At what point does toleration become compromise? How do you draw the line between toleration and compromise?

6. Was there any idea from the chapter that, as you continue to grow in your faith, would help you become a more tolerant person?

For the Leader

Ask your group to discuss the following: If Jesus were on your college or university campus, what might he do to develop tolerant behaviors and foster unity in the midst of diversity?

Prayer and Meditation

Lord,

I confess that some folk just get on my nerves.
I confess that my first reaction is seldom to pray for those people.
I confess that peace and reconciliation are not always my first priority in relationships.

Protect me from the need to always be right.
Protect me from the blindness that can come from a self-righteous attitude.
Help me to overcome the inability to forgive.

Lord, I look at the world and it frightens me.
It seems that we are always on the brink of some kind of dispute, some kind of unrest.
It seems that our social relations are so fragile.
Old hurts are just beneath the surface. Differences and misunderstanding are close at hand.

Lord, equip me with the ability to tolerate others.
Furnish me with the tools for building peace and reconciliation.
Grant me the ability to rise above my circumstances and the issues at hand,
So they do not control my heart,
My actions,
My attitude.

Amen

Chapter 12

Mission Behaviors:
The Need for a Mission Statement

Remember your Creator during your youth: when all possibilities lie open before you and you can offer all your strength intact for his service. The time to remember is not after you become senile and paralyzed! Then it is not too late for your salvation, but too late for you to serve as the presence of God in the midst of the world and the creation.You must take sides earlier—when you can actually make choices, when you have many paths opening at your feet, before the weight of necessity overwhelms you.

Jacques Ellul

I find the great thing in this world is not so much where
    we stand,
as in what direction we are moving.
To reach the port of heaven, we must sail sometimes with
    the wind
and sometimes against it—but we must sail, and not drift,
    nor lie at anchor.

Oliver Wendell Holmes

Getting Lost on the Way to the Cross

Fran was the kind of student any teacher would love to mentor. She had a thirst for learning, an eagerness to read, and a sincere desire to pray. On many occasions Fran would show up at our campus Bible study early to seek additional recommendations for books to read and Scriptures to explore. Fran was earnestly trying to build a foundation for a life of passionate devotion and service to Christ.

Fran also loved to ask questions. As a relatively new Christian she wanted to know everything about Christian faith. "What did Jesus mean when he called people to be the 'light of the world'?" "Is there a difference between a disciple and a believer?" "Why did Jesus have to die?" The questions were endless. Her curiosity was contagious. Fran's insatiable desire to grow spread like wildfire among others in the group. Like great athletes who bring everyone on their team to a new level of playing, Fran had the same effect. She was a teacher's dream student. A teacher could not ask for a more encouraging situation.

As Fran continued to grow during her junior year of college, the new seeds of faith that had been planted in her life began to move her in the direction of serving other people. She spent a weekend in a soup kitchen in Los Angeles. She became involved with an outreach program for teenagers at a local high school. Fran also began to reach out to others on her college campus, especially non-Christian international students who represented other worldviews and faith commitments. As a new Christian, Fran was showing remarkable signs of maturity and understanding of what it meant to follow Christ.

What made Fran so unique is the fact that she came from a non-Christian Korean family. Her father had died, leaving her mother to raise Fran and provide for her daughter. The mother earned a meager salary by working at a Korean restaurant as a kitchen helper. The hours were long and hard. It was grueling work, but Fran's mother did it without complaining because she was providing a better opportunity for her daughter. But watching her mother work so hard was difficult for Fran. She hoped that one day a way could be made for her mother to retire, put away the scrub pads, and enjoy the remaining days of her life.

One day this growing disciple was confronted with a very difficult decision. Fran found out that her mother had arranged for her to be married! This was not a complete surprise to Fran. Within some traditional Korean families, prearranged marriages are still the custom. However, for a young woman who was developing a very sincere and committed relationship with Christ, the announcement of a prearranged marriage would be Fran's most difficult challenge as a new believer. This would be the first major confrontation between the values of the new kingdom to which she had subscribed and the values of her culture.

The man chosen for Fran was older and considered by her family's customs to be an excellent choice. He had already obtained his Ph.D. and had been offered a good research position at a local university. The pay would be terrific. Not only would he be able to provide for his own family, but he would be able to look after Fran's mother as well. For someone who wanted to settle down, buy a home, raise a family, and live comfortably, her preselected mate would be perfect.

There was a serious problem for Fran. The man chosen for her to marry was not a follower of Christ. Although Fran's future mate did hold loosely to a Buddhist philosophy of life, he was more of a humanist—a person who believed that life's answers are found in the abilities of the human race and that the chief goal in life is to work hard and live comfortably. He believed Christianity to be a foolish and idealistic enterprise. Although he was not vehemently opposed to Fran's faith, he certainly did not share her passion and zeal to grow as a disciple of Christ. With the undeniable reality of God's presence and Spirit at work in her life, for Fran the idea of marrying someone who was not passionate about living his life for Jesus created a severe conflict of interest. Fran was in the middle of a tug of war between her culture and her faith.

But there was another reality confronting Fran. At twenty-eight years of age, Fran's biological clock was ticking. One of her life goals was to have children and raise a family. Not being particularly—as our culture defines it—attractive, Fran believed that her opportunities for marriage were few. Deep inside she began ask some tough questions: Would there be other opportunities for marriage if she turned her back on this man? Would God provide a spouse if she refused the opportunity her mother had created? What would be the repercussions within her Korean community if she snubbed this tradition?

Being blackballed from the Korean community was one of the biggest fears Fran would face. If she did not accept this arranged offer of marriage, Fran would be shunned by the community that had given her much of her identity, sense of history, and sense of belonging as she adjusted to life in the United States. Besides the loss of community, saying "no" to her mother and relatives would have other serious repercussions. Not only would her mother be devastated if she didn't accept the marriage, but denying this opportunity for financial security would force her aging mother to continue working long, hard hours at the restaurant—hours and work that were taking their toll on her health. The decision facing Fran had a string of consequences that would affect not only her life, but also the lives of others.

The Moment of Decision

Sitting in a McDonald's restaurant across from the main campus, Fran and I drank coffee and talked about the decision she was about to make. Deep down inside Fran knew that if her new-found faith was to grow and mature, she would have to turn her back on the marriage and her community. Much like disciples who had to choose between the security of their families and their fishing businesses and or the challenge to follow Jesus, Fran was confronted with a difficult choice. I reminded Fran that the most difficult aspect of Christian discipleship is the choices one has to make. The Bible is loaded with examples of individuals who had to choose between "common sense" and faithfulness to God. I recalled the furnace experience in the Old Testament of Shadrach, Meshach, and Abednego—three young men who were faced with tremendous cultural and societal pressure to conform to the expectations of the day. Their culture told them to kneel down and worship an idol of the king. Their faith told them that they could not worship both an earthly king and the Creator of the universe. The young men had to make a choice. But it was in choosing the way of God that their faith would be made stronger. It was in choosing to remain faithful that they would experience God in new, fresh, and dynamic ways. And it was ultimately in choosing the way of Yahweh that their world would get the opportunity to see the power of the one true God. Just like iron is tempered in a hot furnace, the faith of Shadrach, Meshach, and Abednego was tempered in the furnace. Their obedience resulted in a stronger faith that ultimately brought their community to conversion. Their obedience turned a king who was bent on self-worship to a king who could say, "Praise be to the God of Shadrach, Meshach, and Abednego . . . for no other god can save in this way!" (Dan. 3:28–29).

Fran was standing at a critical place in her development of faith, a place where the road divided. Fran would either walk the road of her culture and of the apparent security it would bring, or she would have to step out in faith and trust that God would honor her devotion and take care of her maternal needs and the needs of her mother. Like the saints throughout the history of the church who faced difficult choices of faith and obedience, Fran was at the crossroads and needed to make her choice.

When the time of decision ended, Fran chose to marry the Buddhist man. The forces of culture and familial expectation were too intense. Common sense and practicality prevailed. Watching her walk down the aisle, dressed in her wedding gown, toward a man who did not understand her spiritual thirst for God was extremely disheartening. All the months of Bible study, questions, and prayer seemed irrelevant. Fran's earnest learning and searching would not be fostered in her new home. With no encouragement from her new husband, it seemed inevitable that Fran would slowly walk toward the day when her dreams of serving God would vanish and her vibrant spiritual journey would become a distant memory.

After the wedding I did not hear from Fran for a number of years. Via the grapevine I caught wind that she had had children. But I had no real details on what was happening in her life. Did her husband ever convert? Despite the hostile environment, did she continue to grow in her faith? Did she ever go to church? To my surprise, I received a letter from Fran one day. In her familiar handwriting, Fran wrote about the children she had birthed. She told me about the nice home she lived in. She told me about the nice stuff her husband was able to buy. And then the tone of the letter shifted. Fran shared how she often looked back on her days in college as the best years of her life. She reminisced about our Bible study and how God was so real in her life during those days. Although she had the security of a home, the company of children, and a partner who provided, there was a profound and nagging emptiness deep within her soul. Fran had it all but lacked everything. By reading between the lines of her letter, I sensed that her life was full of regret. The furnace experience had come and Fran had walked away from the opportunity to be tempered. At the crossroads, Fran had opted for the sensible choice. She had capitulated to the pressures of culture and the voices of common sense that surrounded her.

Unfortunately for Fran, this point of critical decision came at a time when her faith was still forming. Still very young and newly converted, Fran had lost her bearings because she had not yet clarified the non-negotiables in her life. She had been introduced to Christian faith, she had embraced it as a lifestyle, but Fran had not had the opportunity to establish the pillars on which she would build a life of discipleship. The values and core commitments of what would guide her life had not yet crystallized. Fran had not created a "mission statement" for her life that would provide guidance during difficult times and keep her honest to the unique and special life God was calling her to live.

Jesus Had a Mission Statement

For young disciples of Christ, there is nothing more crucial than developing a life mission statement. The importance of adopting a personal mission statement is underlined by the fact that Jesus begins his public ministry by reciting his mission statement. After being tempted in the desert for forty days, Jesus returns to Galilee to start an incredible three-year ministry of devotion and service to God's kingdom. Jesus begins his ministry by articulating what his earthly ministry would look like. In his inaugural sermon, Jesus stands in front of the congregation, recites a passage from the prophet Isaiah, and lays out the plan God has given him to guide his choices. In a sense Jesus publicly announces: "This is what my life and ministry will be about for the next three years!"

> "The Spirit of the Lord is on me,
> because he has anointed me
> to preach good news to the poor.
> He has sent me to proclaim freedom for the prisoners
> and recovery of sight for the blind,
> to release the oppressed,
> to proclaim the year of the Lord's favor."
>
> Luke 4:18–19

What is interesting about Jesus' mission statement is that it incorporates a number of principles that we see consistently surface through his ministry. Although the mission statement does not tell the reader exactly where, when, what, and how Jesus will perform his ministry, the mission statement does give the reader an idea of Jesus' priorities for making his life and ministry decisions.

The Spirit of the Lord Is on Me

The first principle learned from this mission statement is that Jesus was not the final authority in his life. Jesus articulated that the Spirit of the Lord was on him and that he was anointed by God to perform his ministry. From the very beginning it was understood that Jesus' call to ministry was not a decision he made apart from his relationship with God. Jesus' preaching, proclamation, healing, and releasing of people in physical and spiritual captivity were all motivated because of his connectedness with God. Jesus was not a solo operator, in charge of his own destiny and ministering on self-determined power. The power and authority bestowed upon Jesus was given by God because of the partnership Jesus had with God.

Any Christian who takes the time to create a mission statement must recognize that mission must come from God. God is the giver of mission. We do not create our own mission and then ask God to endorse it. We do not just sit down with a few noble ideas, list the pros and cons, and then decide which idea makes the most practical sense. We do not let the anticipated job market act for God and then tell us what we should or should not do with our lives. The disciple of Christ asks God to breathe a mission into our hearts and mind. We ask God to be the giver of the dream. Only when God is the giver of the mission can the mission be fulfilled. Only when God is the giver of the dream can the dream become reality.

Lest I sound too abstract and lofty, one must ask: "How does God breathe this 'dream' into us? How does this vision and mission for our lives get communicated to us?" Biblical evidence suggests that God uses multiple channels and vehicles to communicate this vision and dream to people. Personal communication with God, interaction with other mature Christians, the study of Scripture, and the present historical context are all found throughout Scripture as ways of helping God's people discern their calling in the world. David was *chosen* for his kingly responsibilities by God's human spokesperson of the day, Samuel. It is the "word of the Lord" that came to Jeremiah and lodged itself deep within his heart and conscience, propelling him into the life of a prophet. Moses was called directly by the voice of God to respond to a specific historical reality. The ways God's people receive their life mission cannot be reduced to one specific formula. When God gives a mission to an individual, it can come from a variety of sources.

If Jesus' life is used as a model of how he gained his sense of mission and calling, we discover that there are some significant and important events that shaped his thinking. First, it is no coincidence that Jesus spent time in isolation prior to the launching of his public ministry. Although we know little of what happened with Jesus during his forty-day wilderness experience, we do know that throughout Scripture "wilderness" is frequently associated with a place where God speaks to people. Beginning in the Old Testament, we learn that it is in the wilderness that God shapes a ragtag group of slaves into a covenant people. We also learn that it is in the wilderness of Babylonian captivity that God reconnects with a people who have forgotten what it means to live as God's chosen people. Wilderness is a place where people connect with God. It is in the wilderness that Jesus develops a clarity of mission and ministry. I do not think that it is an accident that the Gospel writer Luke has Jesus returning to Galilee immediately after his time in the wilderness

(4:14) and preaching his inaugural sermon to the hometown crowd. Jesus gains his vision during an isolated time of prayer, solitude, and temptation.

But prayer, solitude, and temptation are not the only sources that seem to inform the clear articulation of Jesus' mission. The fact that Jesus' mission statement is an exact quote from the Old Testament also supports the notion that the mission was informed by Jesus' understanding of the Old Testament Scriptures. Jesus was steeped in the great themes and stories of God's revelation to the people of Israel. And because of Jesus' deep understanding of the Old Testament, Jesus understood the heart of God. Jesus understood God's concern for the poor, God's passion for righteousness and justice, and God's concern for the salvation of the world. In essence, when Jesus shares his mission with the people of Galilee, he shares a mission that captures the essence and heart of the God of Abraham, Isaac, Jacob, Moses, and the prophets.

Throughout the history of the Christian church, disciples of antiquity have crafted their life mission through the influence of multiple sources. William Wilberforce, the great English abolitionist who spent much of his life fighting the injustices of the British slave trade economy, received his life direction through a friend and mentor, John Newton. When Wilberforce was debating whether to abandon public office and go into full-time ministry, Newton helped him to clarify his vision and remain as a voice and conscience for the British parliament. Newton reminded his young friend that "The Lord has raised you up to the good of His church and for the good of the nation." Newton encouraged Wilberforce to use his gifts for God's kingdom in dismantling a hideous trade that destroyed thousands and thousands of God's children. It was this very defined life mission that helped Wilberforce persevere after years and years of being a solo prophetic voice and suffering numerous political defeats. In Wilberforce's life, God used the historical reality of the slave trade and the life of John Newton to clarify his life mission and calling.

Mission statements must be developed through the channels God uses to guide and inspire those devoted to discipleship. As disciples we must be open to these different sources offered by God to inspire the mission and dreams of people. Therefore, a truly Christian mission statement must find consistency with the truth of Scriptures, is confirmed by the body of believers, and is inspired by the Spirit.

Where Jesus Spent His Time

Jesus' mission statement also reveals that his life and ministry would be spent working with certain kinds of people. Although the mission statement does not specifically spell out the neighborhoods, the age groups, or the ethnic groups that Jesus would direct his efforts toward, the mission statement does tell us that Jesus will seek out the poor, the captives, the oppressed, and those who have physical and social limitations. Jesus' mission suggests that he will direct the majority of his time and energy toward people who have needs and who have little power. According to the mission, Jesus' life will not be spent with the "church folk" and the upwardly mobile. Instead Jesus' life decisions will be biased toward the disenfranchised and those who have been cut off from the Temple because of the social stigmas they carry.

The Gospel narratives affirm the consistency between Jesus' mission statement and his ministry. Throughout the ministry of Jesus we catch numerous glimpses of Jesus having dinner with prostitutes, healing lepers, and bringing God's grace and love to those who have been pushed to the fringes of society and excluded from opportunities to worship God. Time after time, we meet a Jesus who is focused on caring for people who are described in the Isaiah passage.

What Did Jesus Do?

The last thing the mission statement teaches the reader is the style of ministry Jesus performed. Jesus' mission clearly delineates that his ministry is about teaching, preaching, healing, and proclaiming a new message that would bring freedom to people who needed to be set free. Through parables about grace and God's love, Jesus preached a new and radical message of unconditional love. The Sermon on the Mount and the story of the prodigal son are just a few reminders that Jesus was a preacher. The healing of the demonic and the cleansing of those with leprosy are reminders that Jesus was not just a preacher but that he also proclaimed this new message of liberation through his actions. And by bringing sight to blind people, by stopping the hemorrhaging of a bleeding woman, and by raising a dead girl to life, Jesus confirmed that part of his mission was to heal people. Consistently the Gospels reveal a man who exercised the ministry of teaching, the ministry of preaching, the ministry of healing, and the ministry of proclaiming. Jesus stayed true to his mission and calling.

Did Jesus Follow His Mission?

The real value of a mission statement is whether it actually guides and helps people make their decisions. With so many things vying for our attention and energy, it is critical to realize that we cannot do everything. Jesus did not do everything. Because Jesus was fully human he was limited by the same things that limit all people. Therefore Jesus had to make real-life decisions. One of the tools that helped Jesus make those real-life decisions was the mission statement he articulated at the beginning of his ministry. Jesus built his decision-making around his mission.

When reading the Gospel accounts we frequently see Jesus fulfilling various elements of his mission statement. Jesus stays true to sharing the good news of God's love with the poor. When confronted with the reality of where to begin his ministry, Jesus chooses the city of Capernaum (Mark 1:21). It is in this city of Capernaum, which was known as one of Israel's poorer cities, that Jesus plants his initial ministry roots. From the very beginning of his public ministry, Jesus is guided by the principle found in his mission statement—God has anointed him to preach good news to the poor.

Jesus also had to choose which "dinners" to attend, whether he should spend all his time in the Temple, where he should spend his nights, which disciples should get a little more attention, and whether he would obey the "letter" of the Jewish law or the spirit of the law. Jesus had to make choices. Without the guidance of a Spirit-inspired mission, Jesus could have wandered in the desert and become a recluse who wrote journals on spirituality. Jesus could have stayed within the safe confines of the organized religion of his day by engaging in theological discussions with the scribes and religious leaders. And yet repeatedly, throughout the Gospel narratives, Jesus finds the very people he came to serve. The actions of Jesus align themselves with the ideals set forth within his mission statement.

For many readers these earthly decisions of Jesus may seem very ordinary and mundane. The casual reader might argue that Jesus' life was simply a spontaneous response to the needs around him. I would argue that if Jesus was simply "available" to all the needs of those who wanted a piece of him, his life would not have had the kind of focus it needed to produce the results it did. For example, if Jesus spent all his time healing the sick and never fulfilled his mission as a teacher to his disciples, the foundation for the Christian church would never have been established. As disciples of Christ who desire to live lives that bear tremendous fruit for God's kingdom, we must realize that these ordinary real-life decisions as to how we focus our time are absolutely critical. The question for the aspiring disciple is this: If the perfect man—Jesus—needed a mission statement to help keep his course, how much more do we need a mission statement to guide our lives?

What Guides Your Decisions?

Some of the most difficult and serious questions asked by collegians are, "What is God's will for my life?" "Where does God want me?" and "What should I do with my life after graduation?" These are all difficult questions. There is no simple answer. Unfortunately God does not miraculously pick us up and place us exactly where our gifts, talents, and passions can be utilized for the kingdom. We must begin a journey of obedience that will eventually lead us to the location (or locations) where God wants to place us.

While on this journey of obedience, we make everyday choices as to where we should invest our time, energy, and resources. The decisions we make affect our lives in incredible ways. Besides our common sense, and an innate notion of what is good and what is bad, something is needed to inform these decisions. Lampposts are needed to provide light and direction for the journey. Mission statements are critical for staying on course.

College is an important time of life to begin the process of formulating a mission statement for our lives. While we explore different areas of study, different vocational opportunities, and different career choices, it is critical not to let this period of life sneak by without taking time to reflect, pray, and develop a mission statement. But how exactly does a person begin the process of creating a mission statement that is relevant and inspired by God? How does a person begin to fit together ideas, interests, and Scripture passages into a dynamic mission statement that will help us to keep our lives on course?

A Way to Begin

One helpful and critical way to begin the process of creating your mission statement is to dialogue with wiser, older people who are living lives of vibrant faith. One of the great gifts of being a Christian is the privilege of being part of a larger family of people. Within this family—both dead and alive—are lives worth learning from. Although mission statements need to be anointed by God's Spirit, mission statements need not be created only between you and the Lord. The formulation of mission statements should involve friends and elders who know you well, are committed in their faith, and will help you focus your scattered ideas.

As initial ideas, visions, dreams, Scriptures, and pieces from conversations begin to settle within you, pick up a pen and begin to craft a statement for your life. Your initial draft may be half a page, a paragraph, or a few sentences. One student I know simply adopted Micah 6:8 as the mission statement for his life—"God has showed [Me], what is good and what the Lord requires of [Me]. To act justly and to love mercy and to walk humbly with [My] God." For this particular student, his daily life decisions all revolve around the questions "Does this decision promote justice in my world and in my relationships?" "Does my decision demonstrate mercy and compassion to the people in my life?" "Am I walking humbly with God?" Other students have developed much more complex statements that isolate the different areas of their lives (family, career, relationships, and so forth) and have developed short mission statements for each of the areas.

After completing an initial draft of your mission statement, find someone who knows your heart and your passions and let that person read it. Ask him or her to make comments, add ideas, and refine your statement. It may be a pastor, a professor, a missionary, an author, or another Christian leader. Comments from wise and more mature people can be invaluable.

A Second Step

Another idea helpful in developing your mission statement is to read Christian writers who you respect and who bring biblical truth to life. One writer, for example, who offers some very practical wisdom in making significant life decisions is Frederick Buechner. In his book *Wishful Thinking: A Theological ABC*, Buechner shares some wonderful insights on how one should go about shaping a mission statement and making significant life choices.

> There are different kinds of voices calling you to all different kinds of work, and the problem is to find out which is the voice of God rather than society, say, or the super-ego or self-interest. By and large a good rule for finding out is this. The kind of work God usually calls you to is the kind of work (a) that you need most to do and (b) that the world most needs to have done. If you really get a kick our of your work, you've presumably met requirement (a), but if your work is writing TV deodorant commercials, the chances are you've missed requirement (b). On the

other hand, if your work is being a doctor in a leper
colony, you have probably met requirement (b), but if
most of the time you're bored and depressed by it, the
chances are you have not only bypassed (a) but probably
aren't helping your patients much either. Neither the hair
shirt nor the soft berth will do. The place God calls you
to is the place where your deep gladness and the world's
deep hunger meet.[21]

The opportunity to give your skills, gifts, and education to Jesus
so these skills can be used to meet a deeper hunger in the world is
a privilege. It is an even greater opportunity when meeting this
hunger brings you deep gladness. One way to ensure that you do
not get swept away by the current and the voices of the world is to
read books by wise people who can give you words that will help
you create the kind of mission statement that will have insight
from outside the circle of friends you presently draw from. Sometimes an author can help us see things in new and fresh ways.
Sometimes God can use certain authors to inspire and challenge
us to dream dreams that we would never have dreamed otherwise.

A Student with a Mission

Not too far from Philadelphia is a Christian liberal arts college
named Eastern College. The mission of this small private
school is to educate Christian young people in ways that challenge them to go out into the world and make a difference for
God's kingdom. One of their special graduates is a young man
named Bryan Stevenson.

After graduating from Eastern, Bryan had the opportunity to
attend Harvard Law School. When the first-year law students
were surveyed as to what they were going to do with their law
degrees, close to 70 percent said they were going into public law.
The students had noble ambitions. They were going to use their
skills as lawyers to improve the world and fight for the poor. During their second year of school students began getting job offers
in the mail from top law firms across the country. One by one the
idealistic young lawyers were seduced into careers with big pay-
checks. By the time Bryan graduated, only two from his class had
stayed true to their earlier calling. Bryan was one of those students.

As an African American who graduated at the top of his class,
Bryan had every major law firm in the country asking him to join
their team. Fortunately Bryan had a mission in life that ran deeper
than money and prestige. Fortunately Bryan's committed mission

in life had been so indelibly seared into his conscience and heart that he could not be distracted by the voices of the world.

While in law school Bryan had the opportunity to do a summer internship in the southern United States. What Bryan quickly discovered was that in the South the majority of men on death row did not have adequate legal representation. Frequently these men had been given lawyers who had never tried a capital case—many had not even tried a criminal case! Bryan was appalled by the reality that these men had been sentenced to die without being given a fair trial. Fortunately his God-given indignation grew into a conviction. Out of his intern experience ideas and convictions began to settle in Bryan's heart. God began to speak to Bryan. The beginnings of a mission statement started to emerge. Bryan would combine his God-given gifts as a lawyer with a growing conviction for justice for the poor and under-represented.

When Bryan left Harvard he took a job as the director of the Alabama Capital Representative Resource Center, which represented death row inmates in Alabama. He was offered a salary of $50,000 but took only $18,000 because he thought the center could not afford the additional cost.

Today Bryan still works defending death row prisoners in Alabama. He works seven days a week, from 8:30 A.M. to 11:30 P.M. He lives simply in a one-room apartment with hardly any furniture. Not only has he given his heart and life to setting the captives free, but Bryan has become a national advocate for prisoners on death row. He carries a heavy caseload himself, supervises five young lawyers, and raises $200,000 per year for their salaries. It is a heavy load for someone only thirty-two.

When Bryan was interviewed by the *Washington Post* for a front-page magazine article called "Mystery of Goodness," a rather jaded and cynical press was caught off guard by the authenticity of such a committed young man. When asked why he would "waste" his career fighting cases that he would seldom win, Bryan said the following: "I want to be a witness for hope and decency and commitment. I want to show in myself the qualities I want to see in others." For Bryan a life that acted consistently with his heartfelt beliefs, his mission statement, was what he desired most.

Over the years Bryan has remained true to his mission. While others have given lip service to helping the poor, Bryan has remained faithful to the mission he began to establish while in college: justice for the poor, a witness of hope for the hopeless, a champion of decency and fairness, all undergirded by unswerving commitment. This is what Bryan Stevenson believes and lives. This is why a legal system is now being reexamined and changes are being made. One man with a mission statement. One man with the courage to remain true to that mission.

Beginning with the End in Mind

In Steven Covey's best-selling book, *Seven Habits of Highly Effective People*, he challenges his readers to begin the process of developing life mission statements with "the end in mind." Although Covey comes at the process from a more secular perspective, the metaphor he uses to drive home the point is powerful. Covey asks his readers to imagine that they are at a funeral. The church is full. People are crying. There is a line to view the body. You decide to get in the line and file past the open coffin. To your utter surprise and shock you see that the body is you! It is your funeral. At this point Covey suggests that numerous people will get up to speak about your life. There is a colleague from work, someone from your church, a family member, a fellow student, and a host of other people who represent various areas of your life. The question Covey directs to his readers: What would each of the speakers say about you? And what would you want each of the speakers to say about you? Covey wants his readers to begin the process of crafting a life mission statement with the end of their lives in mind. Do you want your colleagues to talk about how you encouraged them, how you listened, and how you demonstrated God's love in the workplace? Or do you want to be remembered as the one who was always trying to make himself or herself look good for the next job promotion, always in a rush, or always impatient? Covey believes very strongly that if we begin with the "end in mind," our goals and life mission will lead us in the right direction.

For a Christian it is even more critical to go through this process of thinking about the testimonies that will be shared at our funerals. Will the testimonies shared at our funerals reflect a life that embodied the spirit of Jesus? Will people share about how we were generous with our blessings and compassionate toward those with little? Will person after person stand up and attest to how you encouraged them, loved them, and challenged them?

Recently I had the privilege of attending the funeral of a ninety-four-year-old Christian woman. First, I was surprised at the number of people in the sanctuary. This was a woman who had outlived all her friends and yet the place was packed with children, young adults, and other elderly people. She had obviously transcended age and had influenced many lives. The most powerful part of the funeral, however, was not the size and diversity of the crowd. The funeral was challenging and motivating because of the testimonies. Mrs. Davies' children shared about her incredible character and selflessness. Her grandchildren shared about how she had influenced them in their growing and sometimes wavering faith. People, both young and old, shared about her generosity and about the impact she had had on their lives. The funeral was incredible. It was truly a celebration of a Christian life well lived. Everybody left the church feeling more inspired to live as a disciple of Jesus. Even in death, this woman's life continued to touch other lives. Ninety-four-year-old Mildred Davies had remained true to her mission. She finished the race committed to her lifelong mission—to live and act as Jesus would want her to live and act. Hers was not a wasted life.

If Jesus Were a Sophomore

"What are you gonna do now?" began my holy Friend. "You have too many choices: Should you go the game? Should you date Susan? What should you do for your spring break? Too many choices and no criteria for making your choices. You're in trouble."

This was the last thing I needed to hear. We kept walking up the path. He liked to join me on my meditative walks.

"The worst thing that ever happened to Christian faith was when people spiritualized Me—when they disconnected Me from really living. It bugs Me when folks only think of Me on the cross. I lived on the earth. I walked on the earth. I had to make choices. It wasn't always easy."

"How did you make those choices?" I asked with great interest.

"I had a sense of where I needed to go. I had a clear sense of what I was called to do. This meant saying no to certain trips and opportunities. After all, I could not be in more than one place at a time," he replied.

"But how did you develop this sense of mission? This clarity?" I asked.

"I prayed. I surrendered My will to God's will. I let God give Me My mission. Once I decided how I was going to focus My life and ministry, it became easier to make decisions. This did not mean that decisions were easy. It simply meant that I had some kind of criteria for making my decisions—like fenceposts lining a road. They kept Me on the right path."

"It sounds like this is what I need," I concluded.

"I would agree," replied my Friend.

It is clear: Jesus had a mission statement. As we read the Gospels, it becomes very apparent that certain behaviors repeat themselves in the ministry of Jesus. We see compassion and healing for the sick and poor. We see teaching and preaching. We see Jesus investing in others and empowering them to serve. Before Jesus launches out on his mission, Jesus sets the course for how his life will be lived. We must do likewise. Without a clearly defined sense of mission, we will waste an opportunity to lead a fruitful life. Without a deeply rooted set of principles governing our daily lives, we will slowly lose our sense of vision and mission. Like a ship without a rudder, we will drift.

God gives us our college years as a gift. Young adulthood is a period of life when one can begin to formulate a plan for the future. Not only is it a time to decide our careers, but it is a time to think about what we want our lives to count for. Furthermore, it is a time to truly seek God and try to discern how God wants us to live our lives. As the late French theologian Jacques Ellul states, we seek God during this period of life not only to ensure our salvation but because soon the "weight of necessity" will overwhelm us. The "weight of necessity" is the cares of the world. As Jesus claims in his parable of the sower and the seed, the cares of the world choke the plants and do not allow them to bear the fruit they were designed to bear. Likewise, without a biblically centered mission statement inspired by the Spirit, the eager disciple will be mesmerized by all the distractions of the world and will be knocked off a kingdom-centered course of activity.

A long journey often begins with a good map. A sturdy house begins with a well-drawn plan. A brilliant play begins with a well-written script. A well-lived, fruitful life begins with a mission statement. Step back from the hectic schedule of everyday life. Begin to pray, meditate, and articulate a life that is built around principles of God's kingdom.

Remember:

During my years of being close to people engaged in changing the world I have seen fear turn into courage. Sorrow into joy. Funerals into celebrations.

Alice Walker

Questions for Reflection

1. Have you ever thought of developing a mission statement for your life? If so, how have you set out putting one together?

2. If you have never put together a mission statement for your life, how would you go about the process of putting such a mission statement together?

3. In the words of Frederick Buechner, "What is your deepest gladness?" What are your unique giftings? What kinds of activities and service stir your passions? How can your "deep gladness" and the world's "deepest hungers" connect?

4. If you struggle with identifying your unique giftings, ask someone who knows you well to help identify some of your gifts and talents.

5. Begin the process of developing a mission statement. Put together a sentence or two that might help guide you as you make choices that will affect your future.

For the Leader

Ask the members in your group to work on their mission statements over the next week and bring them back to the group the following week. As the leader, perhaps you could set up a one-on-one time with each member of your group during the week to listen to their thoughts and offer guidance.

Prayer and Meditation

Lord,

Thank you for the unique and wonderful gift of my life.
Thank you for the way you have put me together.
Thank you for my history that shapes the way I think and the
    way I perceive the world.
Thank you that there is nobody else on the face of this earth like me.
I bring to You ALL that I am—my personality, my loves, my
    passions, my dislikes, my fears, my intellect, my gifts—and
    present them as a living sacrifice.

Take me, Lord—this unique, one-of-a-kind, wonderful creation.
Breathe vision into me. Reveal Your mission for my life.
Bring thoughts, ideas, and Scriptures into my conscience that
    can help give my life direction.
Set my heart ablaze with passion for Your world and Your people.

Lord, there are so many distractions.
There are so many good things to do.
But help me to focus on the things You need and desire me to do.
Give me the courage to say no and to walk away from things
    that will distract me
From the mission You have for me.

Amen

Conclusion:
Where Do We Go from Here?

Just as there are countless varieties of wine, there are countless varieties of lives. No two lives are the same. We often compare our lives with those of others, trying to decide whether we are better or worse off, but such comparisons do not help us much. We have to live our life, not someone else's. We have to hold our own cup. We have to dare to say: "This is my life, the life that is given to me, and it is this life that I have to live, as well as I can. My life is unique. Nobody else will ever live it. I have my own history, my own family, my own body, my own character, my own friends, my own way of thinking, speaking, and acting—yes, I have my own life to live. No one else has the same challenge. I am alone, because I am unique. Many people can help me to live my life, but after all is said and done, I have to make my own choices about how to live.

Henri Nouwen

Axis: a straight line about which a body or a geometric figure rotates or may be supposed to rotate.

A former student recently wrote to tell me about a dynamic church group he had joined. Having recently graduated from college, Jake was thrilled to find a group that took "college-aged" students seriously. The name of the group was "AXIS."

Jake liked the name of this fellowship because it described the significance of early adulthood. Since an axis is an imaginary line around which a body spins, the group contended that the years between twenty and twenty-four would be like a "line about which their whole lives would rotate."

The members of the group realized the significance of this period of life and attempted to focus their attention on creating certain behaviors that would become the center around which their adult lives would "rotate." The group was committed to becoming people who got involved in issues of social justice, who grew in wisdom and knowledge of their faith, who took risks, and who strove to reach beyond their comfort zone. Together this group committed to forming a "center point" for their lives that was filled with habits and patterns reflecting values and a lifestyle consistent with radical discipleship. Establishing this "Kingdom AXIS" was a goal for each of the students.

I wish more university- and college-aged students had the opportunity to be a part of a group with such a clearly defined mission and purpose. I wish more students would embrace the AXIS metaphor as a vivid reminder of the stage of life in which they are living.

A Long Obedience in the Same Direction

Eugene Peterson provides some further hints in his book *A Long Obedience in the Same Direction* as to how students can lead long lives of faithful devotion to God. Peterson contends that it is essential to begin establishing "life rhythms" that prepare disciples for the long haul. Peterson likens the faith journey to an Alpine hiker who must learn to walk in a way that maximizes energy and allows for completion of the climb. Inexperienced hikers begin to climb mountains with vigor and an enthusiastic pace. Unfortunately these inexperienced climbers run out of steam halfway up the hill. To complete the journey one must learn the disciplines of walking correctly. To complete a fruitful spiritual journey, God calls disciples to "walk" in ways that allow growth and an enduring, vibrant spiritual life.

Living in a "fast food" culture that creates an expectation that everything—including spiritual growth—should happen *now* does not encourage young disciples to build the kind of foundation that produces spiritual fruit over a lifetime. Peterson contends that disciples must reorient their thinking by becoming people who develop a more long-term view of spiritual growth. Peterson argues that brief cathartic religious experiences and the promises of Christian "how-to" books are not the diet needed for a life of faithful discipleship. Real spiritual growth is steady, hard-fought, persistent activity. Real spiritual growth involves getting certain fundamentals in place and then building on those fundamentals over a lifetime. In Peterson's words, we need to be about the business of engaging in a "long obedience in the same direction."

In a culture that increasingly honors speed over endurance, the trivial over truth, appearance over depth, security over risk, intelligence over wisdom, and self-contentment over self-sacrifice, it is imperative that contemporary Christian collegians cut against the norms of society by cultivating lifestyle behaviors that create a foundation on which a "long obedience in the same direction" can be maintained. Without the foundational behaviors in place, one cannot even begin the journey.

Peterson cautions those who buy into the cult of instant spiritual growth. He claims that the end result of people who do not develop a "long obedience in the same direction" are people who "live life badly." Peterson adds,

> The puzzle is why so many people live so badly. Not so wickedly, but so inanely. Not so cruelly, but so stupidly. There is little to admire and less to imitate in the people who are prominent in our culture. We have celebrities but not saints. Famous entertainers amuse a nation of bored insomniacs. Infamous criminals act out the aggressions of timid conformists. Petulant and spoiled athletes play games vicariously for lazy and apathetic spectators. People, aimless and bored, amuse themselves with trivia and trash.[22]

How do we protect ourselves from becoming people who live badly, who live inanely, and who live stupidly? As people who are committed to growing as disciples, we must begin the process of cultivating a pattern of living that has deep roots and cannot be hijacked by the pressures and influence of our culture. Cultivating these behaviors must begin now.

If Jesus Were a Sophomore

"Hey Jesus, are you up there?" I call into the darkness.

"Yeah, I'm here. What's up?"

"I've got a question for you. Will you lend me an ear?" I inquire.

"Shoot away," He responds with his usual interest and warmth.

"I know I probably shouldn't ask—some of my friends might think I'm a liberal heretic. But I've just got so many questions," I begin.

"Don't you think God can handle your questions? Asking questions isn't a sign of lacking faith. It takes faith to ask questions. People of great faith have also been the people with the most questions. Don't worry, we can handle your questions up here."

I think I hear Him chuckle. I'm feeling a little better with His response. But it is the questions around Jesus' human nature that always cause me some consternation. These are the questions I was a little afraid to ask. Just how human is Jesus?

"When You were my age," I begin with some trepidation, "did You ever have questions about Your life? Did You ever struggle with Your faith? Did You ever wonder why You were created? Did You ever just want to settle down, get married, and have a couple of kids? Or did You just kind of glide through Your twenties?"

There is silence. I wonder if I had rocked the boat. Had my questions about His human nature been an insult to His divinity?

"What do the Gospels say?" He begins. *I always hate it when somebody answers with another question. I have had professors like that.*

He continues, "I know there are many blank spots, but there is enough to give you a glimpse. I struggled. I wept. I felt people's pain and confusion. I knew that even after feeding thousands of people they would be hungry the next day—I would be hungry the next day. Remember the scene in the garden. I could have walked away from it all. I could have chosen differently. I was not programmed to make that choice. I wasn't coerced. I knew the cost. I knew I would be killed."

"So what advice would You give to me now?" *I beg, desiring clarity for my life.*

"Remember that life is a series of choices. Choices you have to make. Nobody can live your life for you. This is one of great love gifts of God. You are free to use this gift as you desire." *He pauses. His words are cutting to the core of my being. I thirst for more.*

"Now, you can make these choices on your own, or you can involve Me. If you involve Me I will not guarantee an easy life. I will not guarantee a life without questions and doubts and pain. But I will promise you an abundant life. I will promise you an extraordinary life filled with mystery and adventure. I will promise you a life that blesses other people."

I sit there in silence, letting His words soak into my mind and heart. And then comes His climactic conclusion.

"But don't wait. Begin today. Don't let these important years pass you by. No matter how tough the questions, or how deep the struggles, or how complex the relationships you encounter during this period of life—this time is a gift. I can do things in your life now that will be difficult to do later in life. Invite Me to live it with you."

And with these words I close my eyes, think about what my life should be about, and slowly drift to sleep.

Just as Jesus has had an answer for other young saints throughout the history of the church, he has an answer for you. It is no accident that many great Christian leaders like St. Francis of Assisi, Mother Teresa, St. Augustine, Dorothy Day, and Martin Luther King Jr. began to build their "Axis of discipleship" when they were transitioning out of adolescence and entering into early adulthood. It was during this critical period of their lives that these young saints listened to the voice of God and had the courage to begin implementing the disciplines needed to sustain their activity of serving God in the world. It was their obedience at an early age that ultimately led them to become Christians who made a tremendous impact in their world at a later stage in their life.

A fruitful life of discipleship is a life that blesses and changes the world. A fruitful life, however, is not an accident. A fruitful life is the result of an intentional series of choices and decisions that lead us toward God and lead us toward becoming the person God created us to be.

Begin today.

Begin today to live by the question "How would Jesus want me to use these critical young adult years?"

Questions for Reflection

1. What kind of life do you want to lead? When you hang up the sneakers at the end of race, what do you want to look back and see? What will your legacy be?

2. Write down a definition of what you want your life to look like at thirty, at forty, at fifty, at sixty. Keep these definitions.

3. Identify some "behaviors" that you need to begin to establish in your life. Write them down. Talk about them with your friends.

4. Speculate. Imagine. How would Jesus spend his college years? If Jesus were a student on your campus today, how would he act? With whom would he associate? What would he try to learn? With what kinds of activities would he involve himself?

For the Leader

Ask the members of your group to go off by themselves and spend twenty to thirty minutes alone. Give them some blank paper and ask them to construct a dialogue with Jesus about their lives: questions they have; struggles they are experiencing;

directional issues they are encountering. After they write down their conversation, have them share their dialogue with the others in the group, if they feel comfortable doing so.

Prayer and Meditation

Lord,

I want to live my life well.
I don't want to look back and regret how I spent this period of my life.
I want to make choices that help me to grow in faith and in love.

Guide my feet along the path of a long obedience in the same direction.
Help me to establish the kinds of behaviors I need to make this journey.

I don't want to be a lazy spectator,
And live life vicariously through others.

I want to be your disciple, Jesus.
I want to go forth into the world in Your name and in Your service.
Please remind me that You are there when I need direction, courage, and strength.

Amen

Notes

1. Sharon Parks, *The Critical Years* (San Francisco: Harper & Row Publishers, 1986), p. xii.
2. Erik Erikson, *Insight and Responsibility: Lectures on the Ethical Implications of Psychoanalytic Insight* (New York: W. W. Norton, 1964), p. 138.
3. Ibid., p. 139.
4. George Barna, *Prism*, "The Church of Tomorrow," September/October 1997, p. 12.
5. Ibid.
6. Clark Pinnock, *Post American Magazine*, January 1975.
7. Simon Carey Holt, *Theology, News and Notes*, "Finding God in the Ordinary, the Mundane, and the Immediate," March 1999.
8. Thomas Merton, 1965 audio tape.
9. J. D. Smart, *The Cultural Subversion of the Biblical Faith* (Philadelphia: The Westminster Press, 1977) is a great read for any collegian.
10. Daniel Taylor, *The Myth of Certainty* (Waco, Tex.: Jarrell), p. 112.
11. J. Heinrich Arnold, *Discipleship: Living for Christ in the Daily Grind* (Farmington, Penn.: Plough Publishing House, 1994), p. 36–37.
12. George MacDonald, Michael R. Phillips, eds., *The Gentlewoman's Choice* (Minneapolis: Bethany House Publishers, 1987), p. 58.
13. Dietrich Bonhoeffer, *Life Together* (San Francisco: HarperSanFrancisco, 1954), p. 76.
14. G. K Chesterton's *St. Francis of Assisi* (Garden City: Doubleday Image Books, 1957) is a terrific little account of the life of this saint.
15. As quoted in J. P. Little's *Simone Weil: Waiting on Truth* (New York: Oxford University Press, St. Martin's Press, 1988), p. 25.
16. Nicholas Wolterstorff, *Lament for a Son* (Grand Rapids: Wm. B. Eerdmans Publishing Co., 1987), p. 86.
17. Henri Nouwen, *In the Name of Jesus* (New York: Crossroads, 1989), p. 47.
18. Dietrich Bonhoeffer, *Life Together*, pp. 77–78.
19. Oswald Chambers, *My Utmost for His Highest* (London: Marshall, Morgan and Scott, 1927), p. 170.
20. Rodney Clapp, *Families at the Crossroads: Beyond Traditional and*

Modern Options (Downers Grove, Ill.: InterVarsity Press, 1993), p. 139.

21.   Frederick Buechner, *Wishful Thinking: A Theological ABC* (New York: Harper & Row, 1973).

22.   Eugene Peterson, *Run with the Horses: The Quest for Life at Its Best*, (Downers Grove, Ill.: InterVarsity Press, 1983), p. 12.